MW01625675

# Operations Management

Steven M. Bragg

Published by AccountingTools, Inc., Centennial, Colorado.





For more information about AccountingTools® products, visit our Web site at www.accountingtools.com.

ISBN-13: 978-1-64221-322-5

Printed in the United States of America

# Table of Contents

# About the Author

**Steven Bragg, CPA,** has been the chief financial officer or controller of four companies, as well as a consulting manager at Ernst & Young. He received a master's degree in finance from Bentley College, an MBA from Babson College, and a Bachelor's degree in Economics from the University of Maine. He has been a two-time president of the Colorado Mountain Club, and is an avid alpine skier, mountain biker, and certified master diver. Mr. Bragg resides in Centennial, Colorado. He has written more than 300 books and courses, including *New Controller Guidebook*, *GAAP Guidebook*, and *Payroll Management*. He has also written *The Auditors* science fiction trilogy.

Steven maintains the accountingtools.com web site, which contains continuing professional education courses, the Accounting Best Practices podcast, and thousands of articles on accounting subjects.

# Chapter 1
# Introduction to Operations Management

## Introduction

Operations management is all activities related to improving the production and delivery of goods and services to customers. Every item in your home, the car you drive to work, and the desk you sit at in the office is the result of a dense web of operations management activities at suppliers. While the people involved in these activities may not have "operations manager" titles, they are all involved in the operations management process, and are critical to the success of the businesses for which they work. In this book, we describe all aspects of the operations management process and the techniques used to arrive at enhanced results.

## The Nature of Operations Management

Operations management is about resource management. A company has access to a limited amount of resources, and needs to direct their use carefully in order to generate positive cash flows from company operations. The people involved in operations management will have different titles, depending on the nature of the business. For example, a trucking company might call its operations manager the fleet manager, while a publishing company might call this person the editor in chief. No matter what the title, the operations manager is in charge of the vast majority of all operations within a business.

This does not mean that operations management oversees *all* activities within a business. There is also the product development group, which comes up with new products and services that can be offered to the company's customers. Also, there is the sales and marketing function, which communicates the company's product offerings to the addressable market, and takes orders from customers. Operations management lies between these two other functions, converting new product designs into actual products and making them ready for sale to customers.

In addition to these three core areas, most companies are also supported by a cluster of administrative units that handle such matters as accounting, finance, human resources, and information systems. As the name implies, these support functions assist the three core activity areas of the business. There may be some overlap between the administrative units and the core activity areas, depending on how responsibilities are assigned to managers within each individual business.

Operations management will differ markedly, depending on the nature of a business. The classic concept of it is in a manufacturing company, where the procurement, production, and distribution functions are all considered to be part of operations management. However, consider the businesses in the following exhibit, where operations management is not associated with production activities at all.

**Operations Functions in Different Types of Businesses**

| Business Type | Related Operations Functions |
|---|---|
| Advertising agency | Ad campaign development, refinement, and rollout through distribution companies |
| Book publishing | Author acquisition, editing, indexing, layout, printing, distribution |
| Trail building | Volunteer acquisition, permissions management, activity scheduling, safety training |
| Water park | Facility maintenance, activity scheduling, guest safety oversight |
| Winery | Vineyard management, grape picking, grape crushing, cellaring, bottling, distribution |

Operations management may be the competitive driver of a business. For example, a restaurant chain may compete based on the freshness of its food, which is a sourcing function that falls within its operations management group. Or, a rocket-launching company may compete based on the reliability of its rockets, which is a product design and construction function that is also classified as operations management. Or, a business that sells customized products does so through a just-in-time manufacturing process, which lies at the core of the operations management function. All of these organizations base their competitive position on the high quality of their underlying operations management processes.

## Company Size Differences

The various operations management functions tend to be highly refined in a larger corporation, where there are procurement managers, production schedulers, production managers, warehouse managers and so forth who handle each individual segment in the operations process flow. This is not the case in a smaller company, where there are too few staff to allow for a high degree of specialization. Instead, one person may be called upon to handle multiple operations tasks, such as both procurement *and* production scheduling. These less defined situations allow a business to respond more quickly to customer requests, since there are fewer people to coordinate. However, these broad spans of control are also less efficient, because no one is able to become an expert in one narrowly-defined area. Consequently, though they may be more responsive, smaller businesses tend to be less efficient than larger companies, and so may be less profitable.

## Company Type Differences

The clear motivation when engaging in operations management in a for-profit business is to enhance its cash flows and reported profits. This is not the case for a nonprofit business. A hospital, wilderness response group, animal shelter, or arts festival is not directly driven by the profit motive, but rather by its mission statement. For example, an animal shelter may have assigned itself the mission of caring for all animals delivered to it, while a wilderness response group has the mission of searching for all missing persons within a specific geographic area. However, the mission statement of a nonprofit is not the sole driver of its operations management activities, for it still has to carefully husband its resources to provide the mandated services without going out of business. Thus, a nonprofit may not be driven by the need to generate a profit, but it *is* driven by the need to avoid a loss – while fulfilling its mission.

## Business Environment Impacts

The business environment within which a company operates will alter how it chooses to manage its operations. For example, businesses have traditionally been able to conduct operations without having to factor the cost of carbon emissions into their activities, since the cost of carbon was free. This is unlikely to continue to be the case, with many governments starting to contemplate charging for carbon emissions. Similarly, governments have tightened their restrictions on companies in regard to such environmental concerns as groundwater contamination, methane emissions, and employee safety. In addition to these regulatory concerns, customers have greater choice of products due to their worldwide access to suppliers over the Internet, which imposes pressures on both product pricing and product quality. Another change is ongoing trade wars between trading blocks, which have caused the prices of raw materials and merchandise to fluctuate wildly, forcing companies to rejigger their supply chains on short notice. And to impose even more pressure on operations, methods of manufacture have begun to change, as 3-D printing allows for lower-volume production of complex products. All of these issues reflect current changes in the business environment, which are likely to continually force organizations to update their operations management practices.

## The Input-Transformation-Output Process

The core capability of any business is to transform inputs into outputs, which are products or services. The details of this process vary radically from industry to industry. For example, metal stamping operations are needed to produce the casing for a desktop computer, thereby transforming sheet metal into the final casing. Conversely, a wilderness rescue group uses inputs (searchers, airplanes, helicopters, and satellite photos) to develop an output service, which is locating a missing person.

Despite the broad range of differences between the two preceding examples, the types of transformations generated tend to be limited to just a few categories, which are:

- *Materials transformation.* The physical properties of incoming materials are transformed into a different output. For example, animal skins are transformed into leather, while copper ore is transformed into wire.
- *Location transformation.* The main purpose of some companies is to move something from one location to another. For example, a railroad moves coal from a mining site to a power station, while an overnight delivery service moves a check payment from a customer in Los Angeles to a supplier in Chicago. The item being moved is not transformed, only its location.
- *Ownership transformation.* Some companies specialize in aggregating products made by other parties, for distribution to the final customer. For example, a chain of retail stores buys outdoor clothing from a variety of suppliers and offers them for sale through its stores. This represents both a location transformation and an ownership transformation.
- *Information transformation.* A firm may collect raw data and transform it into information that is valuable to its clients. For example, a satellite data collection firm launches satellites that take pictures that can then be used to track crop yields or changes in weather patterns.
- *Customer transformation.* The providers of services literally change their customers. For example, a nail salon buffs the fingernails of its patrons, while a plastic surgeon uses facelifts to enhance the looks of his aging clients.

A business needs certain resources in order to successfully achieve any of these transformations. A common resource type is facilities, such as an operating room for a surgeon, or a manufacturing plant for a producer of cell phones, or a refinery for a producer of oil-based products. It also requires trained staff to operate and manage operations. For example, an overnight delivery service requires truck drivers and airplane pilots, while a train requires an engineer and conductor, and a consulting firm requires a group of trained consultants. The exact mix of personnel required will likely be a blend of highly-trained employees for a few operations (such as software developers) and a mix of less-trained personnel in other roles (such as production line workers).

The output of the process may be either a product or a service. A product is a tangible item, while a service can be either an activity or a process. Thus, a couch, a television and a bicycle are all considered products, while a haircut is a process and a yoga class is an activity. Many businesses provide a combination of these outputs. For example, a software company sells software (a product) as well as consulting and staff training on how to use the software (which are activities). Similarly, a restaurant provides both a product (the meal) and a service (table service by the waiter). And, a car dealership sells not only vehicles, but also financing for those cars and ongoing vehicle maintenance. Some firms go to the extreme of renting out their assets along with support services for the assets, thereby converting their product sales into service sales. For example, several driverless car companies are planning to build cars and then rent them out by the mile to customers. In short, some businesses may lie at either extreme of the products and services continuum, but many lie in between. When this is the case, they have more complex transformation processes, since they are dealing with both products and services.

## The Process Hierarchy

The operations used by a business to transform inputs into outputs are comprised of a collection of processes, each of which conducts a small part of the transformation process. A *process* is a series of interdependent and linked procedures which, at every stage, consume resources in order to convert inputs into outputs. Each successive output is then used as input for the next stage, until an end result has been reached. Thus, the first process in a series is the internal supplier for the next downstream process, while the second process is essentially the internal customer for the first process. A key requirement for improving internal processes is to have this customer-supplier relationship, so that employees have a strong incentive to continually improve the service they provide to their internal customers.

---

**EXAMPLE**

A ski resort is comprised of many processes that are needed in order to successfully transport skiers to the top of the resort and back down it. These include parking lot management, artificial snow generation, snow grooming, chairlift maintenance and operation, ski patrol operations, avalanche mitigation activities, restroom maintenance, and food service operations. All of these processes must function properly in order to create an optimum skier experience.

---

This clustering of processes can be viewed as a *process hierarchy*, which presents a hierarchical decomposition from the core processes down to the individual task level. The number of levels in a hierarchy is determined by the breadth and size of the organization. A large hierarchy might have at its top a set of core business processes, below which are processes, sub-processes, activities, and tasks. For example, a film studio has set construction as one of its core business processes. Below this core process is a set of processes that include site acquisition, site design, site construction, and site safety. Below the site acquisition process is a set of sub-processes that include site location, site leasing, and lessor payments. Below the site leasing sub-process are several activities that include owner contact, lease negotiation, and contract approval. Below the contract approval activity is a set of tasks, including final contract review, contract approval, forwarding of payment terms to accounting, and data entry of contract terms into a contracts database. Thus, a process hierarchy is comprised of a dense web of activities, all of which must work together to transform inputs into outputs as efficiently as possible.

It can be quite a challenge to extract improvements from this multitude of activities. It is usually achieved incrementally by examining each element of a process, implementing a series of minor changes, and measuring the result to see if an improvement has been achieved. An alternative, which we will address in a later chapter, is to use business process reengineering (BPR) to more thoroughly overhaul processes, sometimes replacing them entirely with new technology components. BPR allows a business to dispense with outmoded notions of how transactions should be dealt with, focusing instead on the latest best practices. In either case, constant attention to process improvement results in incremental efficiency improvements over time that can be difficult to replicate, and which form the competitive underpinnings of a business.

## Process Differences

The many processes that comprise operations are all similar in that they transform inputs to generate outputs, but they have many differences beyond this basic underlying capability. The key differences fall into the following four categories:

- *Volume of output.* The activity volumes for some transactions range from one or two per year to thousands per day. For example, a business may only produce a customized product for a special customer once a year, while producing thousands of its best-selling green widget every day. This volume difference drives whether it makes sense to work on efficiencies and acquire specialized equipment, or to accept a low level of efficiency for a process that rarely happens. For example, when a process is being repeated many times per day, it makes sense to work on even the smallest process improvements, since an enhancement representing a fraction of a penny of savings will be repeated many times, resulting in substantial savings for the company. Conversely, when a process takes place rarely, it is not cost-effective to improve it, so management is content to allow it to remain relatively inefficient.
- *Variety of output.* A process may be expected to deliver a broad range of outputs, or the exact same output, every time. Variety has a major impact on the cost of a process, since it is much less expensive to deliver the same thing, over and over again, than to produce a different output every time. For example, when a stamping machine is designed to produce the same part a thousand times a day, the machine operator can probably do so with a high degree of efficiency and with minimal variation in the produced units. Conversely, when a food cart company offers 300 variations on its basic product, with custom graphics, it is quite likely that the firm can only do so profitably by selling at a relatively high price – in order to factor in the high level of inefficiency associated with the many variations incorporated into its production process.

- *Variation in demand output.* A particular process may have wildly variable process volume, where many transactions must be processed within a short period of time, followed by fallow periods when there is minimal demand. Other processes face a much more consistent demand level over time. This difference has a major impact on process efficiency, since a process with a consistent demand level is much more amenable to ongoing tweaking to improve its efficiency. Conversely, a process that experiences high levels of variability in demand is constantly ramping up and scaling back the staffing required for it – which means that process knowledge is lost when employees are shifted away from the process, and new people have to be trained up when process demand eventually increases again. A good example of this is a restaurant located at a seasonal destination; the owner has to lay off most of the staff during the off season, and hire new staffers just prior to the beginning of the peak season.
- *Visibility to customers.* When a process is directly experienced by customers, its performance level directly impacts customer satisfaction levels, which in turn drives customer turnover and profitability levels. Other processes are relatively invisible to customers, and so errors or inefficiencies in these other areas are less likely to trigger customer revolts. For example, the efficiency of the tellers in a bank allow for customers to be serviced more quickly, so it behooves management to focus considerable attention on teller training. Conversely, the hedging activities of a bank are quite important, but they do not directly impact customers; consequently, management has less incentive to improve the hedging activities than it does the teller operations.

The visibility to customers issue brings up an interesting cost reduction consideration, which is that it pays to reduce the number of processes directly experienced by customers. This is because customer-facing processes can have a strong negative impact on customers if they are not handled properly. For example, a chain of retail stores has dozens of locations, each of which must be fully staffed with appropriately trained personnel who know how to deal with customer demands. In addition, each of these stores needs to be properly supported by a full range of inventory, which calls for a sub-set of processes to anticipate customer demand, order goods before they are sold out, and restock them in the stores. These conditions represent a multitude of opportunities for something to go wrong, annoying a customer. Now consider a web-based store that sells the same products. Customers buy through one site and their orders are processed by a single, highly-trained team of distribution personnel. In the latter case, the company has pared down the visibility of its processes to customers, forcing them to buy from and be serviced by a single company operation. Because of this more focused approach, it is much easier for the web store to deal with customers, which reduces customer turnover and therefore increases its profits.

---

**EXAMPLE**

The Wakatobi Dive Resort in Indonesia is arguably the best scuba diving resort in the world. It achieves this status by focusing on those processes seen by its customers, which include personalized dive master service for each guest, butlers for guests in the larger suites, and flights into the resort on a private plane, which lands at a resort-built airport near Wakatobi. However, the cost of this high level of service is an equally-high price, which the resort must impose in order to pay for the extensive array of processes that are visible to its customers.

**EXAMPLE**

Amazon sells a massive range of products to customers, and is one of the best-known customer-focused companies in the world. And yet, it has very few processes that are actually visible to customers. Orders are placed through its website, so there is no interaction with Amazon employees at this point. Also, orders are routed to the nearest Amazon warehouse, where the orders are filled and sent out for delivery, and typically left at the front doors of customers. Throughout this process, it is quite unlikely that a customer will ever meet an Amazon employee. The only point at which personal interaction is expected is when calling Amazon with complaints. Their customer care representatives are trained in dozens of processes to handle customer issues – but this is still only one process area that deals with customers. Because of the limited amount of customer-facing processes, Amazon is able to focus on high levels of efficiency in its operations, allowing it to drive down costs to a much greater extent than is possible for its retail competitors.

---

To summarize, if the managers of a business want to drive down costs by improving its processes, they can engage in the following activities:

- Minimize the number of processes that are used infrequently, since they are inherently inefficient. Instead, structure the business to perform a smaller number of high-volume transactions that are more amenable to cost reduction.
- Standardize the outputs generated by the business, so that they can be produced in greater volume, which drives down unit costs.
- Structure the business to have more stable and predictable demand levels, so that the business can retain employees and their knowledge of the business, while also maintaining a high level of asset utilization.
- Focus customer contacts on a narrow range of processes, so that management can focus on enhancing the performance of all other processes that customers do not experience.

The preceding summary does not in any way imply that a business should always follow the indicated rules, only that doing so will allow a business to drive down its costs. Thousands of businesses have taken the opposite path in order to provide highly customized service to their customers, but at high price points – it is difficult to provide unique products and services to customers at low prices, while still generating adequate profits.

## Operations Manager Activities

The enhancement of operational activities begins with the operations manager. What does this person do to bring value to a business? The exact nature of the job will depend on the functional area over which the person is given responsibility, but will likely encompass the following four classic management areas:

1. *Planning*. The manager needs to consider the capabilities of the business in comparison to those of its competitors, and decide upon a strategy that gives the firm a good chance of earning above-average profits. This strategy is then used as the basis for a detailed set of plans to be implemented within the operational areas of the business. For example, if the manager of a summer resort in the mountains decides to set up cross-country skiing facilities to expand the operation into a full-year resort, he will need to develop plans for obtaining clearance from the nearby landowners, cutting trails, arranging for snowmaking operations, obtaining rental skis, hiring cross-country ski instructors, and weatherproofing the facilities for winter use.
2. *Organizing*. The manager needs to obtain the financing, assets, and personnel needed to implement the plan, and then develop processes that will utilize these resources in completing the goals stated in the plan. This can be a massive endeavor, so the manager will likely need to assign work to others and grant them the authority to proceed with targeted tasks. For example, the manager who decided to develop a cross-country skiing capability needs to decide which brands of rental skis to carry, how to service them, how to sell them off at the end of the season, what types of equipment rental plans to offer guests, and the price points at which they will be rented.
3. *Leading*. As part of the planning and organizing process, the manager needs to lead the organization. This involves motivating, communicating, guiding, and encouraging employees and anyone else involved in the work. The manager will need to provide coaching assistance to subordinates, and assist them in resolving any problems encountered. For example, the manager of the cross-country skiing operation will need to assist employees in deciding when to use the resort's limited water rights to make snow, as well as to work with staff to develop a third-shift track grooming schedule, so that trails are ready for guests first thing in the morning.
4. *Controlling*. The manager needs to set up a measurement system to ensure that desired results are actually being achieved. If not, he or she will need to take corrective action to ensure that the firm's plans remain on track to be achieved. For example, the manager of the cross-country skiing operation tracks first-year guest totals, and finds that the actual numbers signing up are 20% lower than stated in the plan. He can work with the marketing department to offer next-day discounts to generate a short-term boost in the guest totals.

These management activities are an essential element of operations management, since managers are expected to target specific areas of improvement within company operations, develop plans to achieve these improvements, and follow through on the plans. This is a never-ending process that takes up much of the time of operations managers.

## Summary

Operations management represents both the competitive advantage and primary source of risk for a business. If done well, operations can look like a finely-tuned machine that generates desired outputs exactly when needed, in the exact amounts and the correct configuration, while minimizing the use of resources. If handled poorly, operations can drive a company straight into bankruptcy through inefficient resource usage, uncoordinated processes, and low-quality outputs. Through the remainder of this book, we will examine the tools an operations manager can use to provide a sustained competitive advantage to a business.

# Chapter 2
# Operations Performance

## Introduction

How well are the operations of a business performing? There are many numeric measures for it that can be used to compare the results of operations to historical results, as well as to the reported results of other businesses. We delve into some of these measures throughout the book; however, in this chapter, we go beyond these common analyses to address alternative measures that may be even more important to judging operations performance.

## The Importance of Operations Performance

The operational components of a business likely represent almost all of its asset investment, and probably employs the bulk of its personnel, too. Therefore, the performance of operations is critical to the survival of the business. If operations are well run, a firm will have happier customers, positive cash flows, and much better prospects for the future. If operations are not well run, the company will have ongoing financial problems, unhappy customers, higher employee turnover, and a damaged reputation in the marketplace. Consequently, senior management needs to have the correct measurement systems in place for monitoring and enhancing its operations.

The measurement systems are not just those recommended by the company's accountants – who tend to be excessively focused on financial measurements. Instead, management also needs to consider such factors as product quality and reliability, the time required to ship orders, the time required to respond to customer issues, the time required to repair products in the field, and so forth. This does not mean that such financial measures as product line profitability and the return on assets are not important, only that other measures are needed to gain a more comprehensive view of the performance of operations.

When a company has just been formed, management is much more likely to focus solely on financial metrics in order to ensure the short-term survival of the business. Once the organization is on a more secure financial footing, its measurement orientation tends to expand, to encompass the environmental and social impact of the entity. We address the concept of corporate social responsibility in the next section.

## Corporate Social Responsibility

Corporate social responsibility is the viewpoint that a business should be more aware of its impact on society and the environment. The intent is to deliver positive outcomes

for all stakeholders in the business that result in long-term sustainability, not just a positive return for its shareholders. A *stakeholder* is any person or entity that has an interest in a business or project. Stakeholders have a significant impact on decisions regarding the operations and finances of an organization. Examples of stakeholders are investors, creditors, the government, employees, and the local community.
The actions taken should extend beyond the narrow interests of the firm and go beyond the basic requirements of the law. There are many aspects to corporate social responsibility, which include the following:

- A low carbon footprint, perhaps coupled with actions to clean up the environment [local community impact].
- Employing significant numbers of people from the local community, rather than offshoring work [local community impact].
- Engaging in philanthropy, especially in the local areas where a business has facilities [local community impact].
- Engaging in volunteer events, perhaps by allowing employees to do so on company time [local community impact].
- High service and quality levels [customer impact].
- At least conforming with minimum government regulations, if not performing at a substantially higher level [government impact].
- Dealing with employees in the most ethical manner possible [employee impact].
- Fair pay scale, in relation to local wages [employee impact].
- Minimizing the amount of repetitive work [employee impact].
- Good working conditions [employee impact].
- Long-term orders to enhance the reliability of order placements [supplier impact].
- Early notice of purchasing requirements [supplier impact].
- On-time payments with minimal deductions [supplier impact].
- Return on investment [investor impact].
- Profitability and cash flows generated [investor impact].

Not only does this approach result in an improved environment, it also enhances the image of the organization with its stakeholders, who will then be more likely to support it. Further, people may be more willing to work for such an organization, which enhances the quality of its employees. In addition, having a reputation as a good corporate citizen can enhance an organization's brand image, which may lead to increased sales. And perhaps most importantly, the concept of corporate social responsibility can generate a long-term benefit for a business, and so should be incorporated into its long-term strategy.

When management installs a measurement system that incorporates the concepts of corporate social responsibility, it is much more difficult to judge the overall success of the business, since it now encompasses internal operations, the impact of those operations on the environment, and its impact on the community. In the following sections, we cover these different views of performance.

## The Triple Bottom Line

The triple bottom line refers to the financial, social, and environmental results of a business. Each of these results focuses on a different activity – generating a financial return for investors, having a positive impact on people, and having a positive impact on the planet. The intent behind this manner of reporting is to make corporate managers more aware of their responsibilities outside of the more traditional focus on returns to investors. In short, management needs to recognize that its actions have an impact on society and the environment, which should be incorporated into strategic and tactical decision making.

A difficulty with this more comprehensive method of reporting is the difficulty encountered in quantifying results for the last two areas. For example, how does one measure the sustainability of a business? *Sustainability* focuses on meeting the needs of the present at an acceptable profit level without compromising the ability of future generations to meet their needs. This is a necessarily qualitative measurement, so it is essential to formulate a measurement system and stick to it over many years, in order to create a baseline for measurement in future years. Examples of the actions that may be taken to reduce the environmental impact of a company's operations are:

- Handling of waste material produced by operations
- Making products easy to disassemble for future recycling
- Reducing energy consumption in the materials handling and distribution processes
- Reducing energy consumption in the production process
- Reducing water and air pollution in the production process
- Using recyclable materials in product offerings

Ideally, a company that structures its operations to produce a balanced set of triple bottom line results is in a good position to account for the total cost of running its operations. However, there is a natural conflict built into the triple bottom line concept, which is that the owners of the business are primarily interested in its financial results, since these results directly impact the value of their holdings and the dividends they receive. Thus, given the ownership structure of most businesses, it is likely that financial results will continue to be the most heavily weighted part of the triple bottom line.

**EXAMPLE**

Here is a summary of the triple bottom line report for Unilever, a well-known global corporation, based on its most recent sustainability report:

- *People (social impact).* Unilever has focused on improving health, well-being, and livelihoods for millions. The company has initiatives targeting gender equality, fair wages, and safe working conditions across its supply chain. In 2024, Unilever reported that it empowered over three million women through training and support programs. Additionally, it improved health and hygiene for over a billion people through its products and community outreach.
- *Planet (environmental impact).* Unilever has committed to achieving net-zero emissions by 2039. In 2024, it made significant progress by reducing its carbon footprint by 30% across operations and using 65% of renewable energy. The company also emphasized sustainable sourcing, reporting that 85% of its agricultural raw materials were sustainably sourced. Unilever reduced plastic waste by introducing recyclable and reusable packaging solutions.
- *Profit (economic impact).* Financially, Unilever reported a revenue increase of 7% compared to the previous year, demonstrating that sustainable practices can align with profitability. Cost efficiencies from waste reduction and energy savings contributed positively to its bottom line. Unilever also invested in local communities, supporting smallholder farmers and local suppliers, which strengthened its supply chain resilience.

Overall Impact Unilever's triple bottom line approach reflects a balanced focus on people, planet, and profit, showcasing how sustainability initiatives can drive long-term business success while making a positive impact on society and the environment.

## Operations Performance at the Strategic Level

Most measurement systems used in operations are compiled and acted upon on a daily basis, which means that the vast majority of them are targeted at issues well below the strategic level. However, when designing a measurement system and focusing the attention of front-line managers on specific issues, senior management can make sure that these issues support the strategic direction of the company. For example, if management wants to position the company as a purveyor of extremely high-quality production machinery, it needs to place particular emphasis on manufacturing very high-quality equipment that simply does not break down. It may be less concerned with cost savings within operations than attention to high-quality products, so it designs a measurement system that tracks multiple aspects of product quality, including raw material rejections at the receiving dock, failures at specific points in the production process, and failures reported by customers. Conversely, it does not design measurements that reward the procurement staff for sourcing cheaper parts, since it does not want them buying parts that may have lower quality levels.

As another example, picture a company that has a strategy of becoming the low-cost provider within its industry, so that it can gobble up market share. To do this, management develops an operations performance measurement system that focuses employee attention on sourcing low-cost parts, maximizing the length of production runs (to avoid expensive line changeovers) and automating tasks to minimize the labor component of product costs. In this case, the measurement system is entirely different from the one just described for a quality-focused business, since the strategy is oriented in a different direction.

We have just described how strategic considerations are used to drive which measurements are chosen. This concept can be turned around when it comes to the impact of operations on revenue, where operational enhancements can drive increases in sales – which is a strategic consideration. For example, when operations are designed to provide customers with high-quality products, built to their specifications and within a short turnaround time, these features have a strong tendency to increase revenues, even in the absence of any specific marketing activities. When operations are conducted in this manner, it makes sense to measure those aspects of operations that are increasing sales, such as the time period from order placement to delivery and the number of product failures per million.

Despite the differences in orientation in the preceding examples, any organization needs to give *some* attention to costs. Even when the strategic focus is elsewhere, an organization cannot stay in business if it operates inefficiently. Consequently, even a high-end jewelry store chain that is clearly focused on excellent customer service will still monitor its costs closely and investigate unexpected cost overages. This is essential when the profit percentage is relatively low, since even small cost reductions can have an outsized impact on profit levels. For example, picture a business operating in a competitive industry, where profit margins are 5%. This means that it generates profits of $50,000 on every $1,000,000 of sales. If it can shave expenses down by just $25,000 per $1,000,000 of sales, it can increase its profit percentage by 50%. If management were to instead try to obtain the same $25,000 of additional profit by increasing revenues, it would have to generate an additional $500,000 of sales – which would probably be difficult to achieve in a competitive industry. Thus, close attention to costs is essential, even when the main strategic thrust of a business is elsewhere.

In addition to the cost consideration, how management chooses to use its operations-related assets has a major impact on the required asset investment in the business. When operations can be configured to minimize asset usage, this means that the business requires a smaller overall asset investment, which improves its financial position, allowing senior management to adopt strategies that can employ financial resources elsewhere.

**EXAMPLE**

Grubstake Industries produces trench digging machinery for the construction trade. Some of its production processes require investments in very expensive automated machining tools, which soak up roughly half of the company's total asset investment budget each year. The industrial engineering manager investigates alternatives and finds that a nearby machining shop would be willing to take over the most expensive machining tasks in exchange for a 5% increase in the cost of the parts. Though the production cost would increase, the required production investment would decline so much that management would be able to invest in a new product line, which would generate far more profit than the cost increase associated with the production outsourcing option. Accordingly, the company outsources the targeted production function, sells off the related machining tools, and invests in the new product line.

## Operations Performance at the Operational Level

Since operations are central to the functions of a business, they need to be monitored at a detailed level every day. These measurements are irrespective of the strategic direction of the business, and fall into the same general categories of performance objectives, which are described in the following sub-sections.

### Quality

*Quality* is defined as conformance to customer expectations. This means that the product or service delivered to the customer is exactly as expected or better. Thus, if the customer expectation is for an electric automobile to carry four adults and four pieces of luggage 250 miles per charge, then meeting those expectations is the goal of the manufacturer. Conversely, the customer perceives low quality to be an excessively small vehicle that travels a shorter distance between charges.

Internally, quality also refers to the minimization of errors, so that parts and completed products are manufactured within specifications at all times. By keeping production within specifications, costs can be substantially reduced, since less staff time is needed to correct mistakes, and fewer parts and products must be scrapped. This is a particular benefit when you consider that the more senior staff are usually assigned to the remediation of faulty units, and they are the most expensive employees in the operations area. In short, quality has both an internal and external impact for a business.

**EXAMPLE**

Milford Sound, maker of hi-fi audio equipment, defines quality as producing speakers that provide a well-balanced range of sound at the high, medium, and low audio ranges for its customers. From an internal perspective, Milford maintains tight control over its production process, so that all speakers are manufactured within tight tolerances. Doing so results in only one speaker in 100,000 being rejected for being out of specification. These different aspects of quality show the external and internal benefits of focusing on quality.

**EXAMPLE**

An automobile dealership defines quality as having a spotless showroom, a quiet waiting area for customers, a well-stocked snack area, and maintenance turnaround time that matches the times quoted to customers. From an internal perspective, the dealership defines quality as being able to repair customer vehicles within one day, without needing to deal with any follow-up issues.

---

## Speed

*Speed* is defined as the total elapsed time period between when a customer orders a product and when it is delivered. This performance objective benefits a seller in several ways. First, customers are more likely to buy a product when they know they can receive it in short order; they may even pay a premium for it. And second, receiving a product more quickly may resolve crucial issues for a customer, such as being able to repair equipment more quickly. In the latter case, building a reputation for speed can build quite a loyal following, making customers more likely to return for additional purchases.

Internally, speed in the materials handling and production processes reduces the amount of time that inventory stays on the premises, since the duration of production jobs is reduced. When this is the case, the company has a reduced need to invest funds in working capital, which minimizes its need for financing. In addition, because inventory is held for a shorter period of time, the business reduces its risk of inventory obsolescence. Inventory is routed through the firm so fast that it has no time to become obsolete. Further, since jobs can be completed so quickly, there is less need to forecast very far out into the future, which reduces the risk of making incorrect forecasts for goods that will never be sold.

---

**EXAMPLE**

Ultimate Cabinets makes custom-designed cabinets for the most discerning customers. Early on, it found that existing operations were only able to manufacture custom cabinets with a lead time of eight weeks, which caused problems for contractors who needed the cabinets for short-duration kitchen renovation projects. Ultimate's operations manager overhauled the system by installing a just-in-time system, where the requisite wood products were only ordered from a nearby supplier upon the receipt of customer orders, with delivery expected the following morning. In addition, the number of in-process jobs was reduced, to increase the focus on the remaining jobs, which in turn meant that raw materials spent less time waiting in queues and more time being transformed into finished products. The outcome of these changes was a production process that only required four days to create cabinets. This massive speed improvement greatly increased customer satisfaction with the company, increased the volume of orders, and also cut the company's investment in working capital by 30%.

---

**Dependability**

*Dependability* is defined as delivering products or services on the expected date specified by the customer. This means that products are delivered neither too soon nor too late, but rather within a specific delivery window. This is an especially important performance objective when customers are operating their own just-in-time production systems, since they need inbound deliveries to slot into their production lines within very tightly-defined periods of time. In these situations, dependability can be the single most important performance characteristic for customers.

---

**EXAMPLE**

A South American city that is famous for its long commute times hires a bus company to provide on-time service for its citizens, so that they can commute to and from work within a reasonable amount of time. The government decides to contract with a bus company that offers quite a low bus fare. However, it soon becomes apparent that commuter times are lengthening, because the bus company is saving money by stretching out the service intervals on its buses. This results in much more frequent bus downtime, so that bus service becomes more unreliable.

After the contract with the bus company expires, the government contracts with a much more expensive bus company that guarantees on-time bus service. This turns out to be a hit with commuters, whose commute times decline precipitously. The commuters reward the city government by voting the mayor back into office.

---

In the preceding example, dependability is much more important than the price being charged.

Dependability is also a critical element of the operations *within* a business. When a portion of a process can be relied upon to always deliver its scheduled output on time, this makes it much easier to complete the entire output of the process. For example, when an upstream workstation feeds parts into a bottleneck operation within the production area, those parts *must* arrive on time, or else the unit volume running through the bottleneck will decline, which has a direct impact on the profitability of the business as a whole. In this situation, employees will have to scramble to enhance the output of the upstream operation, which takes them away from their other tasks, where they could have been more productive. In this case, the uncertain dependability of one workstation has a significant negative impact on the business as a whole.

## Flexibility

*Flexibility* is defined as being able to make whatever internal changes are needed to respond effectively to the outside environment within a short period of time. It is needed in the following situations:

- *Broad product mix.* In some industries, individual product sales totals may be relatively small and vary by season, so that the seller must continually alter the mix of items being produced. A highly variable production mix calls for a high degree of flexibility, as equipment is continually reset for different production requirements. Also, the materials management staff needs to order and maintain in stock a broad range of raw materials and components.
- *Short product cycles.* When the competitive environment mandates that products be replaced with upgrades on a regular basis, operations must be able to continually churn out these new products. This requires the ability to continually source new products, retool production lines, and roll them out through a variety of distribution channels.
- *Variable quantity levels.* Some products experience highly variable sales volumes, such as snow shovels towards the end of the year and air conditioning units just prior to the summer months. When this is the case, operations need to scale up drastically to meet demand spikes, and just as quickly drop back down or even stop operations entirely. This calls for the ability to bring in a large number of personnel for short periods of time, as well as to maintain sufficient production capacity to handle peak production loads.

One of the best examples of flexibility is the concept of *mass customization*, where a business is able to produce large volumes of goods while at the same time modifying them to the needs of specific customers. Doing so keeps costs relatively low, while still offering sufficient customization to meet the needs of most customers. This ideal state is achieved by limiting the number of customization choices allowed to customers, so that the most common customization requests can be accommodated, while still allowing the firm to achieve the low costs associated with mass production.

---

**EXAMPLE**

A home builder allows its customers to make a number of modifications to its basic house model. It can do so profitably, because the basic floor plan does not change. Instead, customers are only allowed to make changes to appliances, fixtures, and trim – all of which are added *after* the basic structure has been completed. This allows the home builder to construct homes on a standardized basis until late in the production process, when customizations are introduced.

---

There are instances in which flexibility is less of a concern from the perspective of performance objectives. For example, in a long-term, commoditized industry that has changed little over a long period of time, the only competitive orientation may be on cost. When this is the case, production operations probably involve very long production runs that call for minimal flexibility.

From an internal operational perspective, flexibility can be of great assistance when there is a problem somewhere in operations, because the staff is more capable of clustering on and resolving the issue within a short period of time. This allows operations to return to normal quickly, so that the normal production schedule can be followed.

---

**EXAMPLE**

The International Widget company suffers a failure in one of its widget stamping machines. Spare parts are being flown in, but the machine will be down for at least two days, meaning that the company will fall seriously behind on one of its customer orders. Fortunately, management has foreseen this problem and held two older stamping machines in reserve, rather than selling them off when they became too inefficient for regular operations a few years ago. Further, four people in the paint shop were cross-trained on stamping machine operations as part of the company's ongoing cross-training program. By bringing the reserve machines online and staffing them with the backup employees, International Widget has enough flexibility to overcome the machine failure problem.

---

## Cost

Our final performance objective is *cost*, which is the expenditure required to create and sell products and services. It is an especially important consideration in industries where products are not easily differentiated, so that customers purchase based primarily on price.

The areas in which costs can be driven down will vary, depending on the type of business. For example, in a labor-intensive operation, the focus would be on minimizing the amount of labor by implementing procedural efficiencies, maximizing employee time on production activities, and implementing automation when it makes sense to do so. Conversely, in a business where the main cost is raw materials, the cost-saving focus shifts to reducing transport costs, minimizing scrap and spoilage, and using concentrated purchasing to obtain volume discounts from suppliers.

The other performance objectives usually have an ancillary effect on cost. For example, high quality reduces the error rate, and therefore the amount of labor expense needed to fix errors. Similarly, having highly flexible operations allows a business to direct its personnel more rapidly toward problem areas, so that operational difficulties can be fixed at low cost. For a third example, operations with fast cycle times require less on-hand inventory, so the financing cost of working capital is reduced.

## Operations Performance Measurements

The essential feedback loop for operations management is to have a system of measurements in place that monitors the most crucial activities. These measurement outcomes can then be compared to historical results, standards, or the benchmark results of best-in-class businesses to pinpoint those areas within operations that are most in need of an upgrade. The measurements chosen should be linked to the topics already addressed in this chapter, which include quality, speed, dependability, flexibility, cost, social impact, and environmental impact.

There are hundreds of possible measurements that may be applied to operations, some of which are specific to certain industries. In the following sub-sections, we focus on a small number of operations performance measurements that can be applied to most organizations.

Ideally, an operations manager will use a small number of core measurements that do not change, as well as a set of other measurements that are targeted at specific problem areas. Once those areas have been resolved, they can be replaced by other measurements targeted at dealing with a new set of problem areas. When settling upon the ideal cluster of measurements, management will want to have at least a few that trace back to the corporate strategy, to ensure that operations are being improved in areas that will support the strategic direction of the business.

### Defects per Unit

Defects per unit (DPU) is the number of defects divided by the number of products, and is considered the universal measure of quality. Thus, if there are 50 defects in 1,000 units produced, then the defects per unit will be 0.05.

An essential element in any calculation of defects per unit is what constitutes a defect. Merely changing the definition of a defect can have a profound impact on the reported outcome. For example, if a drilled hole has to be drilled with an accuracy of 1/1000$^{th}$ of an inch, then the DPU may be quite high, at 0.20. However, if some variation is allowable, where the drilling accuracy is acceptable with an accuracy of 1/10$^{th}$ of an inch, then the DPU declines to just 0.001. The latter figure may very well be correct, as long as the resulting variability in the drilled hole is still acceptable within the production process.

DPU is a measure of what is wrong with a process; a high DPU is a strong indicator that a process requires significant corrective action. When variations and defects have been reduced, customer satisfaction is increased, which ultimately results in an improved profit number.

### Throughput

An excellent measure of operational speed is *throughput*, which is the number of units that pass through a process during a period of time. For example, if 800 units can be produced during an eight-hour shift, then the production process generates throughput of 100 units per hour.

Throughput can be increased by enhancing the productivity of the bottleneck operation that is constraining production. For example, an additional machine can be purchased, or overtime can be authorized in order to run a machine for an extra shift. The key point is to focus attention on the productivity of the *bottleneck* operation. If other operations are improved, the overall throughput of the system will not increase, since the bottleneck operation has not been enhanced. This means that the key focus of investment in operations should be on the bottleneck, not other operations.

For financial analysis, throughput can be increased by altering the mix of products being produced, to increase the priority on those products that have the highest throughput per minute of time required at the constrained resource. If a product has a smaller amount of throughput per minute, it can instead be routed to a third party for processing, rather than interfering with the bottleneck operation. As long as some positive throughput is gained by outsourcing, the result is an increased overall level of throughput for the company as a whole.

### Mean Time between Failures

A good measure of dependability is mean time between failures (MTBF), which measures the average time that equipment is operating between breakdowns or stoppages. It can be used to help management understand the availability of equipment, which can be a critical issue when there are process reliability issues. It can be used to plan for contingencies that require the repair of key equipment items, especially equipment associated with the bottleneck operation.

To calculate MTBF, divide the total time a piece of equipment has been running during the measurement period by the number of breakdowns that have occurred during that period. For example, a mechanical sorter is designed to operate for 10 hours per day. The sorter breaks down after seven days of operation. The MTBF in this case is 70 hours, which is calculated as follows:

(10 hours per day × 7 days) ÷ 1 breakdown = 70 hours

The calculation is more complex when multiple breakdowns occur. For example, the same mechanical sorter breaks down twice in a 7-day period. The first breakdown occurred 20 hours from the start time, and took two hours to repair. The second breakdown occurred 40 hours from the start time and took two hours to repair before it was again operating normally. This means that the total uptime period is the sum of 20 hours of uptime, followed by 18 hours of uptime, followed by 28 hours of uptime. Given this information, the MTBF calculation is:

(20 hours + 18 hours + 28 hours) ÷ 2 breakdowns = 33 hours MTBF

By taking steps to increase MTBF, one can increase the uptime of equipment. This is especially important for equipment that must be in continuous operation. Operations managers can use periodic maintenance checks and preventive maintenance to minimize the number of failures.

### Time to Market

A representative measure of flexibility is time to market (TTM). This is the period of time between when the first ideas are formed for a new product and when it is eventually made available to consumers. It is especially important in industries where products are outmoded quickly. Time to market is also a valuable measurement for maintaining consistent product design schedules, so that products are rolled out at a predictable pace. TTM is useful for maintaining control over costs, since shorter projects generally tend to absorb fewer costs.

There is no standard measurement for TTM, since it can be difficult to determine the starting date for the measurement period. It may be the date when an idea is initially formulated, or when it is approved for development, or when it is fully funded, or when the assigned development team starts work. There may be months or even years between initial idea formulation and project staffing, so these differences are important. This is also a problem on the back end of a development project, though the range of possible values is smaller. The ending date may be when engineering passes the design to manufacturing, or when the first copy is shipped, or when it is first bought by a customer. The best approach may be to adopt whichever start and stop dates are being most commonly used within the industry, so that the firm's TTM results can be compared to the reported results of competitors.

---

**EXAMPLE**

Zara has mastered the time to market concept by reducing the typical fashion industry lead time of 6-12 months to just 2-4 weeks. It does so with the following techniques:

- *Rapid design and production.* Zara's design team continuously monitors fashion trends and customer preferences. When a new trend is identified, their designers quickly create new items. Using a streamlined production process, Zara can move from design to finished product in as little as two weeks.
- *In-house manufacturing.* Unlike many competitors who outsource production to save costs, Zara keeps a significant portion of its manufacturing close to its headquarters in Spain. This allows for faster turnaround times and more control over the supply chain.
- *Efficient logistics.* Zara's logistics network is optimized for speed. Their central distribution center in Spain can ship new items to stores worldwide twice a week, ensuring that fresh products hit the shelves quickly.

For example, when a new fashion trend was spotted at a major fashion show in Paris, Zara's team quickly designed similar items and had them available in stores within three weeks. This rapid response not only captured customer interest while the trend was hot but also minimized unsold inventory.

By mastering time to market, Zara maintains customer excitement, ensures that stores always have the latest trends, and achieves higher sales with fewer markdowns. This strategy has been a key factor in making it one of the largest fashion retailers globally.

---

## Productivity

One of the most essential performance measurements is *productivity*, which is used to measure the efficiency of an individual or process. To calculate productivity, divide total output by total costs consumed, where output is usually defined as revenue.

Productivity is commonly measured on a trend line, to see if the cumulative impact of ongoing training and process improvements are enhancing the ability of a person or business to generate greater output at the same or a reduced cost. There are many ways to enhance productivity. Here are several possibilities:

- Automation
- Employee empowerment to make more decisions at the local level
- Employee training
- Outsourcing to lower-cost providers
- Process improvements
- Product redesigns to make products easier to manufacture

These productivity improvements may focus on reducing costs, increasing output, or a combination of the two. Thus, outsourcing to lower-cost providers enhances productivity through cost reduction, while product redesigns to make them easier to manufacture enhances productivity through increasing output. Other examples are:

- A computer manufacturer shifts its inbound call center to India, in order to increase productivity by reducing costs.
- An automobile manufacturer sets up a two-tiered pay structure that pays lower wages to new employees, in order to increase productivity by reducing costs.
- A contract manufacturer opens up a third shift in order to increase productivity by increasing the volume of units produced from its facility.
- A manufacturer invests in high-speed robots in order to increase productivity by expanding the number of units produced.

The productivity concept may be refined down to a comparison of a single input and a single output, rather than measuring it for operations as a whole. For example, a refrigerator production facility could compare the number of refrigerators produced to the number of employees. Or, an airplane manufacturer could measure the number of airplanes produced to the number of employees. This *single-factor productivity* measurement is usually focused on the primary inputs and outputs of a business. Thus, it would make little sense for an oil refinery to measure productivity by comparing the amount of oil produced to headcount, since its main input is the asset investment in the refinery.

---

**EXAMPLE**

The Hail Correction Institute repairs hail damage to cars. It typically repairs 400 dents per week. Each of its seven employees works 40 hours per week. The company's total labor expense per week is $7,680, and its total overhead expense is $1,500 per week. The Institute's labor productivity (a single-factor productivity measure) is calculated as follows:

400 dents ÷ 280 total hours worked = 1.43 dents fixed per hour

The multi-factor productivity of the Institute is calculated as follows:

400 dents ÷ ($7,680 labor cost + $1,500 overhead cost) = 0.044 dents per dollar expended

---

### Return on Invested Capital

The return on invested capital compares a firm's return on capital to its cost of capital. If the comparison yields a positive number that exceeds the current inflation rate, this means that the firm is doing a good job of allocating its funds to operations that yield a reasonable return. Conversely, if the return on invested capital is negative, this means that the company is destroying its own capital. A business that can consistently generate a positive return on invested capital is well-managed and so is more likely to be a reasonable investment choice for an investor. The return on invested capital is calculated as follows:

(Net income – dividends) ÷ sum of all debt and equity = Return on invested capital

The calculation should be based on the operating results of a business, excluding the financial effects of all one-time or unusual events. This approach yields a truer picture of the ability of a firm to profitably invest funds in its operations.

This calculation is most important in industries that require a large amount of capital spending, such as oil refineries. In a business that requires little capital spending, such as a services business, the calculation is not a critical issue when evaluating an organization's performance.

---

**EXAMPLE**

The operations manager of the Corregidor Manufacturing Company wants to calculate the return on invested capital for the business. He knows that the firm's net income for the last year was $1 million, it paid out a dividend of $200,000, and it has debt of $7 million and equity of $4 million. This results in the following return on invested capital calculation:

($1 million net income - $200,000 dividend) ÷ ($7 million debt + $4 million equity)

= 10.9% return on invested capital

---

## The Measurement Tradeoff

One concern to consider when setting up a measurement system is that performance improvements in one area may reduce performance in another area. For example, if the target is to reduce raw material purchasing costs, this is usually done by promising suppliers to purchase in greater volumes in order to obtain volume discounts. However, doing so increases the inventory investment, which requires a larger amount of working capital. Similarly, installing a just-in-time production system will increase inventory turnover, but may increase delivery charges from suppliers, who now have to make daily deliveries to the company, rather than the more infrequent deliveries that had previously been the case. Consequently, management has to decide how it chooses to balance measurements that compete with each other. This will require management to trade off improvements in some areas for performance declines in other areas.

## The Efficiency vs. Variety Tradeoff

Another concern when developing a measurement system is to decide upon the level of product or service variety being offered, since more variety causes an increase in operations complexity, which in turn causes efficiency levels to decline. This is a strategic choice. Every time there is a question about whether to increase or reduce the number of products being produced, management needs to evaluate what this change will do to operations complexity, and therefore the impact on efficiency levels. Once this expectation has been set, management will be in a better position to evaluate the results of its measurement system. For example, if a new product line is added, management needs to understand that this added complexity may have a negative impact on such measures as throughput time, the return on invested capital, and productivity.

## The Efficiency vs. Customer Service Tradeoff

Another issue for an operations manager to consider is whether to emphasize the efficiency of operations or the level of customer service provided. For example, a grocery store manager may choose to only staff a single checkout counter. Doing so reduces the labor cost of the checkout operation, but also worsens customer service, since customers may be queued up in front of that checkout counter for a prolonged period of time. Conversely, all checkout counters could be staffed, which massively shortens customer wait times, but which also drastically reduces staff efficiency. The store manager will probably need to decide how large a customer queue is acceptable (such as two people in front of a checkout counter) before opening another counter with a backup staff person whose primary responsibility is in a different part of the store. The likely outcome is that the measurements for staff efficiency and customer wait times will need to be balanced against each other, where the optimal outcome is located within a relatively narrow performance range.

## Summary

We have shown in this chapter that the measurement of operations performance is a balancing act, where the selection of one area for a targeted improvement may have a negative impact on performance in a different area. Also, management needs to understand that measurements should support the strategic direction of the business, while also focusing on the key performance objectives of quality, speed, dependability, flexibility, and cost. This means that the measurements chosen should address many different aspects of operations.

For more measurement opportunities pertaining to operations, see the author's *Business Ratios Guidebook* book and *Constraint Management* book.

# Chapter 3
# Operations Strategy

## Introduction

The purpose of a firm's operations over the long haul is to provide it with a strategic advantage. This means that every element of operations must be properly aligned with the stated strategy of the business. This is a critical issue, since the tactical responses of management to day-to-day events will tend to jerk the focus of operations around in a relatively random manner, giving the company no long-term strategic posture. Consequently, operations managers need to have a firm grasp of the organization's strategy, along with a set of decision guidelines to follow that support the strategy. They can then consult the guidelines whenever making decisions, so that tactical choices are in approximate alignment with what senior management wants to do over the long term.

In this chapter, we cover the forces that impact the formulation of operations strategy, as well as how strategy is developed and modified.

## The Nature of Strategy

*Strategy* is a plan of action that is targeted at achieving a major aim. Strategic plans tend to be longer-term, and may extend multiple years into the future, depending on the nature of the business. For example, the strategic plan for a power company may need to extend a decade into the future, since its plans must encompass the development of electricity-generating facilities and an electrical grid for its customers. Conversely, the strategic plan for a company situated in an entirely new industry may not extend more than one year, since the market is still developing and could branch off in unexpected directions. Examples of several highly simplified strategies are:

- *Retail chain*. To develop an online store, serviced by regional warehouses that can deliver to any customer in North America within two days.
- *Automobile manufacturer*. To enter the sport utility vehicle market with a mid-sized offering within three years, to be sold in the European and Asian markets.
- *Hotel operator*. To double the number of properties within ten years, focusing primarily on vacation destinations around the world.
- *Utility company*. To increase the proportion of renewable energy sources to 40% of the total amount of electricity provided within 10 years.

When properly formulated, strategy is not as simple as the examples we just stated. It should involve a comprehensive pattern of decision making that is applied to every part of a business, so that even the most minute aspects of operations are working in concert with the general strategic direction of the organization.

## Operations Strategy

Operations strategy is that portion of the overall corporate strategy that is designed to enhance operational capabilities in support of the overall strategy. When fulfilled properly, operations strategy should be a key driver of the competitive advantage of a firm. The degree of success in formulating and implementing operations strategy can be described as being along the following continuum:

1. *Currently negative.* Current operations harm the organization. Products and services are provided late or incorrectly, and tend to drive away customers. In this situation, the best operations strategy is to avoid making mistakes, so that operations do not harm the business.
2. *Benchmarking.* The company is comparing its operations metrics against those of benchmark companies, in an effort to implement best practices. The objective is to raise performance levels to the point where operations are comparable to those of competitors. At this level, operations are at least not giving customers a reason to go to competitors.
3. *Market leading.* Operations have improved to the point where they are the best in the industry. At this point, operational performance is clearly supporting the strategic direction of the company.
4. *Strategic foundation.* Operations have improved to such an extent that they form the foundation for the company's overall strategy. At this level, competitors view the company as being so innovative and proactive in implementing new services that it is clearly the business to beat in its industry.

An alternative view of the preceding performance continuum is that operations are constantly struggling to meet the demands of the market, which are constantly changing, and so it can never be expected to perform so well that it actually leads corporate strategy. This viewpoint suggests that operations can never be the *foundation* for a company's strategy. Instead, its best hope is to advance beyond having a complete suite of best practices, which makes it no worse than any of its competitors. This viewpoint assumes that a firm's marketing and new product development processes are the true drivers of strategy.

The view that operations can never be a leading driver of strategy is suspect, for several reasons. First, the operations area is comprised of a multitude of processes, all of which can be tweaked to enhance their performance; in total, this can result in an overwhelming competitive advantage for a business in terms of its quality, speed, dependability, flexibility, and cost that is quite difficult to replicate. And second, in markets where there is not a great deal of product or marketing innovation, operations may be the only advantage that a business has over its competitors.

## Top-Down Alignment of Operations Strategy

The most common method used to develop strategy for operations is for the senior management group to develop the corporate strategy based on outside conditions. This is done via a review of competitor positions, expected regulatory and technological changes, and so forth. Based on this analysis, senior management decides how to orient the business and allocate funds between the various business units. Under this approach to strategy development, operations managers are then told to develop their own strategies that support the overall corporate strategy, including a complete suite of plans and budgets. At this point, the support functions, such as accounting, human resources, and information technology, develop their own plans to support the plans developed by operations. In short, this hierarchical approach is initiated at the top of the organization and then trickles down through the business. Under this approach, the operations area is charged with converting senior management's strategy into a set of plans that can reasonably be expected to be implemented.

---

**EXAMPLE**

The senior management team of International Envelope, Inc. decides that there is a rich opportunity for the company to become the low-cost envelope producer, allowing it to grab large chunks of market share and drive competitors out of the market. This strategy is presented to the operations manager, who needs to devise plans for acquiring high-volume envelope production machinery, including opening production plants around the country and in other countries (to shorten delivery times and therefore delivery costs). This will result in massive excess capacity in the short run and a decline in profits, but these issues are considered secondary to the strategy of achieving market dominance.

If the senior management team had instead devised a strategy of narrowing the focus of the business to a small, highly-profitable niche for odd-sized envelopes, the operations manager would instead need to devise plans for selling off all equipment *not* associated with odd-sized envelopes and potentially shrinking the number of production plants to just ones adjacent to the customers needing these envelopes.

---

When used properly, the operations manager can give feedback to senior management regarding the areas in which the corporate plan may be difficult to implement. This iterative loop can be used several times, to make it easier for the final version of the corporate strategy to be translated into a practical set of operations plans.

## Alignment of Operations Strategy with Market Conditions

A different perspective on the development of an operations strategy is to base it on the intended market position of a business, rather than the strategic direction set by senior management (as was the case in the last section). This approach can work well, since it focuses directly on the needs of customers. Operations planning should be in alignment with the needs of the firm's most important customers. Thus, if a key customer needs very rapid deliveries, the operations plan should be focused on just-in-time production or large finished goods inventories that can be used to deliver complete orders on short notice. Or, if customers demand customized solutions, then the operations plan should provide for a high degree of flexibility, so that product designs and production operations can be adjusted on the fly.

When the business model of an organization depends on being able to win a number of one-time orders (as is frequently the case with large capital projects), it can make sense to focus the operations strategy on meeting the threshold purchasing requirements of customers, and in particular on those few characteristics that will assuredly win customer orders. For example, if a government requires that a construction contractor bidding on a contract have documented capabilities in plumbing installations, then the operations plan needs to ensure that the requisite expertise is available, such as having five master plumbers on staff. This can be considered a threshold requirement. Or, if a key requirement for winning a government bid is to have completed at least three housing projects on a military base within the past three years, then the operations plan needs to obtain such contracts, even if doing so will incur a loss for the business. By focusing on those specific areas that are more likely to gain sales, the operations manager can also ignore those areas that are *least* likely to ensure sales success.

Another way to adjust operations to match the market perspective is to tailor operations to gain sales in specific market segments. For example, if a company were targeted at the governmental fire suppression market, it could develop fire trucks with varying features to sell to local fire stations, while offering vehicle customizations to meet local needs (such as urban versus rural fire departments). If the key qualifiers for making sales into these markets are price and time to delivery, then the operations manager could set up plans targeted at keeping costs low and delivering fire trucks within a short period of time.

Yet another way to configure operations from a market perspective is to tailor operations to maximize sales and (especially) profits from the different phases in the life cycles of its products. The *product life cycle* refers to the different stages that a product passes through over time. There are four stages in this cycle, which are:

1. *Introduction phase.* In this phase, a business is trying to build market acceptance for a new product. The market is poorly understood and it is not certain that customers will like the features being offered, so operations needs to be able to reconfigure products on short notice that incorporate different features, until the most acceptable product configuration is achieved.
2. *Growth stage.* If the company is able to gain market acceptance for a new product, it must contend with rapid growth in customer demand. The obvious impact on operations is the need to meet that demand by bringing more capacity on line, while maintaining high quality levels. Competing products are

likely to appear at this stage, so it is also important for operations to drive down costs, so that the company can meet the price points being offered by competitors while still maintaining healthy profits. It is also likely that additional versions of the product will be released in order to build out a complete product line, which increases the level of complexity that operations personnel must contend with.

3. *Maturity stage.* Following the initial growth phase, demand will eventually level off. There are many competitors in this phase, so the primary task is to defend market share. This is done by differentiating based on market features, which tends to increase the complexity of operations. Also, there is ongoing, downward pressure on product prices, which will call for increased attention to cost reductions in order to maintain adequate profit margins.
4. *Decline stage.* Demand for the company's original products will eventually decline. When this happens, competitors will increasingly compete based on price, which will drive down profits across the industry. In this situation, operations will need to focus increased attention on cost reductions and productivity improvements, in order to maintain profits at a reasonable level. The operations manager will also need to gradually scale back the related production capacity as sales levels decline. Further, it will be necessary to gradually withdraw the product from some distribution channels, focusing on those remaining niches where the product still generates an adequate profit. Eventually, the operations manager will need to conduct an orderly product termination, selling off excess inventory and shutting down production lines in the most cost-effective manner.

The duration of a product life cycle depends on the market. In some cases, a product may last for decades, while other products may have a life span of less than a year.

## Alignment of Operations Strategy with Operational Experience

An alternative approach is to develop operations strategy based on information provided by the front-line staff of the company, such as its sales personnel and customer service department, who are constantly talking to customers and so can provide the most up-to-date market information. A business that uses this bottom-up approach may still develop a "corporate level" strategy, but it is one which really just formalizes the recommendations made by front-line employees. In this situation, senior management takes the advice of employees lower in the organizational hierarchy to decide where to allocate resources most effectively. In this case, operations planning tends to be more short-range to medium-range, based on the changes recommended by employees. This approach is more likely to result in changes to strategy on short notice as market conditions change, which means that operations planning also tends to span a relatively short period of time.

This bottom-up approach to strategy development is more likely to result in small niche strategies to take advantage of smaller opportunities in the marketplace that have been spotted by employees, rather than a broad-based change in direction. This means that the overall corporate strategy can be somewhat muddled-looking, though it may also result in quite satisfactory profits.

## Alignment of Operations Strategy with Internal Capabilities

As noted earlier, it is possible that operations can provide the primary source of strategic advantage for a business. In this case, management deliberately cultivates operations processes and resources in order to enhance specific capabilities. Ideally, this focus should be on core competencies. A *core competency* is a singular advantage that distinguishes the performance of an organization. It should be exploited to give an organization a competitive advantage in serving its customers; doing so gives an entity the ability to generate an above-average profit over the long term. Such a competency could, for example, involve the skill level of employees, a technical capability, or a unique process flow. When core competencies are properly built into a marketing campaign to improve brand recognition, customers are more likely to pay above-average amounts for a company's products and services.

Management should be well aware of the core competencies of a business, and continually strive to protect and enhance them. A management team that is unaware of core competencies is more likely to unknowingly allow them to lapse over time. Conversely, it may not make sense for management to waste time concentrating its efforts on areas of the business that are not core competencies; in such cases, it can make sense to outsource functional areas or processes to third parties.

Here are several examples of core competencies:

- The ability to manufacture custom products to customer specifications within a short period of time.
- The ability to deliver goods to customers on short notice and to difficult-to-reach locations.
- The ability to conduct field repairs within a short period of time at any customer location.
- The ability to constantly replace existing products with enhanced replacement products.
- A production process that massively reduces the number of flaws in finished goods.

These core competencies may be based on an underlying factor, such as an organizational structure that allows for the use of multi-functional teams to develop new products, or the use of process experts to continually enhance targeted processes. These underlying factors may not be readily apparent to the casual observer, but are essential to the conduct of operations.

By focusing on core competencies, a business is essentially building barriers to imitation, because it is so difficult for new market entrants to replicate these competencies.

When developing a set of core competencies, it is equally important to have a firm knowledge of operational constraints. If there are bottlenecks within any operations process, they represent a clear limitation on the ability of the company to increase its sales. Thus, even if management wants to target a specific market niche by enhancing certain competencies, its efforts will fail unless all related constraints can be overcome. For example, if a book printer wants to develop a new line of glue-bound "perfect" paperback books, it will not be able to do so if its existing printing facility is already operating at capacity. Instead, it will need to either acquire an expensive new printing facility, increase the capacity of the existing facility, or outsource the work.

Another area to consider, beyond core competencies and constraints, is the unique resources available to a firm. When a company has access to resources that are not available to competitors, this can represent a powerful competitive advantage. For example, a maker of Styrofoam cups is able to produce them at a lower cost than anyone else, because it has built proprietary manufacturing equipment and protected the equipment with patents. Or, a company owns the rights to a mine that produces a "rare earth" mineral, for which there are only three mines in the world; it can retain all mineral production for its own use, so that competitors have to bid for this scarce resource from the other two mines. As a final example, a chip fabricator has spent billions of dollars building a fabrication plant that can produce eight-nanometer chips, and has developed the infrastructure needed to efficiently produce the chips. It is extremely difficult for competitors without the requisite experience, infrastructure, or financial resources to build a comparable plant, so the company has a resource that is limited to only a few similar plants anywhere in the world.

In short, the development of core competencies and resources, coupled with a detailed knowledge of operational constraints, can be a powerful driver of operations-based strategy.

## Strategy Integration

While any one of the preceding strategic formulation tools can result in an adequate strategic plan for operations, the most refined approach is to compare them for commonalities and differences, as well as to compare them to customer requirements and the expected competitive positions of competitors. This results in several iterations of strategy formulation, hopefully resulting in a plan that will provide the best possible competitive advantage to a business.

A good tool for reconciling the market conditions and internal capabilities strategic viewpoints is the operations strategy matrix, which lays out the standard operations performance objectives down the left side, with priorities indicated for each objective, based on the market conditions viewpoint. Then a set of strategy decisions are stated in the row across from each objective, based on the internal capabilities of the firm. This layout is useful for clarifying how well a business is able to use its internal capabilities to meet the objectives indicated by its market research. A sample matrix appears in the following example.

---

**EXAMPLE**

Nuclear Containment, Inc. builds containment vessels for a new breed of fusion power plant. These vessels are extremely strong titanium shells intended for spherical tokamak fusion reactors. It is essential for these containment vessels to be constructed perfectly, with very tight tolerances, which means that quality and dependability are the most important criteria in the marketplace. These market requirements, along with the operational capabilities of the company, are noted in the following table. When there are blank cells in the matrix, it indicates that priority levels are too low to make it worthwhile to consider any strategic improvements.

| Performance Objective | Market Importance | Operations-Based Strategy | |
|---|---|---|---|
| Quality | High | Laser-based tolerance measurement | 3-D titanium printing |
| Speed | Low | Team-based design approach | |
| Dependability | High | Sonic resonance analysis of completed vessels | Pilot testing on miniaturized models |
| Flexibility | Low | Iterative design approach | |
| Cost | Medium | Target costing teams | Titanium blending with vanadium and aluminum |

---

The contents of this matrix can be adjusted to arrive at a reasonable degree of alignment between the externally-derived and internally-based sources of strategy development. When the market clearly demands a high level of performance in one or more of the objective areas, then management will need to focus its attention on enhancing internal capabilities to support those objectives. The shifting of resources to support targeted internal capabilities will necessarily draw resources away from those internal capabilities that are targeted at objectives to which the market is assigning a low level of importance.

When management upgrades operational capabilities to support the strategic alignments indicated by this matrix, the company will be in a good position to at least maintain its market share, if not increase it.

Another visual tool for judging a proposed strategy is the importance/performance scale, which plots the importance of an improvement priority on a scale, alongside its current performance rating. This approach is useful for quickly determining which improvements are well behind expectations, and so are in the most need of a priority fix. The following exhibit contains a sample importance/performance scale for a set of improvement priorities for a company that manufactures activewear clothing. In the example, it is apparent that the company is in need of serious performance improvements in its usage of four-way stretch fabrics, as well as in its use of multi-colored print designs, since the current performance ratings in these two areas are well behind their associated importance ratings.

**Sample Importance/Performance Scale**

| Planned Improvement | 1 | 2 | 3 | 4 | 5 |
|---|---|---|---|---|---|
| Four-way stretch fabric usage | | | o | | × |
| Integration of body mapping technology | × | o | | | |
| Use of digital printing | o | × | | | |
| Use of multi-color print designs | | o | | | × |
| Use of natural blends | | o | × | | |

Key: × = Importance rating       o = Current performance rating

Another way to judge a strategy is to examine how the company's resulting capabilities will match those expected of competitors during the period covered by the strategic plan. Competitors will also be enacting their own strategic plans, so management uses its contacts and publicly-available information to estimate where capabilities will be within the industry over the next few years. Management can then evaluate its initial drafts of the strategic plan to see if planned operational enhancements will be behind, comparable to, or in advance of those of competitors over the next few years. This analysis may call for additional adjustments to the plan to concentrate resources on the areas that appear to be most competitively critical in the future.

A further way to judge a strategic plan is to analyze those operational capabilities that are clearly behind those of competitors, to see if this deficiency is really a problem. In many cases, customers do not put much value on one or more of the performance objectives, which allows management to deliberately starve these operational components of resources, so that they can be more profitably applied elsewhere. For example, customers may not have a strong interest in being able to obtain customized products, so the business can minimize this capability in favor of driving down costs, which is of more interest to customers.

The inverse of the last point is to review resource allocations to see if the firm's capabilities are excessive in certain areas. For example, it may be that the firm has developed an astonishing ability to deliver orders with far greater speed than its competitors, within one hour of order placement. However, if customers do not care about speed once deliveries are being made within one day of order placement, then it is possible that resources need to be shifted away from this operational capability and toward other performance objectives that are more important to customers.

## Summary

An operations strategy should be closely tied to the overall goals and objectives of a business. To do this, one should examine whether the operations strategy addresses all important issues at the corporate level, whether the actions to be taken support each other, and whether the most critical issues have been targeted and are receiving an adequate amount of resources. Answering these questions will likely require several iterations of the planning process, but will result in a highly effective operations strategy.

# Chapter 4
# Product and Service Innovation

## Introduction

If a business wants to generate above-average profits, then one of its most critical tools for doing so is being able to develop a system of product and service innovation. Doing so can yield sustainable revenue and cost advantages, which can then be used to engage in further innovation to extend the positive effects. Operations managers are not directly responsible for product and service innovation (that usually falls on the engineering manager), but they are usually asked to be involved in the process, if only to provide advice regarding how proposed innovations can be manufactured or provided in some other way to customers.

In this chapter, we examine how to structure a system of innovation, where to concentrate the firm's efforts to achieve better results, and how to deal with a number of additional factors that can either enhance or torpedo the outcome.

## Innovation Theory

The underlying concept behind the need to engage in innovation is to get better-performing and less-expensive goods and services into the hands of customers. This can be accomplished by a combination of changes in product design, the manufacturing process, and the value chain. This concept is derived from three assumptions, which are:

- *Unmet needs*. We assume that consumers have unmet needs that are waiting for a solution. Businesses need to constantly invest in innovation to discover these needs.
- *Value-based competition*. Businesses compete with each other based on the value of their offerings to consumers, where value is the ratio of product quality to price. Thus, innovation is needed to continually increase the level of value being offered. The usual outcome is either a commitment to offer the lowest price (with innovations targeted at cost reductions), or develop a high level of product quality (with innovations targeted at product features).
- *Business partner engagement*. In order to discover unmet needs and deliver value to consumers, a business needs to develop relationships with its business partners to conduct research, develop products, source parts, produce goods, distribute them, and provide after-market servicing. This requires varying degrees of trust-building between the parties, which will change over time as the organization's product mix evolves.

A potential problem with this classic view of innovation is that companies tend to pursue the best opportunities first, so that later innovation efforts are targeted at issues that are more likely to yield diminishing returns. This means that, *if* everyone is equally competent at the innovation process, then their pursuit of declining returns should result in approximate parity over the long term. There are multiple ways out of this trap, which are:

- *Pursue new markets*. Companies can pursue entirely new markets where there is no competition, allowing them to generate significant returns for long periods of time.
- *Refine innovation*. Not all companies are equally good at innovation. Some do not engage in it at all, while others have flawed processes. Consequently, a highly-refined and actively-supported process can deliver a long-term advantage to a business.
- *Embed with customers*. The company can provide a service so perfectly targeted at customers that they see no reason to switch their allegiance elsewhere, no matter how innovative the competition may be. This approach requires a business to develop deep relationships with its customers; this will likely result in a high level of information sharing with them, giving the company in-depth insights into what they need.
- *Create new value*. In most industries, innovation tends to cluster around specific areas, such as process improvements in the oil and gas industry. This tends to result in everyone coming up with the same innovations, which results in no competitive advantage. Instead, the company can come up with new areas in which to compete, such as when Cirque du Soleil altered the traditional circus away from animal acts and toward acrobatic feats. These fundamental shifts in how to perceive a market can result in significantly enhanced odds of generating unusually high returns.

The preceding trap avoidance recommendations are especially important when you consider that, in many established markets, the amount of revenue to be gained from each incremental innovation improvement tends to decline, because product cycles are shortening, leaving companies with less time in which to recoup their costs before the next iteration of products hits the market. Hence, the need to improve the innovation process.

## Innovation Strategy

An organization's strategy can be thought of as a commitment to achieving a specific goal. The best strategies are designed to align the activities of each functional area of a business toward reaching the targeted goal. While there might be a great deal of attention paid to integrating the efforts of the traditional business areas in order to push a strategy forward, this is rarely the case with innovation. Instead, innovation tends to produce an assortment of unrelated best practices that have a modest impact on operations throughout the business. These improvements rarely have a direct impact on the corporate strategy, since there was never any intent for them to do so.

A better approach is to devise a more structured approach to innovation, where there is a coherent set of processes in place that mandate the areas in which the company is especially interested in looking for innovations, and the funding processes used to ensure that the best alternatives are provided with sufficient resources. Having such a system in place is especially important when there is limited funding available, since management needs to pick which innovation opportunities to provide with funding, where those decisions are based on how each one relates to the corporate strategy.

It can be useful to identify the areas in which business innovation can occur, in order to direct management's thinking into those areas where innovation will be most beneficial to the business. This approach is also useful for identifying neglected areas that could benefit from an enhanced level of innovation. The following areas can be used to segment the various opportunities:

- *Branding*. Where the company creatively leverages its brand, as Richard Branson did by applying the Virgin brand to a vast array of businesses.
- *Custom solutions*. Where the company structures itself to offer tailored solutions to each of its customers. Any consulting firm uses this approach.
- *Customer experience*. Where the company completely overhauls the customer experience to make it as unobtrusive or delightful as possible. The high-end Mandarin Oriental hotel chain is firmly centered on this approach.
- *Development platform*. Where the company bases its product offerings on a central platform, from which it creates derivative products. Car companies operate in this area, where they build multiple car models on top of a single engine and drivetrain configuration.
- *Distribution channels*. Where the company finds unique channels to sell its products, such as high-end watches sold at ports of call for cruise ships, or kiosks in airport concourses.
- *Process efficiency*. Where the company increases its internal efficiencies in order to reduce costs. For example, Toyota's just-in-time production system greatly reduces its costs.
- *Product innovation*. Where the company devises unique new products and services, such as the iPhone.
- *Revenue sharing*. Where the company takes a share of the earnings from customer interactions. Mastercard and Visa use this approach by charging a fee whenever anyone uses one of their credit cards.
- *Supply chain*. Where the company creates a streamlined information flow back through its supply chain, so that parts and goods can be delivered as seamlessly as possible. For example, Dell Computer has long had a highly-refined system for acquiring parts on short notice from its supply base.
- *Underserved niches*. Where the company seeks out underserved market niches and fills them, usually with a high level of service and/or customization in order to ward off competitors.

When a business applies innovation to several of the preceding areas at once, then the profit effect tends to be multiplied. For example, Tesla has leveraged its battery technology into an array of products, while applying its brand to additional products, such as the Powerpack and solar roof tiles. Further, its distribution channel is direct to the customer, which goes around the traditional approach of selling through distributors.

Having an innovation strategy in place can be immensely useful when management is confronted on an almost a daily basis with requests from all over the company to engage in such activities as the acquisition of a new order entry system, the rollout of a new distribution channel, the acquisition of a promising start-up company, the development of a new product to fill out an existing product line, and so forth. By applying the strategy to these requests, management can focus on which ones will be of the most use in advancing the overall company strategy.

Ideally, an innovation strategy should allow management to focus on the following key areas when investigating innovation investments:

- *Value creation for customers*. An innovation should deliver some type of value for the company's customers, either by saving them more or providing them with new features for which they are willing to pay money. The targeted outcome might address such areas of interest to customers as durability, convenience, and cost reduction.
- *Profit creation for the company*. An innovation should allow the company to continue earning a profit. This might involve the development of a product ecosystem (combined with service and support) that customers will not be inclined to depart from. Or, innovation might be targeted at developing a sustainable cost advantage, to fend off products from lower-cost countries.
- *Types of applicable innovations*. The corporate strategy might mandate that innovation activities be targeted at a very specific part of the business, so that the results directly support the direction in which the company wants to go. For example, a distributor's strategic direction might mandate that innovations be focused on the development of a seamless ordering system for customers, while an open-pit mining company might be more interested in innovations surrounding the automation of ore transport from the floor of the mine to the surface.
- *Broad perspective*. The corporate strategy could incorporate a broad perspective on the areas in which innovation can enhance the business. Thus, one should remain open to the possibility of addressing areas of innovation that competitors are ignoring, such as enhancing the customer experience in a coffee shop or enhancing customer service in a car dealership.
- *Redefinition of the business case*. The corporate strategy could be redesigned to change the rules of the competitive game. This can be done by defining *who* customers are, *what* products should be offered to them, and *how* products should be offered to them.
- *Identification of uncertainties*. The corporate strategy should involve the identification of technical and market uncertainties, and address how to learn more

about them. This approach is useful for prioritizing which uncertainties are the most important, developing a list of alternative outcomes for those uncertainties, and then testing them in order to resolve the uncertainties.

Innovation strategies will likely change over time. This is because any strategy is really just a hypothesis regarding the behavior of a targeted market, which might not prove to be valid. If customers, competitors, regulators, or technologies behave in unexpected ways, then a strategy will need to evolve to adapt to these realities.

Another viewpoint on innovation strategy is that it also involves the inverse – getting *rid of* business activities in order to free up the cash needed to invest in new innovations. This typically involves an examination of emerging trends to deduce changes in customer tastes, demography, regulatory, and political issues. Examples of such trends are switching away from blue jeans and toward yoga pants, or switching away from sedans and toward SUVs, or switching away from plane travel and toward anything more environmentally friendly. In particular, management needs to investigate the following issues on an iterative basis:

- On what conditions does our current success depend?
- Which of these conditions might change in the future?
- How can we prepare for these changes?

An examination of these issues can reveal insights into whether a company should exit certain business lines and focus its attention elsewhere.

---

**EXAMPLE**

A company that builds high-powered racing boats notices an increasing trend among customer inquiries, to see if the firm builds more environmentally-friendly electric boats. Management decides to exit its primary line of business over the next few years, and focuses all of its attention on building electric racing boats instead.

In this case, management spotted early indications that buying behavior was turning in a new direction, and decided to change the company's product offerings to match that behavior.

---

The grand strategy associated with exiting lines of business can fall into multiple areas, which are:

- *Specific timeframe*. Continue selling the current set of products and services for a specific period of time, and then switch over to new ones as of a predetermined date. This option is most likely when there are only a few possible alternative paths to take, and management is confident that it can predict the future with a relatively high degree of probability.

- *Early mover*. Continually examine the market for incipient changes in customer preferences, and be ready to innovate at once, moving away from the existing lines of business on short notice. This approach requires a significant investment in a range of innovations, in order to take advantage of being an early market entrant. This also means having high margins, since the firm may need to recoup its investments quickly if product lifespans prove to be short.
- *Researcher*. Have people in the marketplace, constantly looking for ideas that have been developed elsewhere, but which can be acquired or licensed for immediate use by the company. This approach works well if the company has developed a strong capability to bring ideas to market within a short period of time, and has the cash to acquire ideas from third parties. It is also helpful if the company can jump on new ideas quickly, before others recognize their value and drive up their price. In this case, a company may be more inclined to stay in its existing lines of business for as long as they generate enough cash flow, in order to fund outside acquisitions. When cash flows decline, these businesses are shut down.

Which of the preceding options to select is based on a variety of factors, including the financial position of the business, the staff time that is available for dealing with multiple initiatives, and how much the corporate culture is associated with existing products and services.

An innovation strategy must be properly funded. This means that the capital budgeting process is configured to grant funds on short notice to strategically-valuable projects, and that the funding allocated to innovation is always sufficient to pay for all projects that support the innovation strategy. Further, funding needs to be targeted at actual strategic innovations, rather than the favored projects of the various departments. This may call for mandated funding in targeted areas, such as 40% of all innovation funding for radical innovation projects.

---

**EXAMPLE**

The senior managers of a consumer electronics company see a long-term need for an innovation leap to a new technology platform, and communicate this need to the management team. After a year, little progress has been made. At that point, investigation into innovation funding reveals that the production manager demanded robotic production line investments to cut his costs, which in turn were driven by pressure from the accounting department, which wanted to preserve margins. In short, the long-term needs of the business were being sacrificed to meet short-term requirements.

---

A final point favoring the use of an innovation strategy is that it streamlines the process for deciding which proposed projects should be pursued and which should be dropped or deferred. When everyone knows the criteria for project selection, there tend to be far fewer arguments about whether a funding proposal should proceed.

## Strategic Innovation

It appears that we have merely swapped the words in the section header from the title in the preceding section. However, this topic is entirely different; in this case, we are looking at the use of strategic experiments within a business. A *strategic experiment* is a risky new venture being run within an established business. It is usually intended to be a multi-year investment in a market that is not well defined, and for which there is no obvious way to earn a profit. This situation arises most commonly in an emerging industry, where no one has a good idea of what the final outcome of the market will be. In this situation, the company that learns from its strategic experiments the most quickly will be the one most likely to capture the market.

When engaged in strategic innovation, a business will likely find that its initial expectations concerning a new market are incorrect – sometimes by orders of magnitude. To add to the ambiguity, it can be extraordinarily difficult to design strategic experiments that yield clear outcomes, because key variables cannot be perfectly isolated. For example, will increasing the price of a product by 50% really yield a clear outcome that sales therefore declined by 20%, or was the change in sales also impacted by seasonal sales differences or because the company changed its store location? Further, the outcome of experiments may take several years to become fully visible, and even then, the results may be ambiguous. Given these issues, managers should focus on the following factors to glean the maximum amount of information from a strategic experiment:

- *Focus on critical unknowns*. These are typically the cost structure needed to succeed in the market, the impact of technology, and the size and segmentation of the market.
- *Focus on the underlying assumptions*. Assumptions are used to build financial models for a new market. Rather than focusing on whether the initial set of revenue and expense assumptions turned out to be true, look instead at the assumptions used to derive these models. Refining the assumptions will lead to better modeling. For example, when entering a new market, it is impossible to know the number of customer support staff needed for every $10 million of sales; this is something that can be learned through a strategic experiment.
- *Focus on trends*. Examine the rate and direction of change, such as 10% increases in sales from quarter to quarter, rather than trying to predict exact revenue or expense amounts. Trends are relatively easy to derive, whereas predicting exact revenue or expense figures in a new market is nearly impossible. A markedly different trend than the amount expected could be grounds for a change in strategy.
- *Focus on leading indicators*. Identify any leading indicators linked to the market, since they provide early warning signs about whether the company's assumptions are realistic. For example, a leading indicator in the market for asteroid mining is likely to be the market price of the commodities to be mined

– if these prices fall too low, then the cost-effectiveness of asteroid mining will be called into question.

- *Focus on updates.* Review the outcomes of strategic experiments quite frequently, such as on a monthly basis. The markets being investigated are likely changing rapidly, so management needs fresh information to evaluate performance and decide whether a strategic shift is needed. This approach can also keep a business from investing too much in a market that turns out to be smaller than expected.

The outcome of a strategic experiment is a strategic innovation, which represents a significant departure from historical practice in one of the following areas:

- *Design of the value chain.* A classic example is Dell Computer's sale of computers to customers, *after which* it built them. This resulted in negative working capital requirements, since it was paying its suppliers well after it received cash from its customers.
- *Conceptualization of delivered value.* For example, rather than selling completed jet engines to airlines, engine manufacturers sell hours of operating time to the airlines, and provide all ancillary services as part of this arrangement, such as engine monitoring and maintenance.
- *Identification of customers.* For example, Grameen Bank pioneered the extension of microlending to the poor in India, which was a market that had previously been completely ignored.

## Closed Innovation

The traditional approach to organizing a system of innovation was to adopt the stance that all innovation must come from within. This meant that a business would hire the best and brightest into its own research lab, from which amazing product and process improvements would periodically emerge. Each of these improvements would then be commercialized, thereby funding yet more research and development spending – and so on. The company would then have complete control over the product, so that it could produce, market, and sell it using its own employees. Further, it would legally protect its intellectual property with patents, so that no competitors could benefit from it. In short, only the initial funding would be needed to pay for a research and development function, after which it would pay for itself.

---

**EXAMPLE**

A classic example of closed innovation is Bell Labs, the research and development subsidiary of AT&T. Founded in 1925, Bell Labs operated under the philosophy that the best way to innovate was to hire the brightest minds and conduct all research and development in-house. They invested heavily in their own labs, recruiting top scientists and engineers to work exclusively on projects for AT&T's telecommunications business. This internal focus led to some of the most significant technological breakthroughs of the 20th century, including the following:

- *The transistor.* Invented by William Shockley, John Bardeen, and Walter Brattain, the transistor revolutionized electronics and earned a Nobel Prize in Physics.
- *Information theory.* Claude Shannon developed the mathematical foundation for digital communications, which is still used today in data transmission and compression.
- *Laser technology.* Arthur Schawlow and Charles Townes developed concepts leading to the laser, transforming telecommunications and data storage.
- *UNIX operating system.* Created by Ken Thompson and Dennis Ritchie, UNIX became the backbone of modern operating systems.
- *C programming language.* Dennis Ritchie also developed C, which remains one of the most widely used programming languages globally.

This approach worked due to the following factors:

- *Deep specialization.* By keeping R&D in-house, Bell Labs fostered a culture of deep specialization and long-term research projects without immediate commercial pressures.
- *Knowledge sharing.* Researchers worked across disciplines, allowing breakthroughs in one area to rapidly influence others.
- *Significant funding.* As part of a regulated monopoly, AT&T could fund Bell Labs generously, ensuring sustained innovation efforts.

This approach, however, was costly and relied heavily on the financial backing of AT&T's monopoly status. As the telecommunications market deregulated, the model became less sustainable, illustrating one of the downsides of a purely internal innovation strategy. Despite the challenges, Bell Labs' focus on internal innovation earned it 9 Nobel Prizes and left a profound impact on modern technology.

---

While this approach can still be used, it suffers from a few problems. First, there is a strong market for researchers, so a competitor can hire them away, along with detailed knowledge of the company's intellectual property. Second, this process does not necessarily result in a predictable stream of profitable innovations. Instead, there may be long – quite long – intervals between the introduction of commercially viable products, so the research and development group might require substantially more funding than had initially been expected. And finally, just because a business has a long history of excellent product development does not mean that an upstart competitor cannot appear and quickly take away a large chunk of its business. Consequently, the closed innovation concept does not always work as well as might be expected. This brings us to the next topic, which is open innovation.

## Open Innovation

When management decides to engage in an enhanced level of innovation, there is a tendency to invest significant resources internally, so that any solutions developed are entirely home-grown. This may seem like a major competitive advantage, since the innovations developed are not available anywhere else. Further, these innovations can represent a significant amount of intellectual property. Despite these obvious advantages to internal development, it can make even more sense to look outside the company for innovation ideas. Doing so provides the firm with access to a vast pool of knowledge that could not be replicated with any amount of internal investment, and so is more likely to result in a significant leap in performance that would not have otherwise occurred. Also, it can be much less expensive to tap into the research work already completed by other parties, rather than attempting to replicate it in-house.

There are several ways to engage in a more open innovation regime, including the following:

- *Benchmarking activities*. A business should institute an ongoing process of searching for better practices outside of the firm. This may involve perusing research papers, traveling to best practice businesses to see their operations, attending conferences, and so forth. A larger company might consider investing in its own network of scouts, to actively search for new ideas.
- *Cross-subsidiary sharing*. In a larger organization, one subsidiary may develop an improvement that should be shared across the organization. Doing so still keeps the knowledge relatively proprietary, while maximizing its usage within the organization. This is an especially useful approach when the subsidiaries make similar products, so innovations are more likely to be applicable across the organization. Cross-subsidiary sharing can be accomplished with a formal knowledge sharing program, including periodic meetings, plant tours, and a best practices database to exchange information.
- *Implementation speed*. When using innovations found outside the company, this implies that the company will only be catching up to what is already being done elsewhere. However, by increasing the speed of innovation implementation over that of competitors, the firm can still experience a competitive advantage, even when everyone is merely accessing the same best practices.
- *Leading off-the-shelf software*. Many of the more sophisticated off-the-shelf software packages already include best practices that the software providers have learned from their interactions with hundreds of customers. These packages are available for all parts of a business, including systems for warehouse management, customer relationships, and (at a more expansive level) enterprise resource planning systems. By fully installing these software packages and considering all options available, management can significantly improve company operations.

- *On-site tours.* It can be quite helpful to conduct in-depth customer tours of the company's facilities, so that employees can learn from customers regarding exactly what they want. This can lead to additional changes in the methods of production and product designs that are more in line with customer expectations.
- *Licensing.* When the company develops something that is outside of its normal area of production, marketing or distribution expertise, it can license the rights to a third party. Doing so ensures that some revenue will still be gained, even if the firm does not exploit the knowledge internally. This approach can be expanded through the enforcement of a company policy that requires all ideas to be licensed out if they are not used internally within a certain number of years. Doing so frees up the value associated with the ideas. Conversely, the company may elect to license outside knowledge for use internally, in which case it will need to pay licensing fees to someone else.

In regard to the last point about licensing innovations to other parties, this is a logical outgrowth of the market positioning, resources, and management interests of a company. There may be significant differences in how companies even in the same industry view these factors, so that certain innovations may be more applicable to one business than another. Consequently, a business might develop an interesting concept, but does not believe that it fits the pattern that has proven to be successful for it in the past; rather than struggling with rolling out the idea, they hand it off to another party (for a fee), so that the business still profits from it to some extent.

## Incremental Innovation

Incremental innovation occurs when management elects to make small, iterative improvements. This approach has a high success rate, since innovations are built upon business models that already work, and which have an existing pool of customers. Also, these "tweaking" changes tend to be relatively inexpensive, so a business can generate reasonable returns from incremental innovations, with a relatively low risk of failure. A further advantage to engaging in incremental innovation is that these changes pile up – a series of small upgrades to a product over a period of time could result in a product that is considered a game changer when compared to the competition.

There is an investment philosophy associated with incremental innovation. Since each incremental innovation effort is not that expensive, a business can develop a broad-ranging portfolio of small individual bets on innovation. A few will not generate a return, but most should do quite well. This is a better alternative than investing a large amount in a small number of innovation initiatives, since just a few failures here will result in a drastically reduced return on investment.

A good way to create a more effective incremental innovation campaign is to apply the principles of target costing to research and development activities, where a project team investigates the cost required to improve a product, and how much more customers will be willing to pay for the resulting incremental improvement. The result is a replacement product that generates more value for the company. A variation is to create value through cost reduction, where an innovation results in a less-expensive product that will generate a higher profit margin for the company.

A highly targeted approach is to build incremental innovation on top of a more disruptive innovation. For example, Amazon's release of the Kindle e-book reader (definitely disruptive) was followed by a number of improvements, including a touch screen and several sizes of readers (all incremental improvements). The initial version of a disruptive technology tends to be a bit rough, which presents the opportunity for a series of incremental improvements.

Businesses tend to confuse the concept of incremental innovation with issuing a massive number of slightly different product variations, in hopes of conquering every possible product niche. While this approach may increase sales in the short term, it also creates a substantial logistical challenge, since the company must now maintain a much larger number of stock-keeping units, which may adversely impact its profits. A better approach is to maintain roughly the same number of products, but to retire older and less profitable versions when more profitable replacements are rolled out.

## Innovation Development

Once basic research has been completed, the innovation process moves into the development phase. This can be a difficult one for many companies, which flounder through the process of converting ideas into viable products. The following activities can be used to improve the odds of creating products that will be accepted by customers:

1. *Develop multiple prototypes*. Construct a set of simple prototypes (possibly just drawings) that represent several variations on the underlying idea, and test them with customers. Based on their input, construct a minimally-viable prototype and present it to customers again – this will likely shrink the range of viable prototypes. This process is needed to resolve uncertainties about the product offering, which reduces project risk. Also, prototypes are not only cost-effective, but also time-effective, for they require far less time to construct than a completely operational unit. They can be used to answer a number of questions, such as:

    - Would a customer use this product?
    - What would be the manner of usage?
    - How much would a customer pay for it?
    - Will the product work as intended?

2. *Conduct a pilot test*. While still minimizing costs, convert the best of the prototypes into a pilot test, focusing on those key features that are of the most interest to customers.

3. *Bring in customers.* Management can regularly bring customers into its innovation labs, so that they can see the team's prototypes and give immediate feedback on them. Doing so massively increases the number of iterations that development teams can conduct.
4. *Gain customer commitments.* The real proof that an innovation is likely to succeed is when prospective customers are willing to put some skin in the game, such as by putting down a deposit to be one of the first owners. Conversely, if no one is willing to do so, or even be placed on a mailing list to be notified when the product is released, then there may be a customer acceptance problem.
5. *Simplify the concept.* A product that has been refined down to its essentials is much easier to roll out, and within a reasonable time frame. Conversely, as layers of complexity are added to a product, it becomes more difficult to produce.
6. *Standardize.* To reduce the associated complexity for operations personnel, review the product to see if any components can be designed into it that are already being used within the company. Doing so reduces the variety of raw materials and parts that must be ordered and inventoried. Also, see if the range of product versions to be offered can be reduced, in order to simplify production planning, inventory storage, and distribution requirements.
7. *Construct a business model.* Develop and test each part of a business model, addressing such factors as price points and how to acquire customers. From an operations perspective, it is especially important to evaluate whether the company has the in-house capabilities to deliver the product. Another issue to discuss is the extent to which operations will need to be reorganized in order to deliver it.
8. *Prioritize.* There are many competing activities going on in a business at any given time, so management needs to prioritize action around the new product rollout, assigning personnel, money, and other resources to it in sufficient amounts to improve its odds of success.

All of the preceding steps need to be addressed before scaling up the concept into a full-blown product rollout. Even after this has occurred, management still needs to focus on operational efficiencies, since the product will not succeed over the long term unless it can be manufactured at a competitive price that still results in a reasonable margin. A good way to maintain a focus on operational efficiency is to periodically engage in benchmarking activities, to see how other organizations are dealing with the same processes.

## The Role of Operations Performance Objectives in Innovation

In previous chapters, we discussed the performance objectives of the operations function, which are quality, speed, dependability, flexibility, and cost. What role do these objectives have in the innovation process? We make note of the key considerations in the following bullet points:

- *Quality*. When creating an innovative new product, quality usually refers to building a product that exactly meets the design specifications. This means that the operations staff has to set sufficiently tight design tolerances to ensure that what customers buy is what the design team intended. This is a more critical issue when products may impinge upon the health of customers (such as pharmaceutical products), and is less of a concern with single-use or disposable products.
- *Speed*. Time-based competition has become the key form of competition in some industries, where successful companies are able to release the latest iterations of their products at a rapid clip. This is very much the case in the fields of consumer electronics and some types of clothing. The rapid release of new products confers several advantages on a company, including being the first to market and being able to take advantage of the latest technology or fashion trends. Conversely, being late to market will likely translate into minimal market share and unusually low sales levels.
- *Dependability*. Dependability is one of the most important operations considerations when designing products, because they frequently incorporate new technology that is relatively unproven. It may also be necessary to use new suppliers for which the procurement staff has no history of performance information. A common outcome is that a new product design is released to production, but the design proves to be difficult to manufacture, and the resulting products are more likely to break down. The risk of poor dependability can be reduced by lengthening the design process in order to test preliminary products more thoroughly, but this reduces the speed at which new products can be released to the market.
- *Flexibility*. Flexibility involves being able to deal with constant change, which is quite likely when new products are being introduced at a rapid-fire clip. As more products are added to a company's offerings, and especially when older products are not retired, the operations manager will likely find it increasingly difficult to maintain a reasonable degree of flexibility. When the cost of implementing a change to a product is relatively low, this is a good sign that operations have a reasonable degree of flexibility. When the cost of implementing a change is high, then operations processes are probably too rigid, and need an overhaul.
- *Cost*. There will be a cost associated with introducing any new product, since there are ramp-up costs linked to locating suppliers, negotiating purchase prices, designing production lines, acquiring production equipment, and so forth. This tends to result in extensive overhead costs until the setup period is over, as well as heightened raw material and transformation costs until the bugs have been worked out of the production process and scrap levels have been lowered.

## Excessive Innovation Effects

It might seem logical to invest in an ever-increasing array of innovations, effectively blanketing the market with lots of new stuff. By doing so, a company can overwhelm its competition, enter lots of juicy new markets, and position itself as an innovation juggernaut in order to attract the best talent. While this approach might initially seem like a can't-lose option that will yield massive revenues, there are a few cautionary points to consider before embarking upon it. They are:

- *Business complexity*. Greatly expanding the range of products being offered means that the complexity of the business has also increased, since there are now more stock-keeping units and product lines to manage, along with the attendant marketing and distribution requirements. In fact, nearly every part of a business is adversely affected when the number of products issued is expanded.
- *Customer service*. With more products comes an inevitable decline in customer service. This is because more service parts need to be stocked, employees need to be trained in how to repair more products, and customers are more likely to require several interactions with the company in order to have their issues fixed. In short, increased complexity worsens the customer experience.

These issues can increase administrative costs substantially, while also driving away customers. To keep this from happening, while still engaging in enough innovation to enhance the business, follow these rules:

- *Establish a vision*. The company should have a clear vision for what types of innovations it wants to pursue. Any suggestions falling outside of this vision are abandoned at once, since they will not support the direction of the company. Thus, an effective vision statement is one that can be used to decide whether an innovation is valuable or should be discarded.
- *Rationalize the product line*. Always be aware of the differentiating factors between each product in a product line, so that customers have a clear progression of choices as they go from the bottom to the top of the product offerings. If any proposed addition does not logically fit into the current product line, then do not add it.
- *Integrate innovations*. When innovations are tightly integrated into a company's current product offerings, the customer experience tends to improve. Accordingly, discuss integration opportunities as part of the evaluation of any prospective innovation ideas. For example, a company could evaluate a customer's needs and propose a complete bundle of products that exactly meets his or her requirements. This approach can mean that a proposed new product that cannot easily be integrated into a company's existing offerings is turned down, even though it might generate revenues.
- *Clean up the internal coordination*. If a new product has unusual administrative, production, or distribution requirements, delay its introduction until the

related issues have been streamlined to the greatest extent possible. This approach usually allows for a higher degree of automation when dealing with customers, too.

- *Talk to customers*. Converse with customers regularly to ascertain their pain points when dealing with the company. If any of these issues are caused by excessive innovation, deal with the underlying issues at once.
- *Make innovators talk to operations personnel*. The people involved in innovation need to talk to operations personnel to gain a full understanding of the grief they are causing elsewhere in the organization. With this feedback loop in place, products can be adjusted to fit more seamlessly into company operations. A variation on the concept is to establish cross-functional teams that are embedded in the innovation process, which has the same result.

## Innovation Metrics

In this section, we focus on a number of metrics relating to innovation, including the economical usage of design platforms and existing components, as well as the time required to develop products, and the percentage of new-product sales. However, before settling upon one or more of these metrics as your ideal innovation measurement, consider the needs of the organization and then pick the measurement that best addresses those needs. This selection process should take some time, since there is a risk of publishing metrics that incentivize employees to do the wrong things. When picking measurements, consider the following issues:

- *Measurement duration*. Measure for the long term, rather than the short term. Some innovation effects will not become significant for a long period of time, so it is essential to not rely exclusively on short-term monthly or quarterly measurements.
- *Level of detail*. Innovation cannot be managed at the level of detail used for other processes, so do not measure it too tightly. For example, a measurement targets the incremental improvement in the return on innovation investments, and is used to cut off investments below a specific threshold level (as is the case with many capital budgeting systems). However, innovations may have a layering effect, where one innovation builds upon the positive effects of a prior improvement. If so, using a hard cutoff for investment approvals may not be a good idea.
- *Motivational impact*. Before rolling out a measurement, consider that what gets measured directly impacts what gets done, and what gets done directly impacts who gets rewarded. Thus, altering measurement systems has a direct compensation impact on employees, which will alter their behavior.
- *Linkage to strategy*. Any measurements selected should directly support efforts to achieve the company strategy as it relates to innovation. For example, a strategy of being first to market with a new automated teller machine should be supported by measures that focus on the time required to complete the project, without being sidetracked excessively by other issues.

In the following sub-sections, we describe a number of measurements that can be applied to innovation-related activities.

**Allocation of Investments**

The decision to invest in an innovation project is a major one, since there may be limited funding available, and not all proposals can be funded. When this is the case, it can be useful to categorize the proposals into such classifications as product line extensions and breakthrough projects. By doing so, management can look at the overall allocations of funding into the various categories and decide whether they meet the risk profile of the business. For example, a 90% allocation to product line extensions is quite conservative, with only 10% of the funding allocated toward "swing for the fences" breakthrough projects. It can be useful to track these allocation percentages over a period of time, to gain a better understanding of management's acceptance of risk.

---

**EXAMPLE**

A new CEO has been hired into Aerial Taxi Corporation. He notices that the firm has not generated much of a return on its investments in innovation over the past few years, so he has an analyst create an overview of the firm's investments over the past five years, with investments aggregated into the breakthrough product and product enhancement categories. The results appear in the following table.

| | 20X5 | 20X4 | 20X3 | 20X2 | 20X1 |
|---|---|---|---|---|---|
| Breakthrough products proportion | 62% | 60% | 55% | 51% | 40% |
| Product enhancement proportion | 38% | 40% | 45% | 49% | 60% |

He then compares this information to the following analysis, which shows the return on investment for the two classifications:

| | 20X5 | 20X4 | 20X3 | 20X2 | 20X1 |
|---|---|---|---|---|---|
| Breakthrough products ROI | 3% | -17% | 2% | 5% | -12% |
| Product enhancement ROI | 16% | 11% | 23% | 15% | 18% |

From these analyses, it is apparent that his predecessor was desperate to achieve a breakthrough product success, and so kept pouring more money into an innovation category that had historically yielded very low returns. He takes immediate steps to drastically alter the investment strategy in favor of more product enhancements.

---

A variation on this concept is to track the allocation of investments into projects that are targeted at products to be offered in entirely new markets.

### Design Cycle Time

In some industries, a distinct competitive advantage can be gained by designing new products within the shortest possible period of time. By doing so, a business can launch products ahead of competitors and gain market share.

To calculate design cycle time, subtract the design start date from the product launch date for each product. Note that this time period encompasses not only the work of the product design staff, but also the time required to procure components, manufacture goods, distribute goods in preparation for sale, and launch a marketing campaign. Thus, the responsibility for design cycle time rests with many departments, not just the product design team. The calculation is:

Product launch date – Design start date = Design cycle time

If the design cycle time is aggregated across all products, a number of minor product updates could artificially give the appearance of an extremely rapid cycle time. To avoid this skewed result, differentiate between minor updates and major new products, and measure their cycle times separately.

A possible issue with an excessive focus on design cycle time is that products may be released to the market before they have been fully tested, possibly resulting in excessive warranty claims or even product recalls. Thus, it can be useful to review the trend line for warranty costs in conjunction with design cycle time.

---

**EXAMPLE**

The president of Grubstake Brothers is concerned that the Japanese competition is developing new backhoes at a much faster pace than Grubstake, resulting in lost sales. He initiates sweeping product development changes, with the following results in design cycle time:

| Year | Average Design Cycle Time |
|---|---:|
| 20X1 | 304 days |
| 20X2 | 291 days |
| 20X3 | 268 days |

Thus, over the three-year measurement period, the company has succeeded in shrinking the average cycle time by 12%.

---

### Number of Design Platforms

The most efficient way to develop a range of products is to use a common design platform as the basis for as many products as possible. Each design platform has a common set of parts, can be produced by a production line that is specifically constructed for it, and is supported by a group of experienced design engineers. This leads to the following advantages for each product developed using an existing platform:

- A smaller incremental investment in inventory, since many of the component parts are already in stock.
- Less time to ramp up production, since the manufacturing capability already exists.
- Less risk of warranty claims, since the underlying platform has already been tested by users.
- Less time to design new products, since designs may only be slight tweaks of existing products.

Clearly, measuring the number of design platforms can be a key consideration for a company that wants to rationalize a wildly proliferated set of products. A variation on the measurement is to track the number of products using each design platform.

---

**EXAMPLE**

A new CEO has just been hired to run Grizzly Golf Carts, which is known for its robust designs catering to overweight golfers. The CEO comes from a lean manufacturing background where vehicle designs are based on the minimum number of design platforms. He finds that Grizzly offers 30 models based on 15 different design platforms. He immediately slashes 10 of the products, because they not only have poor sales, but also operate on unique platforms. Of the remaining 20 models, he orders the staggered redesign of 14 models, so that they are based on one of the five remaining platforms. At the end of this process, the CEO expects to have 20 models that are based on five platforms, for an average of four models per platform.

---

### Reused Components Percentage

A company can reduce the complexity of its operations by using the same components in multiple products. Doing so yields the following benefits:

- Fewer items to maintain in the inventory records
- Can purchase a smaller number of items in bulk, resulting in volume purchase discounts
- Fewer suppliers to deal with
- Less likely to have obsolete inventory items, since parts can be repurposed if a product is eliminated
- More historically-based knowledge of component failure rates

In short, there are many reasons to push the design staff in the direction of creating new products that reuse existing components.

To calculate the reused components percentage, aggregate the number of existing parts in the bill of materials of a new product and divide by the total number of parts in the bill. Ideally, the existing parts listed in the numerator are only those that have been specifically approved in advance for re-use in new products. The formula is:

$$\frac{\text{Number of existing parts in bill of materials of new product}}{\text{Total number of parts in the bill of materials}}$$

This measurement only works if the engineering department has issued a comprehensive bill of materials.

If too much emphasis is based on this measurement, there may be a tendency for the design staff to not experiment with new materials or suppliers. To mitigate this concern, consider assigning some of the staff to an ongoing review of replacement components that can be adopted throughout the company's various product lines.

---

**EXAMPLE**

The Black Cat Ladder Company has a strong incentive to reuse existing parts for new ladder designs, since some components have been certified to not collapse – a key element of a ladder. Consequently, when the design manager envisioned a No Slip ladder, the reused components percentage was mandated to be at least 85%, with new components only being allowed for the grid pads used on the ladder steps to reduce slippage. As a result, 34 parts out of 38 were reused, which is an 89% reused components percentage.

---

## Percentage of New-Product Sales

One way to force employees to continually develop new products is to set a target for what proportion of sales will come from new products, typically on a rolling basis that looks back anywhere from one to three years. Doing so forces them to look for larger product opportunities that can have a notable impact on sales.

To measure the percentage of new-product sales, divide all sales related to new stock-keeping units by total net sales for the measurement period. We use the creation of a new stock-keeping unit as the most likely threshold for a product being considered sufficiently new that it is given a separate identification. The formula is:

$$\frac{\text{Sales from new stock-keeping units}}{\text{Total net sales}}$$

This measurement is most commonly used in markets where there is such intense competition that the only way to maintain sales is to continually release a stream of new products. If the marketplace is instead a staid one, it may not be necessary to place such a focus on new product sales.

---

**EXAMPLE**

Dude Skis manufactures wide skis most applicable to powder skiing. The buyers of these skis are a fickle lot, basing their decisions mostly on the graphics laminated to the tops of the skis. Consequently, Dude must continually issue new models with different graphics in order to appeal to its buyers. The company targets having 75% of its sales come from new models each year. In the most recent year, $3,400,000 of its total sales of $4,850,000 were from the sale of new ski designs. This represents a proportion of 70% of new models, which is below the corporate target. Accordingly, the company hires an additional graphics designer to develop more ski graphics.

---

## Summary

An effective innovation program can have a spectacular effect on the financial results of a business, but it can be quite difficult to achieve, and even more difficult to maintain over the long term. To achieve good results, management first needs to focus attention on those areas of the business that are most likely to profit from innovation, which means that it weeds out improvement suggestions that do not support the strategic direction of the business. Then it needs to decide whether it will only work internally on innovation activities, or whether the organization should be open to input from the outside, which may include paying for improvements that originate elsewhere. Next, it needs to decide how much funding to make available for innovation activities, which should include a discussion of the apportionment of investments among more-risky and less-risky projects. And finally, management needs to create a well-designed system for fully implementing any new innovations, including their roll-out across the organization within a reasonable period of time. A measurement system will be needed, so that management can keep tabs on the progress of the various projects, how innovations are contributing to revenues, and so forth. If these activities can be organized properly, then a business has gone a long way towards making itself a competitive force in its chosen markets.

# Chapter 5
# Operational Structure

## Introduction

The operations segment of a business is just part of a larger supplier network that is probably comprised of several tiers of suppliers, where a cluster of second-tier suppliers feed parts to the company's first-tier suppliers. It is the job of the operations manager to create a supplier structure that optimizes company operations. This structure addresses how much work will be performed by suppliers, how the supplier network will be configured, where suppliers and company operations will be located, and the amount of capacity built into the network to deal with changes in demand. These are critical decisions, since they impact the competitiveness of a business over the long term. We discuss the structure of operations throughout this chapter.

## The Nature of a Supply Network

A *supply network* is a cluster of suppliers that assist a business in adding value for customers by manufacturing and delivering products. Besides manufacturing activities, a supply network also consists of a flow of information back and forth between the company and its suppliers to address such issues as the timing and amount of deliveries, as well as component designs for new products.

A supply network can be extended to include a firm's customers. Those customers to which it sells directly are considered the firm's first-tier customers. If those customers sell on to other parties, then these other parties are classified as second-tier customers. For example, a manufacturer of watches may sell them to a watch distributor (its first-tier customer), which then sells them to retail stores (which are second-tier customers).

The following exhibit illustrates the broad range of a supply network for a manufacturer of precision watches.

**Supply Network for a Watch**

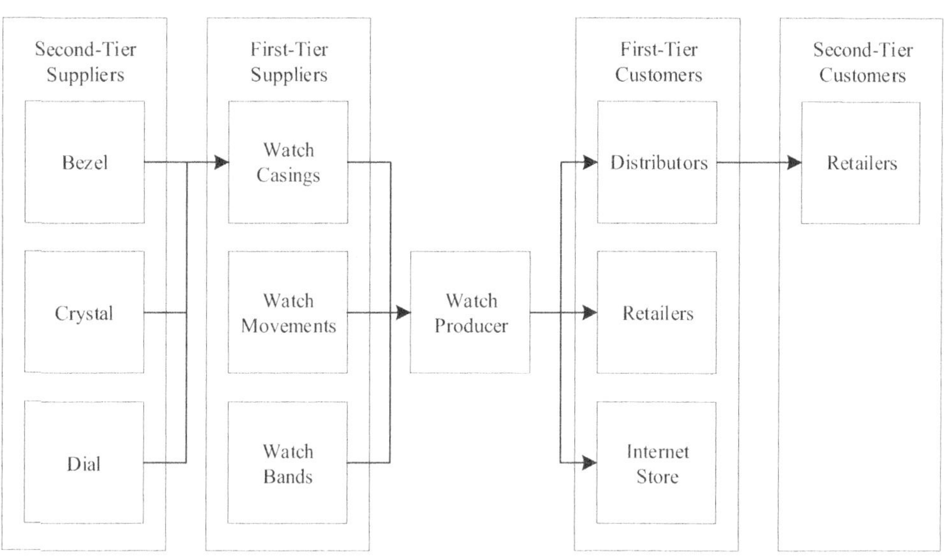


A prudent operations manager will want to delve into the circumstances of second-tier suppliers, rather than relying on the assurances of the first-tier suppliers regarding the performance capabilities of the second-tier suppliers. The reason for doing so is that any number of problems may be hidden within the ranks of second-tier suppliers, such as employing under-age children, running manufacturing facilities in fire traps, and being located in flood plains that could result in the sudden closure of their operations. Unless the company is fully aware of these issues, it cannot take steps to protect itself. Similarly, a business can learn more about its second-tier customers in order to better understand their needs. Doing so allows the firm to develop products that are more closely aligned with the capabilities and requirements of the second-tier customers. Though these intentions are good in theory, it can be difficult to obtain information about second-tier suppliers and second-tier customers from first-tier suppliers and customers, respectively.

When conducting investigations of the supply network, the operations manager should focus in particular on those operations that contribute the most to the key features of the products sold to customers, as noted in the following example.

---

**EXAMPLE**

Hubble Corporation builds observatories to measure the declining orbits of satellites and plot the trajectories of incoming debris. The resolution of its multi-meter telescopes is strongly impacted by the construction processes used on its telescope mirrors. The first-tier supplier that sells it these mirrors uses a set of second-tier suppliers that provide the glass plate for each mirror, grind the glass plate to the correct curvature, and then apply a microscopic silvering layer to the mirror surface. Each of these second-tier suppliers is critical to the ultimate delivery of an observatory in a timely manner, so Hubble needs to obtain status reports from them at regular intervals.

---

The structure of a supply network can be adjusted in a number of ways. Consider the following options:

- *Outsource.* The company could elect to shift an in-house function to a supplier. This makes sense when management wants to concentrate its oversight on core competencies, or when a function has proven to be difficult to manage, or when the function represents too large an investment for the company. When outsourcing occurs, the number of top-tier suppliers increases, and possibly also the number of second-tier suppliers.
- *Take in-house.* Management may elect to do the reverse and take a function back in-house. This is likely to be the case when no supplier has been able to supply the requisite level of service, or when management believes that a function represents a strategically-important or high-risk activity, and so wants more control over it.
- *Concentrate suppliers.* Management may choose to concentrate its business with a smaller number of top-tier suppliers, so that the company has to deal with fewer suppliers. This also makes sense when the company finds that a few suppliers are unusually good at coordinating the activities of second-tier suppliers, which means that some supplier coordination activities can be shifted over to them.

The preceding decisions regarding suppliers, as well as any structural decisions regarding customers, are part of a firm's strategic plan. As such, they should be discussed with senior management and only revised with their concurrence.

## Supply Network Configuration Issues

The configuration of a supply network is one of the more important decisions for the operations manager to consider. For example, a business may choose to concentrate its business with a smaller number of suppliers, in order to shrink its supplier oversight role. Or, if a supplier also becomes a competitor, one must decide whether to continue working with that supplier, or shift the related business to an alternative supplier. Another reason driving configuration issues is the imposition of supplier report cards, which may force the company to drop some suppliers that are not meeting the company's standards. In the following sub-sections, we cover several of the more pressing configuration issues.

## Disintermediation

*Disintermediation* is a reduction in the use of intermediaries between producers and consumers. This involves going around first-tier suppliers and first-tier customers to deal directly with second-tier suppliers and second-tier customers. For example, a manufacturer of custom sinks may be less inclined to sell its wares through a distributor, and instead does so by setting up a web site to sell the sinks directly to customers. Or, the procurement manager of a company does not want to buy a range of commodities from a distributor, and so elects to buy direct from the original supplier, usually in order to eliminate the intermediary profits being imposed by the distributor.

While disintermediation provides a company with more information about its final customers and may result in lower costs when buying from second-tier suppliers, it does impose costs. For example, setting up a web store to sell direct to final customers imposes the cost of maintaining the web site. Or, if the company chooses to sell direct through its own chain of retail stores, it must now invest in building out those stores and supporting them with regional distribution warehouses. These costs may be significant, so companies typically choose customer disintermediation on a pilot basis, rolling out the concept gradually to assess whether the concept is worth pursuing.

Disintermediation for suppliers is most likely to be a valid concept when the material or component being sourced is extremely important to the company, such as when it needs to secure a 100% reliable source, and so wants to deal directly with the responsible second-tier supplier. It may also be useful when the top-tier supplier has proven to be unreliable or to have imposed excessively high fees, so the company wants to eliminate this party from its network. However, instances of disintermediation in the supply chain should be considered an exception, rather than the rule; otherwise, the operations staff will find themselves spending an inordinate amount of time overseeing a vast number of relationships with second-tier suppliers.

## Co-opetition

*Co-opetition* is the act of cooperation between competing companies. Thus, organizations that engage in both competition and cooperation are in a state of co-opetition.

The operations manager needs to watch out for suppliers that could ultimately become competitors. This is an ongoing problem for Apple, which must decide whether to buy microprocessor chips for its phones from Samsung, which is also one of its primary smart phone competitors. If it gives chip designs to Samsung for chip fabrication, this also means that Samsung has the opportunity to review the designs and incorporate certain features into its own designs. Similarly, when a sneaker company chooses to have a foreign supplier manufacture its shoes, it must deal with the possibility that the supplier will then develop its own designs based on the company's sneakers and then go into competition with the firm. The possibility of co-opetition is most likely when a company is dealing with suppliers of significant components for its products. This is a particular problem when the supplier is located in another country, where it may be able to sell knock-offs of the company's products without the company being aware of it, or having any legal remedies for keeping the supplier from engaging in this behavior.

---

**EXAMPLE**

International Bag is a seller of luggage. When a customer buys a product from its website, International sends an authorization notice to the supplier of that bag to ship it directly to the customer, which is a practice known as drop shipping. Doing so keeps all fulfillment work away from International, but also gives the supplier the contact information for the customer, making it easier for the supplier to sell directly to the customer in the future.

---

### Business Ecosystems

A *business ecosystem* is a network of organizations, including suppliers, distributors, and even competitors, that are involved in the delivery of goods and/or services. In this system, there are usually additional parties who provide goods or services on top of or complementary to the company's own offerings; in total, this broad set of offerings increases value for the end customer. For example, any cell phone manufacturer knows that it must develop an app store and attract third-party developers to it, so that phone buyers will have available to them thousands of apps that can then be downloaded to their phones. By developing this ecosystem, a company can massively increase its sales of the core product around which all of these additional goods and services are built. This approach also creates a substantial barrier to entry for new competitors, who must invest in the development of their own ecosystems in order to bring a viable product to market.

For a business to develop a proper ecosystem around its products, it must make a substantial investment to attract third parties who are willing to build around the firm's products, as well as invest in ongoing collaboration activities to build trust between the various parties. This is a multi-year effort that never stops, or else the business ecosystem creating so much value for everyone will gradually disintegrate.

## Capacity Levels

A major structural decision for the operations manager is how much capacity to build into the system. *Capacity* is the maximum sustainable rate of output that an operation can achieve. The amount of capacity limits the revenue that a business can generate. Capacity can be expensive, so maintaining too much capacity will result in excessive labor and equipment costs. Conversely, if capacity is too low, then the business will be turning away sales. Consequently, management needs to continually revisit its estimates of current and future demand to see if capacity levels are adequate. The most difficult situations are when customer demand levels are highly variable, steeply increasing, or steeply falling; in these cases, management may need to devise backup plans for handling excess demand levels, as well as to rapidly reduce capacity on short notice.

Setting capacity levels can be quite difficult in some businesses. For example, a restaurant can be built with room for only so many seats, while a hotel contains a fixed number of rooms. Conversely, in businesses that have few assets, such as consulting, capacity levels can be more easily adjusted by hiring or laying off staff.

When evaluating capacity levels, one must consider the *economies of scale* concept, where unit costs decline as the number of units produced increases. This effect occurs because the pool of fixed administrative and production costs is spread over a larger number of manufactured units. An additional issue that enhances the situation is when variable costs also decline, because volume discounts can be applied to the purchase of large amounts of raw materials. In addition, as a company gains experience with the production of increasing unit volumes, it becomes more efficient at the production process, which drives down unit costs further. However, the economies of scale concept has an upper limit. A business will find that it must incur additional fixed costs as its sales increase beyond a certain point, due to additional complexities inherent in operating a very large business. For example, an organization may find that additional sales require it to distribute goods in distant regions, which increases its transport costs. This means that the cost per unit will begin to increase after a certain point, which is referred to as *diseconomies of scale*.

There can be a substantial penalty for setting capacity levels too low, beyond the prospect of lost sales. In addition, as capacity usage levels approach the theoretical limit, a business will find that its timeliness in providing goods and services declines, because equipment experiences a higher degree of maintenance downtime. In addition, maintenance costs tend to increase when machinery is operated past its recommended service intervals. Further, as the firm requires employees to work additional overtime for prolonged periods, their productivity tends to decline. For these reasons, using most of a firm's capacity, and especially for long periods of time, tends to increase costs dramatically.

While the preceding points regarding economies of scale and the effects of operating near theoretical capacity might seem to indicate that more capacity is better, this is not necessarily the case. A business might find that it prefers to maintain smaller machines that are less expensive and more configurable, so that the equipment can be easily shifted from one production job to another, even though the per-unit cost is higher than if the company had instead acquired a vastly more expensive "monument" machine that could crank out units at a lower per-unit cost. This approach also allows a business to take on smaller jobs and still make a reasonable profit. Thus, the investment in capacity is very much a strategic issue that reflects how management wants to run the business.

An additional concern with capacity is the timing for when it is expected to be brought on line. If it is available for use in advance of the actual need for it, then the company can easily meet all expected increases in demand, so that customer wait times are relatively short. Having extra capacity on-hand also allows the company to meet demand spikes. A further advantage is that, since the capacity is being installed in advance of expected sales, there is time to work through any installation problems and still have the capacity available when needed. However, installing additional capacity in advance will certainly result in an early expenditure of capital funds, which might otherwise have been delayed – perhaps for years. There is also a risk that the business will have invested in much more capacity than it actually needs, which will only become evident over time. Despite these issues, installing extra capacity in advance works well when the company wants to increase market share quickly, at the expense of competitors.

An alternative approach is to deliberately bring additional capacity on line *after* customer demand already exists. This approach makes more sense when the incremental cost to increase capacity is considerable, and also when the company is trying to convey a sense of scarcity for its products, so that customers have to wait a long time to have their orders fulfilled – which is more common for luxury goods. It is also a more conservative approach, where management waits to see how much demand there really is before committing to a capital investment plan. However, a delayed capacity ramp-up also presents the possibility that customers will be turned away, which presents an opening for competitors to take market share from the company.

A further capacity issue is that each incremental increase in capacity represents a lump of fixed costs that have been added to the cost structure of the business. These cost increases trigger a jump in the breakeven point of the firm, so that it takes more sales just to generate a profit of zero. Stated another way, increasing capacity means that it is not profitable to operate at a low sales level, so management needs to be very certain of expected sales before investing in a high-cost capacity addition. The *breakeven point* is the sales volume at which a business earns exactly no money, where all contribution margin[1] earned is needed to pay for the company's fixed costs. The concept is most easily illustrated in the following chart, where fixed costs occupy a block of expense at the bottom of the table, irrespective of any sales being generated. Variable costs are incurred in concert with the sales level. Once the contribution margin on each sale cumulatively matches the total amount of fixed costs, the breakeven point has been reached. All sales above that level directly contribute to profits.

[1] Contribution margin is sales minus all variable expenses, resulting in the incremental profit earned on each unit sold.

**Breakeven Table**

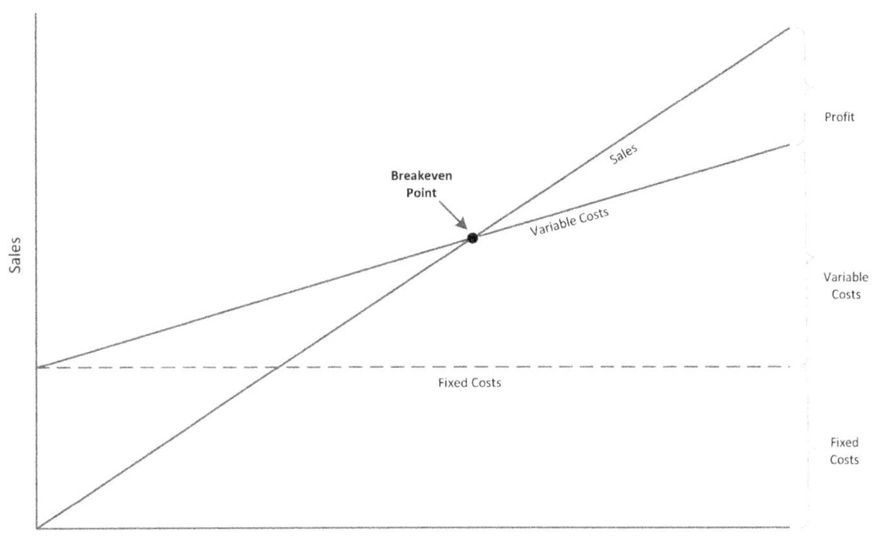


In short, capacity planning is a major concern for any operations manager, who must weigh the benefits of any proposed capital expansion against the offsetting risks of making an investment that will not pay off.

## Operations Locations

The efficiency with which a supply network operates is driven in part by the locations of its operations. If a location is improperly sited too far from key suppliers or customers, then this increases distribution costs and also may make it more difficult to attract employees. For example, if a company opens up a major software programming center in a distant rural location, it will probably have trouble attracting a sufficient number of highly-qualified programmers. Similarly, if a company opens a production facility on the other side of the continent from its most important customer, then transportation costs will soar, while the reliability of delivery times will decline. These are critical issues, since it is quite expensive to move an operation to a new location. Here are several scenarios in which a change in location might be justified:

- *Acquired business*. When a business is acquired, the acquirer will need to examine all acquiree locations to see if they still make sense as part of the supply network of the entire business. This review is part of a larger examination of which acquiree suppliers will be retained, and which of the acquirer's suppliers will be used instead. Also, the acquirer may find that some of its operations are in a better physical location to service selected customers of the acquiree.
- *Customer changes*. When a company's mix of customers changes, it may have to switch locations to be in closer proximity to its newer and larger customers. Alternatively, it may keep its old location and open a new one; this

latter approach is most common when customers insist on local service, as is the case with repair shops and dry-cleaning services.
- *Supplier changes*. When a company switches to a major new supplier, it may consider changing its operations to be closer to that supplier. This is most likely when the input cost from that supplier represents a large proportion of the total cost of its products, or when the materials or components being purchased are so bulky that their transport costs are quite high if the receiving location is situated too far away from the supplier location.
- *Employee locations*. When a company needs large numbers of employees with specific skill sets, it needs to situate its locations where those employees can be found. This usually means building facilities near major universities where the requisite skills are being taught, or near the major cities where these people tend to congregate. These locations are more expensive to acquire and maintain, so companies sometimes split their locations, so that production facilities are located in less-expensive areas and skill-centric facilities are located in the more expensive ones.

The decision to build a facility is a complex one, due to the number of factors involved and the risk of getting it wrong. To improve the odds of building in the correct location, management needs to evaluate the following factors:

- *Capital investment*. Building costs will vary depending on the location, soil composition, road access, utilities access, and risk mitigation. For example, a location in a deeply rural area may involve quite a low land purchase cost, but will call for more expensive utilities costs to run power, water, and sewer lines out to the site. Risk mitigation can be an expensive concern when a proposed facility is located in a flood plain or in an area that is prone to hail, wildfires, or tornados.
- *Cost factors*. When a specific component of the costs of a company's products or services is quite high, it makes sense to locate facilities where the cost of that component is lowest. Thus, call centers are sometimes located in India, because Indians speak English and wage rates are lower there. Or, clothing is routinely produced overseas, with locations moving to whichever country currently has the lowest wage rates.
- *Customer access*. Facilities may need to be located where they are easily accessible for customers. This is a key concern for any service or retail business, such as a hospital, restaurant, or health club.
- *Employee access*. Facilities may need to be located where the most essential employees can easily get to them. This could mean being situated near a major highway, rail station, or bus depot. Or, to access specific skill sets, the location may need to be near a major university that produces the specific types of graduates that the company needs.
- *Governmental factors*. When a proposed investment is quite large, a company may be offered substantial tax breaks by governments that want the company to construct the facility within their jurisdiction. However, at a national level,

the impact of governments can be quite negative, since a government may expropriate company assets or impose restrictions on capital movements, presenting the risk of substantial losses.

- *Labor relations*. Some parts of the world feature excellent labor relations, and some have quite the reverse. When contemplating setting up shop in a new country, it makes sense to explore such matters as the rules pertaining to layoffs, employee participation in management decisions, and how the local culture supports strikes.
- *Security issues*. Does a location have any security issues? This may include the theft of construction materials during the construction phase, as well as the risk of break-ins once the facility has been completed, and personal risk to employees. Some security issues can be mitigated by taking the appropriate security countermeasures, but others may drive away employees, and so should be considered a critical element of the decision process.
- *Transportation costs*. Always consider the cost to transport inputs to the proposed facility, and from there to the company's customers. This may require modeling a standard set of raw material and product flows into and out of the location. It is quite possible that the absence of heavy transport links, such as rail lines or barges, will make transport costs much more expensive.

When selecting sites, a business can become bogged down in the vast number of possibilities, especially when the options include locations in other countries. To reduce the work involved, it can make sense to select a much smaller number of sites, where each one represents a different attribute. For example, a production facility could be located near a major customer, *or* near a major transportation hub, *or* where land costs are very low, *or* where hourly wage rates are very low. The company could find a single location that matches one of these attributes, which limits its analysis to just four locations.

The location analysis process should include modeling using several different scenarios. These scenarios may include the loss of a key supplier or customer, as well as the impact of various natural disasters on each proposed site. By ascertaining the robustness of each location in dealing with these scenarios, one can estimate whether a facility can remain profitable even if a variety of failures impact it.

In the retail industry, there may be only a limited supply of possible locations. For example, a fast food restaurant will only pick sites adjacent to major highway on-ramps and off-ramps. Or, an art gallery will only pick sites on the main street in areas where there are high net worth individuals living nearby. In these cases, the business is forced to wait until a desirable location becomes available, and then decide whether to take it or wait for a different location to become available at a later date.

When evaluating a location change, it can make sense to compare the projected outcome to remaining in the current location. It is quite possible that the analysis will uncover a marginal or even negative benefit to moving from the current location.

## Vertical Integration

A business has greater control over its supply network when it conducts the bulk of the work in-house, rather than shifting the burden over to suppliers. When management wants to take over more of the work, this is called *vertical integration* – where a single business controls different stages of the production process within an industry, extending into the distribution of goods. There are several reasons for following this strategy, which include:

- The acquirer can secure essential raw materials that may be in short supply.
- The acquirer can reduce the total turnaround time of the supply chain, since it now has accurate customer demand information.
- The acquirer can reduce transaction costs, such as searching for and negotiating with suppliers, monitoring their output, and negotiating contracts. Instead, orders can be placed through an internal enterprise resources planning system, which are automatically propagated throughout the acquirer's various businesses.
- The acquirer can take control of the intellectual property of its suppliers, so that it has sole control over how this knowledge is used.
- The acquirer can gather more information about the ultimate customer by acquiring distributors.
- The acquirer can own a limited number of retail outlets in order to gain knowledge about the needs of final customers.
- The acquirer can obtain all of the profits being generated along the supply chain.
- The acquirer can keep its acquired businesses away from competitors, thereby creating a limited form of monopoly.

When a company acquires one of its suppliers, the transaction is called *backward integration*, while the acquisition of a customer is called *forward integration*. For example, a backcountry skiing operation that buys a helicopter rental organization to give lifts to its skiers is an example of backward integration. By doing so, the skiing operation gains access to the helicopters needed for its operations. Alternatively, a clothing manufacturer that buys a women's clothing retail chain is an example of forward integration. By doing so, the manufacturer gains an assured customer and also learns more about the retail chain's customers.

---

**EXAMPLE**

Nautilus Tours is a rapidly-expanding underwater tour operator that bases its submarines throughout the Caribbean, Hawaii, and French Polynesia. Tourist numbers are climbing, since everyone wants to see the coral reefs before they are cooked by global warming.

Nautilus suffers from two problems, which are the supply of shallow-depth viewing submarines and the fees charged by tour aggregators. The supply of submarines is limited, since the company's main provider is allocating its output to several tour operators. Meanwhile, tour aggregators are taking a 20% cut on all tickets sold to Nautilus Tours. To mitigate the submarine supply problem, Nautilus could buy the submarine manufacturer, thereby taking its entire production and blocking competitors from buying the submarines. To mitigate the ticketing fee problem, Nautilus could buy one or more of the tour aggregators. The former is a case of backward integration, while the latter scenario is a case of forward integration.

---

A potential problem with vertical integration is that acquired suppliers now have an assured customer, and so have less incentive to engage in cost cutting and product development, which can eventually reduce the overall competitiveness of the combined company. This problem can be reduced by reserving only a portion of a supplier's output for the company's requirements, thereby forcing the supplier to still compete on the open market for the business of other customers. By also selling to other companies, the supplier has the opportunity to expand its total business, which presents the possibility that it will drive down costs through economies of scale.

Another problem with vertical integration is that the company is making a major investment in other businesses, which increases its fixed cost structure. When this happens, the sales breakeven point for the entire business increases, placing the enterprise at risk of losing money if sales decline below the breakeven level. This risk can be mitigated by only acquiring suppliers and customers selectively, and by avoiding those businesses with high fixed cost structures.

The extent to which a company wants to engage in vertical integration is a key consideration. It is usually sufficient to only do so with the most crucial elements of the supply chain, so that the supplier of a key component is acquired – but not the suppliers of more commoditized components. Similarly, a business might choose to buy a customer, but only one that buys a large part of the company's output, or which has a unique distribution channel. Expanding into every aspect of the supply network is not usually cost-effective, since it means that the company will be buying some companies that have minimal profitability, resulting in a meager return on investment on these acquisitions.

---

**EXAMPLE**

Grissom Granaries operates grain barges and tugboats on the Mississippi River. It makes money by transporting grain from various grain storage businesses along the shores of the river to grain processing facilities located elsewhere. Grissom could choose to engage in backward integration by buying a few grain storage businesses, thereby locking in its grain sources. However, it probably would not want to go back one additional tier in the supply network to buy individual farms, since this presents too much risk during poor crop-growing seasons, or when grain prices decline. Grissom could also choose to engage in forward integration by buying a grain processing facility; however, these companies have second-tier customers, so Grissom would not have visibility into the needs of the final customers for the grain.

---

A final concern with vertical integration is that it increases the company's management oversight role. Management must now spend a great deal of time reviewing the activities of more businesses, setting strategy for them, reviewing budgets, approving funding, and so forth. When this is the case, management's attention is diverted away from the core competencies of the business, which may make the company less competitive over the long term.

In summary, vertical integration is a useful concept when used selectively and targeted at very specific needs of the company. When taken too far, it diverts management attention away from core issues, increases fixed costs, and can make the company less competitive.

## Outsourcing

*Outsourcing* is the practice of sending work to suppliers, rather than completing tasks internally. The main point behind outsourcing is to reduce costs. This can be achieved by sending work to suppliers located in lower-wage areas, or to suppliers that produce in very high volumes, and so can complete tasks at a lower cost per unit. Outsourcing is also useful when management wants to focus its attention on just a few core competency areas (such as product design), and has others deal with less-critical functions. Outsourcing may also be used when a company has proven to be incompetent or inefficient in certain areas, and management no longer wants to spend any resources correcting the underlying issues.

Administrative activities, such as payroll processing and cash management, are most commonly outsourced. However, the concept can also be applied to operations. For example, contract manufacturers are now taking over the entire production processes of their clients, including the sourcing of raw materials and components, and shipping the resulting goods to customers.

The decision to outsource is dependent on a company's performance objectives, which are quality, speed, dependability, flexibility, and cost. For example:

- *Quality objective.* A company is having trouble consistently producing a high-quality marine radio for its customers. It locates a supplier that has long-since engaged in Six Sigma quality programs, and so can assure the company of being able to completely eliminate the quality problem.
- *Speed objective.* A company has been using a material requirements planning system to manufacture goods for its customers, and finds that it cannot deliver any quicker than within five days of order placement. Accordingly, it contracts with a supplier that uses a just-in-time production system instead, which allows it to deliver goods within two days of order placement.
- *Dependability objective.* A company builds strict late delivery penalties into its contract with a supplier, in order to enforce a high degree of delivery performance. Dependability is one of the more difficult improvement areas when outsourcing is used, unless the supplier commits to keeping large amounts of inventory on hand to meet delivery requirements.
- *Flexibility objective.* A company's production capabilities are quite limited, so it is unable to meet the customization requirements of its customers. It outsources to a much larger supplier, which has a broad range of production equipment, allowing it to meet a variety of customization requirements. However, this equipment may be tied up in servicing other clients, so the full benefit of outsourcing may not be realized.
- *Cost objective.* A company wants to reduce its costs, so it contracts production to a larger business that can use economies of scale to achieve lower per-unit costs. The supplier is also located in a low-wage area, so it can maintain lower labor costs than the company could ever achieve.

There are situations in which outsourcing is not advised. When an activity is of strategic importance to the company, it should be kept in-house, so that the firm's survival is not placed in the hands of an outside party. Also, if the company has a store of specialized knowledge in one of its functional areas (such as product design or software programming) then that expertise should be retained on the premises; otherwise, once the related function has been outsourced, it is quite difficult to rebuild. And finally, if the company's performance in a particular area is already quite good, then a supplier is unable to improve on it much, so it would be better to keep that area in-house.

Given the increasing emphasis on protectionism in many countries, it is more likely that companies will outsource only within the countries where their operations are already located, thereby eliminating the effects of any tariffs that may be imposed on goods coming into the country. This approach reduces the ability of firms to access low-wage labor in other countries, which will tend to drive up the costs of their products, making them more expensive for consumers.

As environmental concerns become more important, it is likely that outsourcing will be restricted to relatively nearby suppliers. Doing so reduces the amount of transport involved, and therefore the associated carbon footprint of the trucks, trains, barges, and ships that are involved in the transportation of goods.

## Summary

The structure of a company's supply network is an essential part of its strategy, and also drives how well it is able to provide goods and services to its customers. Operations managers need to consider such factors as altering the number of intermediaries, setting up a business ecosystem, adjusting the amount of in-house capacity, altering facility locations, vertically integrating portions of the supply chain, and outsourcing selected activities. There is no perfect solution – any of these decisions may need to be changed as the mix of suppliers, customers, products, government regulations, labor relations issues, costs, and so forth vary over time.

# Chapter 6
# Process Design

## Introduction

Processes are the core operations of a business, and so play a major role in its ability to deliver goods and services to customers. Being able to design these processes properly is essential to having an efficient and profitable operation. In this chapter, we deal with multiple issues impacting process design, including the volume-variety tradeoff, process types, process inefficiencies, process bottlenecks, value stream mapping, and several related topics.

## The Nature of Process Design

The design of a process involves conceptualizing its layout and flow prior to its creation. It begins with setting the design objectives and then working downward through multiple levels of detail to see if the process will function as planned. It is quite likely that problems will be encountered, resulting in multiple iterations of the design until one can be found that approximately matches the design objectives.

The design of a process is clearly dependent on the design of the product that will be manufactured or the service to be provided. It is quite likely that even a modest change to a product design will require a substantial alteration to the underlying process, possibly making it too difficult or expensive to produce. The reverse may also be true. Consequently, an industrial engineer who is deeply involved in process design should advise every product development team, to ensure an easier level of product manufacturability.

When designing a process, one must also consider that it is receiving information or materials from an upstream process, conducting its own transformation activity, and then sending the results to one or more downstream processes. This interaction means that the process designer has to consider the impact of these other processes on the new process, as well as its impact on them. Otherwise, there will be difficult, error-prone hand-offs at the beginning and end of the process.

A process should be designed to achieve the performance objectives of the business. For example, if a company's basis of competition is to manufacture products at the lowest cost, then it needs to strip every cost-generating activity out of its processes, making them as efficient as possible. This may include stripping out excess capacity, minimizing the amount of work-in-process inventory, and introducing automation to those parts of the process that contain high labor costs. Conversely, if the basis of competition is extremely fast service speeds, then its processes are much more tolerant of costs, because costs are no longer as critical to the performance objective. Or, if the basis of competition is product quality, then error-free processing would be the main focus of attention.

## The Process Volume-Variety Continuum

Processes tend to process activities at high volume and in a very standardized manner, or in low volume and with many possible options. For example, a desalination plant is designed to do one thing very well – convert salt water into drinkable water – and so its processes are designed to be focused on that single goal in a highly efficient manner. Conversely, a law firm that handles many types of law must have a set of processes for each one, to deal with the specifics of each client's case. Process designs tend to be based on this volume or variety orientation, where volume-oriented processes are designed for high efficiency, while variety-oriented processes are less efficient, but are designed to branch off in different directions, depending on the situation.

Processes are not necessarily clustered around either end of this volume-variety continuum; some may be positioned anywhere along it, depending on the volume and variety mix for which they are designed. For example, an automotive dealership has car maintenance procedures for each type of vehicle left with it. If the dealership only services one type of car, then it will need only a few processes, which it can handle in relatively high volume. However, if the dealership elects to take on additional car models, then the number of maintenance processes it has must increase, which drives down the volume for each one, as a greater variety of vehicles are dropped off in the maintenance area by customers.

## Process Types

Where a process sits on the volume-variety continuum determines how it should be designed and managed. The resulting processes tend to fall into one of the following classifications:

- *Project process*. This process is targeted at highly individual projects that require significant degrees of customization and long time periods to complete. It is quite possible that specific activities are not well-defined, and so can branch off in various directions, based on judgments made. For example, a house, a television show, and a custom-built yacht require a project process.
- *Batch process*. This process is designed for smaller quantities, so it has higher volume than a project process, and somewhat less variety. The complexity level may be relatively high, but the amount of uncertainty is lower than for a project process. Once a batch has been set up, the work required to complete all units may be fairly repetitive. For example, a specialist toolmaker of watches develops an entirely new watch movement, uses it to produce 100 watches, and then destroys the design so that no additional watches can be built, thereby enhancing the value of the units that were produced.

- *Mass production process.* This process involves high unit volumes and modest amounts of variety, where the work is highly repetitive. The focus is primarily on maintaining efficiencies in order to drive down costs. A good example of mass production is an automobile production line where unit volumes are high, but it is allowable to insert some variety into the process, such as different car colors and features.
- *Continuous production process.* This process is similar to a mass production process, except that it is designed to operate with no end date in sight and minimal output variety. It tends to require a large capital investment, with a significant proportion of tasks being automated. There are minimal stoppages in a continuous production process; instead, inventory flows straight through the process. An example of a continuous production process is an oil refinery.

The preceding processes show the range of process types, from a pure focus on variety (the project process) to a pure focus on volume (the continuous production process). These processes were targeted at the production of physical goods. The same approach can be applied to the provision of services, where there are distinct differences between services based on their focus on volume or variety. For example:

- *Professional services process.* This process involves the provision of services to a client, usually involving substantial amounts of customization to the needs of the client. For example, a management consultant could assist a client with an examination of its business strategy. Or, an architect designs a custom home that meets the particular needs of a client. This service process focuses on variety.
- *Service shop process.* This process involves the provision of a standard set of services to a client, usually in batch mode where the services are provided to a limited number of customers. For example, a bus tour company offers tours through a scenic area in groups of 40 people, following a standard route and providing a standard commentary. Or, a school offers a standard curriculum to groups of students, based on classroom size. This service process focuses on a mix of variety and volume.
- *Mass service process.* This process involves the provision of a very standardized service to large numbers of customers, typically using standardized scripts or work instructions. For example, the checkout clerk at a supermarket performs the same checkout tasks, over and over again, for hundreds of customers, every day, with minimal variation. Or, the inbound call center for a cable company uses a set of standardized scripts for dealing with calls from its customers. This service process focuses on volume.

Where a process lies along the volume-variety continuum determines the level of resources invested, the technology used, and how jobs are designed. For example, when a company has just started, its inbound call center may be a single part-time person who has no standard script for how to answer company queries. At this point, the process is poorly defined and involves minimal resources. However, as the inbound call volume builds, more employees are assigned to answering these calls, which requires standardized training, a dedicated call center, and standardized scripts for responding to customers. Eventually, at higher volumes, the company chooses to employ an automated system to interact with customers, answer some questions, and route other questions to call center employees. Thus, the volume of calls received drives the amount of resources invested, where high call volumes warrant the increased use of technology.

The operations manager will need to design processes correctly, based on their volume and variety attributes. This means that only a modest level of standardization should be employed for processes that are focused on variety; otherwise, they will appear excessively inflexible to customers. Conversely, a high-volume process should be thoroughly standardized, or else the company is not taking full advantage of the cost-reduction opportunities associated with it.

## Process Design

Once the type of a process has been identified, the next step is to design it in detail. This involves the identification of every activity within the process and the sequence in which those activities will be performed.

The design of a process usually begins with a flowchart, on which is shown each activity, decision point, document, and database into which data is stored and from which it is extracted. There are many possible flowchart symbols, but the ones appearing in the following table are the ones most commonly used.

**Standard Flowchart Symbols**

| Symbol | Discussion |
| --- | --- |
| | **Process:** This is the primary symbol used in a business process flowchart. State each step within a process box. It is possible that a simplified process flowchart will contain no other shapes. |
| | **Decision:** This is used when a decision will result in a different process flow. The decision symbol can be overused. Try to restrict its usage to no more than two per flowchart. Otherwise, the flowchart will appear overly complex. If more decision symbols are needed, consider subdividing a process into multiple ones. |
|  | **Document:** This symbol is particularly useful for showing where an input form is used to collect information for a process, though it can also represent a report generated by a process. |
| 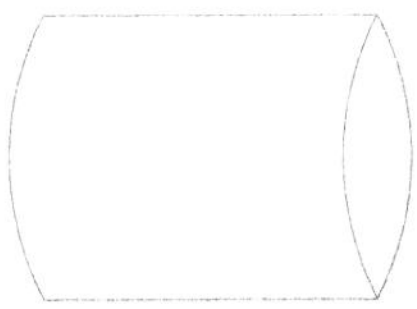 | **Database:** This symbol is used less frequently, and shows when information is extracted from or stored in a computer database. In most cases, the use of a database can be implied without cluttering up a flowchart with the symbol. |

By using the preceding flowchart symbols, one can lay out the structure of a process at either a high level or at quite a deep level of detail. An example appears in the following exhibit, which shows the high-level process for scheduling a customer order into the production process.

**Sample Process Flow for Scheduling a Production Job**

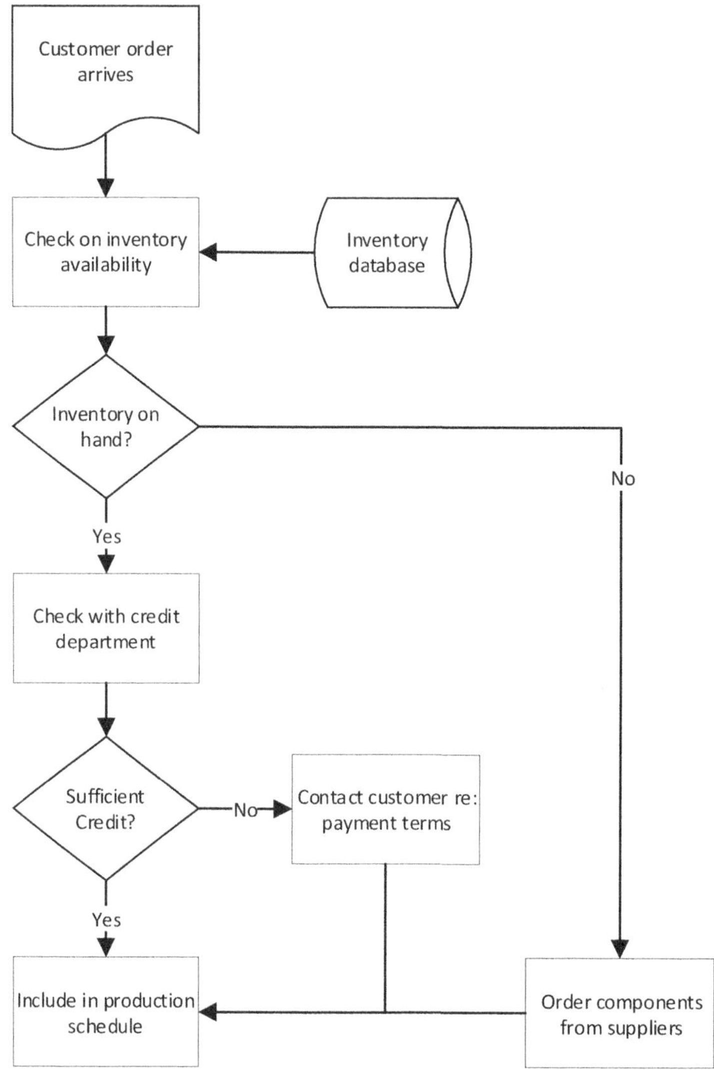


A process will likely be mapped at a more detailed level than what appeared in the preceding exhibit. For instance, the following exhibit contains the process flow for just the first activity shown in the preceding exhibit, which was "check on inventory availability." This more detailed approach can then be used to write a procedure for users.

**Sample Process Flow to Check for Inventory Availability**

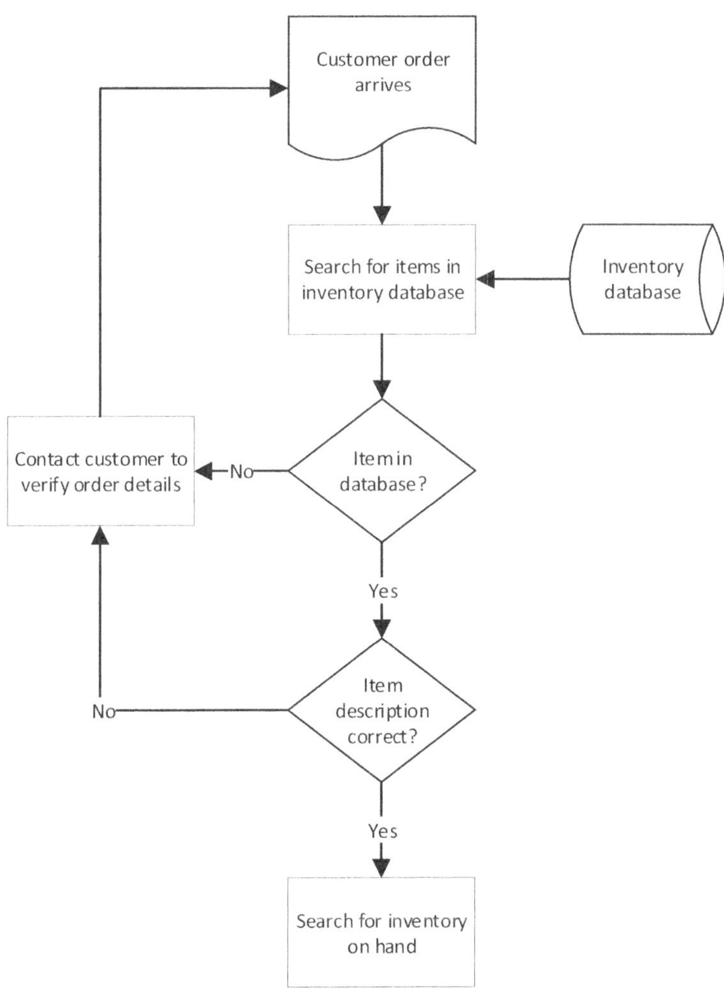


A process may have a high level of interaction with customers. When this is the case, the process needs to be designed to enhance the customer experience to the greatest extent possible. Doing so can avoid the loss of customers who might have a significant lifetime value for the business. Accordingly, customer-facing processes need to be designed with greater care than other processes. This can involve the identification of any touch-points where customers interact with the process, followed by the refinement of those touch-points to enhance the customer experience. For example, a tour company evaluates the customer touch-points for its tours going from Las Vegas to the Hoover Dam. These touch-points include the initial entry to the bus, the introduction by the tour guide, information given during the ride to the dam, discussions about meeting times following the dam tour, and the final talk with customers while returning to Las Vegas. This evaluation may use a point scale, where negative scores are strong indicators of a need for process improvement.

A sample flow chart appears in the following exhibit, where a field service operation clearly identifies those process activities that are highly visible to the customer (and therefore worthy of particular attention) and those that are not.

**Sample Process Flow Emphasizing High Visibility Activities**

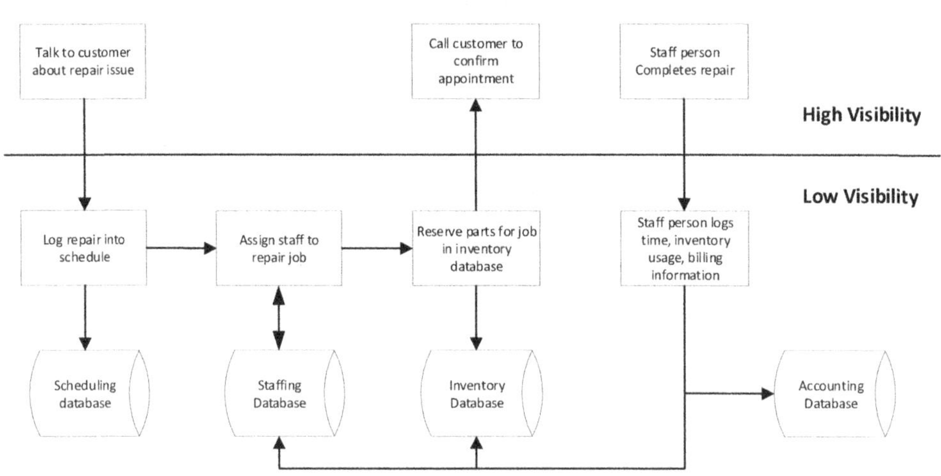


## Little's Law

Little's Law is a useful tool for determining the efficiency of a process that deals with a queue. It calculates the average number of items in a stationary queuing system based on the average wait time of an item within the system and the average number of items arriving at the system per unit of time. Based on the outcome of this calculation, the design of a process and the resources assigned to it may be changed to arrive at a better result. For example, it could be applied to the queue waiting for service in a coffee shop, or the queue of items waiting for rework in a production facility, or the queue of callers into an inbound call center. The formula for Little's Law is:

| | |
|---|---|
| | Average number of items arriving at the system per unit of time |
| × | Average waiting time an item spends in a queueing system |
| = | Average number of items in a queueing system |

---

**EXAMPLE**

Frank owns a coffee shop. He wants to understand the average number of customers queueing in his shop to decide whether he needs to add more square footage to accommodate more customers. Currently, his waiting area can only accommodate 6 customers.

On average, 80 customers arrive at the shop every hour, and spend about 4 minutes there (0.066 hour). Based on this information, the average number of customers queueing in the shop is:

80 customers/hour × .066 hour wait time = 5.3 customers in queue

Thus, on average, only 5.3 customers are waiting in line at any point in time, so it does not appear necessary that more space needs to be set aside for additional queueing customers.

**EXAMPLE**

Frank wants to expand the advertising for his coffee shop in order to bring in 50% more customers. He thinks the queue time can be managed by adding one person behind the counter, which should drop the wait time from .066 hour to .05 hour. Based on this information, the number of customers in queue will change to:

120 customers/hour × .05 hour wait time = 6 customers in queue

The numbers indicate that the increased customer volume will result in 6 customers in queue. If he wants to maintain the queue size at 5.3 customers, he will need to reduce the wait time to .044 hour (calculated as 5.3 customers in queue ÷ 120 customers/hour).

---

## Process Inefficiencies

When designing a process, one must be aware of the many inefficiencies built into it. Usually, a process contains a series of steps that transform inputs into outputs. There will likely be breaks between each of these steps, where there is a wait time before the next processing step begins. The wait time may be much longer than the processing time, which means that the time spent in the midst of a process may be much longer than the sum of the actual processing time required for it. Further, the resources used to conduct processing may be utilized at a rate well below their maximum capacity levels, perhaps because they are only needed for a portion of the units being processed. Given these inefficiencies, processes need to be continually tuned to enhance their productivity levels, based on the types and amounts of inputs to them. This tuning is usually conducted based on a number of measurements that reveal how a process is performing. The most common process-level measurements are:

- *Cycle time*. This is the average interval required to complete a task. Shortening this interval increases the output from a process, which may be needed in order to meet the current level of demand.
- *Work-in-process*. This is the amount of inventory currently being worked on within a process. Accelerating a process means that inventory remains within the process for a shorter period of time, so that the company has to make a smaller investment in inventory in proportion to the sales produced.
- *Resource utilization*. This is the proportion of total time available within a process during which resources are being used. The presence of unutilized resource time indicates that there is excess capacity within a process.

These measures should be monitored regularly, to see if any process adjustments should be made.

---

**EXAMPLE**

The Hail Correction Institute typically requires 80 work hours to process a car that has received hail damage. Of this amount, the owner estimates that only three hours are needed to repair the typical car, including banging out dents and repainting as needed. What happens during the other 77 hours? The Institute spends 30 minutes examining each newly-arrived car, waits three days for an insurance company representative to view the vehicle, then spends 15 minutes negotiating a price with the insurer and 15 more minutes contacting the customer to process payment for a deductible. For the remaining 52 hours, the vehicle waits in queue to be repaired by the Institute's staff.

Even if the wait time preceding the arrival of the insurance company representative is outside of the company's control, it seems likely that the addition of more staff would eliminate some of the queue time thereafter. Doing so pleases customers, and also allows the Institute to clear its backlog, leaving room to generate additional sales.

---

## Process Bottlenecks

A *bottleneck* (or constraint) is an operation that is already operating at its maximum capacity, and so cannot accept any additional work beyond its current production level. A bottleneck drives the total capacity of an entire process, so it is essential to recognize where they are located. A bottleneck can have a pernicious effect on the rest of the process in which it is located, since these other activities are constrained by it, and so may be severely underutilized.

**EXAMPLE**

Pensive Corporation manufactures the Procrastinator Deluxe, a robot used to save labor around the house. The production process involves work at four workstations. The following base case shows that Workstation C can process the fewest units per hour, at 60 units. This constrains the processing speed of the entire operation, resulting in total output of 60 units per hour.

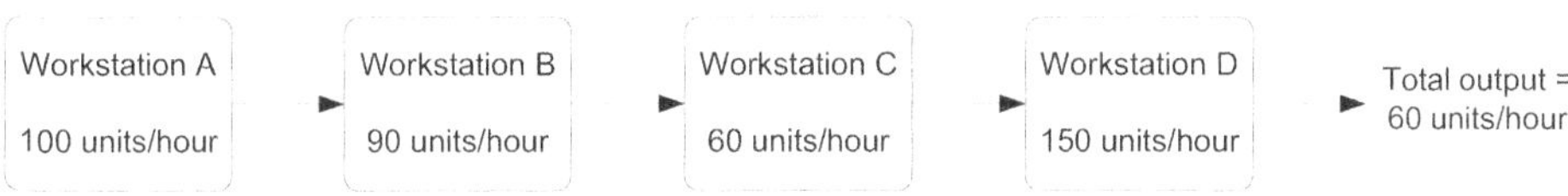


The company's financial analyst conducts an incorrect analysis and recommends that the machines used in Workstations A and B be replaced by higher-capacity equipment. This is done, with the result appearing in the following process flow:

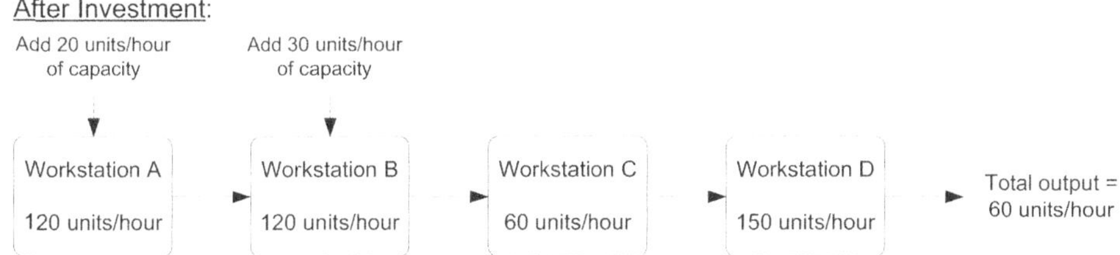


The results are unchanged, since the higher production volume of the first two workstations is still limited by Workstation C. The only changes are that the company has invested in enhanced equipment that it does not need, and which generate an increased amount of inventory that is piling up in front of Workstation C, waiting to be processed.

---

The effects of a bottleneck can be reduced by increasing capacity, outsourcing work, reconfiguring processes and products, and maximizing the efficiency of the bottleneck. Alternatively, the activity level elsewhere in the process can be scaled back, so that capacity levels match what the bottleneck operation can produce.

---

**EXAMPLE**

Global Camper is a manufacturer of motorhomes. Its bottleneck operation is its paint shop. Painting operations can only proceed at a certain pace, so the company can only run 25 units per day through the facility. If the company were to produce more engines, the engines would not contribute to more motorhomes being built; there would only be an increase in the number of engines in storage, which increases the investment in working capital.

The president of the company finds that, since the number of motorhomes produced per day is limited to 25, his next best activity is to cut back production in all other areas if they are producing more parts than are needed for 25 units. Thus, it is better to not optimize in many parts of the business, since there is no need for more parts.

---

## Locations of Bottlenecks

The entire concept of constrained resource optimization is centered on the idea that there must be a bottleneck. Before engaging in such optimization, we must first locate the bottleneck. In a large factory that contains many employees and processes, it can be quite difficult to locate. Consider the following ways to find it:

- *Backlogs*. Every constrained resource has a backlog of work in front of it, since the resource does not have sufficient capacity to keep up with demand.
- *Expediter conventions*. If a company uses expediters to force certain rush orders through the factory, they will likely pile up at the bottleneck, where they are all trying to get their jobs classified first in the queue of work. This clamoring crowd can look like a convention of expediters.
- *Problems*. A bottleneck is overworked, and therefore likely to fail due to a lack of adequate maintenance. Consequently, any resource that seems to constantly require ongoing management attention is more likely to be a bottleneck.
- *Scheduling*. There is usually an ongoing battle over which jobs are scheduled to go through a bottleneck. Consequently, look for areas in the production schedule where the schedule is constantly being revised.
- *Utilization levels*. A bottleneck is in use constantly, so it probably has the highest utilization level in the company, and may involve people working multiple shifts and weekends. If the staff is working in a particular workstation even on a holiday, this is a prime indicator of a bottleneck

There are other areas than the production department in which a bottleneck may be located. Consider the following variations:

- *Engineering*. Any product that is customized will require design work, so a work backlog in the engineering department could indicate that the real bottleneck is the design staff.
- *Procurement*. When there is a high level of industry demand for a specific raw material, the sources of supply may not have caught up with demand, so a business may be allocated a raw material apportionment. This issue can be dealt with by redesigning products to avoid using the constrained raw material, or by offering to pay a higher price for raw materials.
- *Sales*. In a complex selling environment where there are sales demonstrations, sales proposals, and contract negotiations, a backlog anywhere in this process could be the real bottleneck. The problem is most evident when lots of new

sales prospects are being added to locate potential customers, while the same sales volume is still being recognized.

---

**EXAMPLE**

Monk Books produces replicas of famous medieval books. Customers are museums, which keep the fakes available for presentation while the originals are stored in secure vaults. Monk is having a difficult time keeping up with robust demand, and decides to conduct an examination of its processes to locate its bottleneck. The investigation uncovers the information in the following table, which shows the amount of time required to eliminate the work backlog for each of the tasks in Monk's production process:

| Step | Activity | Minutes of Backlog |
|---|---|---|
| 1 | Paper refinishing and coating | 500 |
| 2 | Scribing | 5,900 |
| 3 | Artwork | 6,200 |
| 4 | Paper drilling | 400 |
| 5 | Book stitching | 1,200 |
| 6 | Leather lamination | 820 |

The examination reveals that the second and third steps in the processing - scribing and artwork - have nearly identical backlogs, so either one could be considered the backlog. However, the number of available people who can engage in high-grade scribing is high, while the number of artists capable of applying gold paint to the pages is minimal. Consequently, management elects to bring in several additional staff on a contract basis to reduce the backlog in the scribing area. This leaves the artwork activity as the clear bottleneck of the business, which management deals with by providing the artists with extra administrative support, as well as pencil sketch apprentices to assist with blocking out the basic designs to be painted.

---

It is also possible to designate a resource as the official constrained resource. This is usually a capital-intensive function that the company does not want to invest additional funds in, or an area requiring a large number of highly-paid staff. In this case, management can focus its attention on proper management of the designated area, in order to maximize profitability.

**EXAMPLE**

Alien Battles Company (ABC) creates space battle scenes for science fiction movies. The company's largest expense is the cost of compensation for its computer animators. However, there are a large number of unemployed and highly skilled animators available, so it is not especially difficult to hire the individuals as contractors to ramp up for scheduled movie scenes and terminate their contracts once their work is complete. Instead, the company finds that a large part of its management time is spent in the development of prototype scenes that it can use to land new business. These prototypes require a highly skilled group of programmers who are much more difficult to find than computer animators. Without the presence of a qualified group to support these prototypes, ABC would soon find that its sales pipeline has dried up. Consequently, ABC designates the prototypes function as the bottleneck of the company.

## Process Volume Variability

Over time, a process may experience large swings in volume, either coming into it from upstream processes in the form of supply, or from downstream processes in the form of demand. There are many reasons for changes in process volume, including delays in the arrival of needed information, delayed component deliveries, or changes in the requirements coming from downstream processes. When there is a high degree of variability, it is quite possible for a process to rapidly transition from having a substantial queue in front of it (when demand spikes) to having no queue at all (when demand slumps). When this is the case, one must decide how valuable it is to maintain a small queue size. If it is essential to do so, then the process should incorporate an unusually large amount of excess capacity, to deal with all but the largest demand spikes. Alternatively, if there is a minimal downside to having a long queue, then tolerating it instead of building capacity is a viable option; this is particularly useful when the cost of additional capacity is high.

Process volume variability is not a minor issue, since the associated decisions for how to handle queue lengths can have a profound impact on customers. When there is a process touch-point with a customer that may be subject to a lengthy queue time, one must consider the cost of lost customer goodwill if the decision is made to allow the queue to continue, rather than acquiring extra process capacity to reduce the size of the queue.

## Process Value Analysis

*Process value analysis* involves a review of each step in a process to see if the activity provides value to the customer. If the activity does not provide value, the analysis team looks for ways to eliminate it from the process. By going through a comprehensive process value analysis, a business can strip costs out of the organization while also shortening the duration of the process. When the length of a process is reduced, customers experience a shorter turnaround time for their orders, which increases customer satisfaction levels.

Processes can undergo repeated analyses of this type, where the latest technologies and equipment can be applied to the newest iteration of a process. The concept is also applicable to acquired businesses, where the acquirer can budget for likely cost reductions from a sweeping set of process value analyses.

This analysis might initially appear to be an outstanding way to improve several aspects of an organization, but there is a risk that key control points will be cut out of a process in the pursuit of cost reductions. Consequently, the accounting staff or a controls analyst should be included in the analysis, to advise on how to retain robust controls.

## Value Stream Mapping

*Value stream mapping* (VSM) reveals information about the process steps that a business uses to create value. It can be used to streamline process flows, thereby reducing non-value-added activities. Depending upon the format used, it can point out such information as:

- The work time and wait time required for each step in a process
- The amount of labor needed for a work step, including the identification of overtime
- The error rate by work step
- The downtime by work step

VSM can be applied to any process. The resulting charts can be used to pinpoint areas needing improvement, such as reductions in errors, automation to eliminate staff time, and altered controls to shorten process flows.

The VSM concept is best explained with an example. In the following sample of the timekeeping process, we see that the accounting staff requires only a small amount of staffing and time to process two steps, which are issuing reminders to employees and verifying supervisory approval of time cards. However, the VSM indicates that the controller must allocate more staff to the tasks of reviewing received time cards and summarizing hours worked. These latter two tasks are so time-sensitive that they routinely require the use of overtime to be completed on time. The map also shows a high error rate. Further, the VSM reveals that 25.5 hours are needed to complete this step, which is the lengthiest part of the payroll process.

**Value Stream Map**

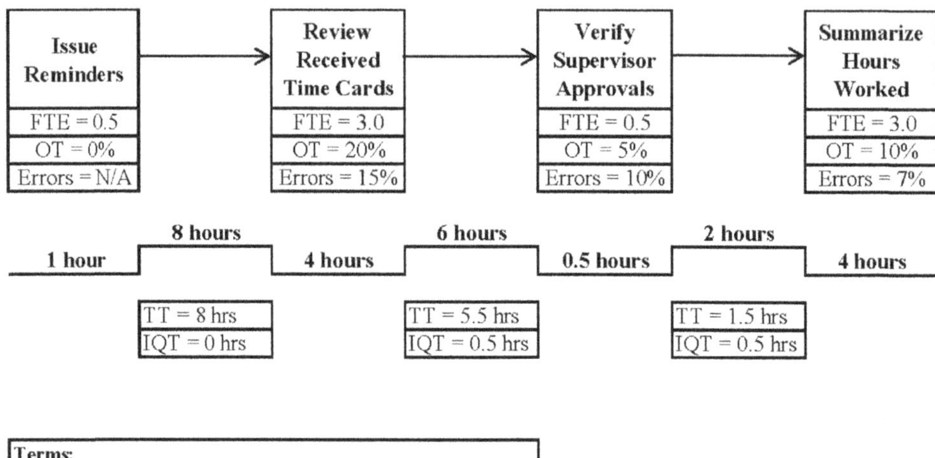


Given the issues shown in the map, it would be reasonable for the manager to implement a more automated method of time tracking, such as a computerized time clock. By doing so, the two bottlenecks in the process can be eliminated, along with overtime and the high error rate. Automation will also likely reduce the total processing time by a substantial amount. The controller might not have realized the severity of the problems with timekeeping without a VSM to clarify the issues.

Value stream mapping is an especially effective tool when used to break down the elements of high-volume processes; these processes are completed many times in a typical year, so even small changes can yield large cumulative benefits. Conversely, there is little point in using VSM to analyze processes that require little time and are only rarely completed, since there is only a modest opportunity for improvement.

## Process Training

Training employees and third parties in how to operate a new process requires more than a simple run-through of the steps involved and a few exercises. In addition, users need to understand how the process fits into the entire picture; that is, how it contributes to the final product issued by the business and experienced by customers. Once users have a clear view of the situation, they are more likely to follow the process flow as it was designed, and to make suggestions for its improvement. This also keeps them from skipping steps in the process that might damage the outcome. Similarly, users should understand what the upstream processes do that feed into their process, so that they can gain a full picture of what the entire linked process is all about.

---

**EXAMPLE**

New employees at Cajun Delights Restaurant are instructed to engage in a blanching process for all vegetables, where the vegetables are scalded in boiling water and then plunged into icy water to halt the cooking process. There was a recent experience where a customer got food poisoning from eating vegetables that had not been blanched. To keep this customer issue from happening again, the manager calls a meeting of the food preparation staff and goes over the need for blanching, why it is important, and the exact steps needed to complete it. Once the staff realizes that skipping the blanching process can transfer organisms on the vegetables to customers, they conduct it without fail. This talk becomes required training for all new hires, too.

---

## Process Standardization

When a business has a large number of locations, it needs to replicate a standard set of processes in each one. For example, the process for making donuts should be identical in a thousand-unit chain of coffee-and-donut shops. Otherwise, management will need to deal with slight variations in the process in each location, which results in slightly different outputs that may be noticed by customers – and not in a good way. Local employees may not like such a high degree of uniformity, especially when they want to exercise some discretion in how they handle tasks. Nonetheless, performing the same process many different ways across an organization will inevitably lead to confusion about how tasks are handled, especially when employees are transferred between locations and find a different set of processes in their new locations.

However, when processes are totally standardized, this also means that there is no room for best practices to emerge at individual locations. To keep this possibility open, a company can require that all locations must first install the company-standard process and run it for several months, to ensure that everyone understands it thoroughly. At this point, employees are allowed to make adjustments to the baseline process in a controlled manner, with outcome measurements to determine whether the changes improve the process. If so, a corporate-level process engineer evaluates the changes and decides whether to roll them out throughout the company.

## Summary

There are many considerations that go into the development of a well-configured process. One should determine the amount of transactional volume it is expected to handle, as well as the variety of outcomes expected from it. Other considerations include the acceptable amount of queue time in front of the process, the impact of bottlenecks, volume variability, the value being generated for the customer, and whether it can be standardized across the organization. Only then can a well-tuned process be devised that adequately supports operations.

# Chapter 7
# Facility Layouts

## Introduction

The layout of facilities involves where to position equipment and personnel within an operation. This has a critical impact on how people work together and interact with equipment, which underlies productivity levels. In addition, facility layout controls how materials, customers and information flow through the organization. In this chapter, we cover the different types of facility layouts, how they can impact operations, and the information needed to decide upon the most appropriate layout.

## The Impact of a Proper Layout

*Layout* is the way in which the parts of something are arranged or laid out. This is a critical factor in the development of efficient processes, but it is also important for how customers form an opinion about their experience with the company, and even for how employees form an opinion about their working environment. Consequently, layout can have a positive impact on many aspects of a business, including the following:

- The efficiency of process flows
- The emotional response of customers to the company
- The flexibility of process flows
- The level of communication among employees
- The level of employee efficiency
- The utilization of space

Conversely, a poor layout can have many negative effects on a business, including lower efficiency levels, inflexible operations, extended process times, and a poor experience for customers. Given these pluses and minuses, it is essential to spend enough time up front to achieve a reasonable facility layout.

## Layout Characteristics

The best layout for a business is the one that meshes most closely with its strategic plan, which means that an excellent layout for one company might be only an average one in another company. Nonetheless, the following characteristics are usually found in a well-designed layout:

- *Flow efficiency*. The layout should minimize the distance travelled by resources as they move through an operation. This is not a firm rule, however, since supermarkets do the reverse, making customers walk to the back of the store for milk, thereby forcing them to walk past other products that might tempt them into making a purchase.

- *Activity spacing.* The activities within a process should be properly spaced apart. In some cases, this means placing activities adjacent to each other, so that operators can more easily communicate with each other. In other cases, it means keeping them far apart, such as when a paint booth operation could contaminate the other processes in a production line.
- *Employee experience.* The layout cannot represent a hazard to employees. Another consideration is productivity, where a proper layout should minimize unnecessary movements. The best layouts supplement these basic requirements with a general look and feel that enhances employee morale.
- *Customer experience.* The layout in a retail environment is primarily targeted at enhancing the customer experience. A properly-designed layout should reinforce the brand image that the company is trying to project.

When devising a layout, it may be necessary to mix and match the preceding characteristics in order to come up with the most optimal approach. For example, if the accountants point out that a certain machine is quite expensive, this may drive a change in a production process, so that several process flows go into that machine; it can then be utilized at a high level. However, doing so muddles the efficiency of the upstream processes that feed into the machine. Thus, there is an efficiency tradeoff to be compared with the high cost of the machine.

## Layout Types

A layout may be derived from one of four general types, where are described in the following sub-sections.

### Fixed Location Layout

In a fixed location layout, the resources being transformed do not move. Instead, the people and equipment needed to perform tasks move as needed to ensure that the resource transformation is completed. This arrangement is needed when the resource being transformed is too large to move, and especially when the variety of tasks to be completed is quite large. However, the fixed location layout usually results in high unit costs, as well as complex project management activities to schedule people and equipment.

For example, a container ship under construction is far too large to move through a production process, so instead it is stationary, while a variety of crews work on it. Similarly, a marble sculpture will remain in one place while the staff in an artist's studio work on it. This approach works well for the project process type that was described in the preceding chapter.

## Functional Layout

In a functional layout, transform*ing* resources are aggregated into one location. This is done in order to increase operational efficiency. For example, in a furniture production company, all planers and sanders are located in one area, while lathes are clustered in another spot, and gluing operations are aggregated into a third area. The functional perspective is found in many retail establishments. For example, an automotive supply store may aggregate belts in one place, hoses in another, and filters in a third location.

With this arrangement, one operator can tend to multiple machines, and it is also easier for maintenance personnel to perform the same services on a cluster of identical machines. However, the flow for resources being transformed can be quite complex, as each one is routed in different directions through the functional areas. There can also be a problem with relatively low utilization levels, as some machines may be idle for extended periods of time. This approach works well for the batch processing that was discussed in the preceding chapter.

## Cell Layout

A cell layout contains a number of transforming resources that are specifically laid out to deal with a certain type of input. Once transformations are completed within the cell, the output may be moved to another cell, where additional transformations occur. This approach can lead to fast throughput, but can suffer from low equipment utilization levels. For example, the intensive care unit in a hospital is specifically configured for that purpose, as is the isolation ward for infectious diseases. In both cases, resources are clustered together to deal with a specific patient condition.

This approach is commonly used in retail stores; for example, in a sports equipment store, a cell layout would mandate that every article of equipment relating to baseball be located in one area, while all equipment related to basketball is located in a separate cluster. With this layout, someone looking for equipment relating to a specific sport (a self-selecting input) can find it within a single cell within the store. This approach works best with batch processing, but can also be applied to a mass production environment.

## Line Layout

A line layout is configured to transform a specific input. It requires an input to follow a pre-arranged route, where exactly the same transformational steps are completed every time. This results in a visually obvious flow that makes it easier to control than the other layout types. It results in the lowest unit costs of all the layout types, but typically involves highly repetitive work, which leads to excessive employee turnover.

For example, a school cafeteria requires students to enter at one end, pick up a tray, and load it with food from a series of food service stations, after which they pay at the other end of the line. Or, dish washing machines are assembled in a standardized production line, where the housing, racks, spray arms, detergent dispenser, control panel and power supply are brought together. This approach works best for either a mass production or continuous flow process.

## Hybrid Layouts

The type of layout used will depend on the type of product or service being provided, the range of possible outcomes from the process, and the expected activity volume. Given the broad range of possible requirements, it is quite likely that some hybrid version of the preceding layout types will be the optimal solution. For example, and as previously noted, a hospital will likely have cell layouts to deal with certain patient problems, such as intensive care and an isolation ward. However, it will also need a line layout for its cafeteria, as well as a functional layout for several of its more generic services, such as diagnostic imaging, general surgery, microbiology, and the pharmacy.

## Layout Selection Criteria

As just noted, the type of layout selected will depend on the volume of inputs going into the process and the variety of outputs expected from it. When a large amount of variety is expected, then the efficiency of the underlying flow is of minimal concern, so it makes less sense to use a line layout. Conversely, if the unit volume through the process is expected to be quite high, then processing efficiency becomes a major concern, which makes the fixed location option a poor one. When volume and variety are both present, then the best choices are likely to be either the functional layout or the cell layout.

Another consideration is the unit cost of the goods or services produced. When the fixed location layout is used, this represents a relatively minimal fixed cost of production, since the resource being transformed is sitting in one place. However, the associated variable cost is quite high, since people and equipment need to be brought to it. At the other extreme is the line layout, where the fixed cost of the layout is very high and the associated variable costs are quite low; in a line layout, a significant investment has been made in equipment that is perfectly positioned to drive down variable unit costs. The functional and cell layouts lie in between the other two layouts in terms of this mix of fixed and variable costs. Based on this consideration, a manufacturer of deodorant would always use a line layout, since it is producing something in high volume on a repetitive basis, with no variability in the expected output, and so can afford the fixed cost to set up a production line. Conversely, a manufacturer of submarines will always pick a fixed location layout, since it is producing in quantities of one, where it makes no sense to invest in the fixed cost of a higher-volume production layout.

The layout choice made may vary over time, either in response to company strategy or the requirements of customers. For example, if management decides to shift into a heavily customer service-oriented strategy, then product and service variety will likely increase, driving the layout choices more in the direction of the fixed location or functional layouts. Or, if the market decides to start buying one of the company's products in massive volume, then the obvious choice is to produce it using either the cell or line layout.

## Layout Impact on Staff

When designing a layout, one of the key considerations in the design is its impact on employees. There are many factors to consider, such as:

- *Colors*. What range of colors do employees consider to be neutral? Which colors do they consider to be annoying?
- *Lighting*. Should ambient light be used? Do employees perform better in direct or indirect sunlight? What level of lighting results in the best work output?
- *Meeting spaces*. Do employees need secluded areas for meetings? If so, should they be standard conference rooms, or would a more informal seating arrangement work better?
- *Noise*. Do employees prefer to work in a noisy environment? Perhaps one with a modest amount of background noise? What if they are unable to function if there is any noise at all?
- *Separation*. Employees are more likely to talk to each other when they are situated close together, with communication levels dropping precipitously when they are further apart. The ideal distance for employees represents a balance of keeping them far enough apart for them to work comfortably, without minimizing the amount of communication to an excessive degree.
- *Temperature*. What is the preferred temperature range for employees? Does this range differ by employee? Should some work areas be warmer or cooler than the average for the facility?

The design factors selected should promote the corporate culture that management wants to achieve. For example, if a business is built around the concept of gathering together to share ideas, then the layout needs to reflect this with many casual meeting areas and more attention to achieving optimal noise levels. Conversely, an organization that focuses on cost reduction is more likely to emphasize compressed work areas and pay less attention to any factors that might increase costs. As another example, when management wants to focus on teams of varying composition, it can design a layout comprised of modular furniture, so that it can be easily pulled apart and reconfigured to meet the needs of the moment.

## Layout Information Requirements

Every layout design must work within certain constraints, including the area within which it will be situated, the amount of money available for it, the time periods during which it can be used, and its adjacency to other processes with which interaction is desirable.

Within these constraints, the designer will likely have to focus on some type of overriding efficiency. For example, in a government office that responds to taxpayer queries, employees will be most efficient if they are parked at their desks, responding to calls. To minimize their travel time, each person should be equipped with a printer and scanner, rather than making them walk to a networked printer or scanner in a distant location. Travel time can be reduced even more by situating bathrooms and an employee snack room as close to them as possible. Further, if they need to consult information stored in filing cabinets, the best option is to digitize the files, so that this information can be accessed from their computers, without having to get up. In short, when travel time is a key consideration, the goal is to minimize the instances in which travel is required at all, and to minimize the distance traveled when it is necessary to do so.

When attempting to reduce employee travel time within a process, it can be useful to conduct a traffic analysis, where the number of point-to-point trips by employees are counted within the process, as well as to and from adjacent processes. This analysis, when laid out visually, can be useful for designing a more efficient layout that reduces travel times. For example, the following exhibit contains the current layout of a procurement department, showing the number of trips between different locations within and outside of the department.

**Sample Traffic Analysis – Unadjusted**

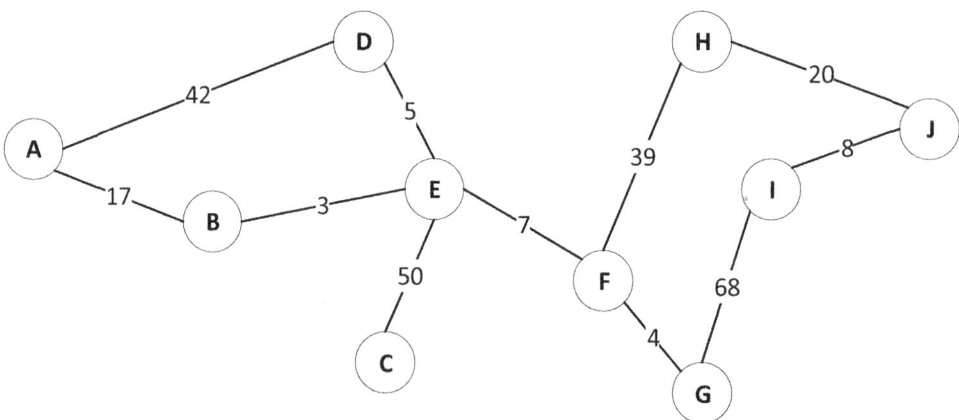


The situation can be improved upon by revising the layout of the department, so that the locations experiencing the highest travel volume are located closer together. Doing so does not reduce the number of trips, but it *does* reduce the total distance travelled. A possible revised format appears in the following exhibit.

**Sample Traffic Analysis – Adjusted**

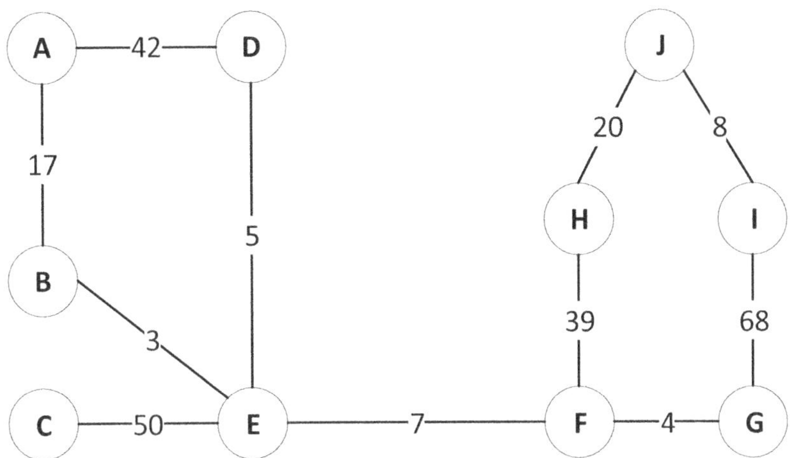


In addition to traffic analysis, it can be useful to engage in cluster analysis, to see if any activities naturally cluster together. This information is especially useful when deciding which machines to incorporate into a production cell for the processing of certain families of parts. The following exhibit illustrates the concept, where a grid shows which machines are used to process various families of parts. In the exhibit, there does not appear to be any particular clustering of machines that would result in an efficient cell configuration. However, when rearranged to shift the crosses in the exhibit to the diagonal line extending from the upper left to the lower right corner of the matrix, this clarifies that there are several coherent groupings of machines that may be clustered into production cells (as denoted by the shaded areas).

**Initial Cluster Analysis**

| | | Component Families | | | | | | | |
|---|---|---|---|---|---|---|---|---|---|
| Machines | | 1 | 2 | 3 | 4 | 5 | 6 | 7 | 8 |
| | 1 | × | | × | | | | | |
| | 2 | | | | × | | | × | |
| | 3 | | | | | × | × | | |
| | 4 | | | × | | | | | × |
| | 5 | | | | × | | | × | |
| | 6 | | × | | | × | × | | |
| | 7 | × | | × | | | | | × |
| | 8 | | × | | | × | × | | |

**Sorted Cluster Analysis**

| | | Component Families | | | | | | | |
|---|---|---|---|---|---|---|---|---|---|
| Machines | | 7 | 4 | 3 | 8 | 1 | 5 | 6 | 2 |
| | 2 | × | × | | | | | | |
| | 5 | × | × | | | | | | |
| | 1 | | | × | | × | | | |
| | 7 | | | × | × | × | | | |
| | 4 | | | × | × | | | | |
| | 8 | | | | | | × | × | × |
| | 3 | | | | | | × | × | |
| | 6 | | | | | | × | × | × |

For example, machines two and five could be clustered together to produce component families four and seven, while machines three, six, and eight could be clustered together to produce component families two, five, and six.

Though the preceding exhibit for cluster analysis appears to make a clean resolution inevitable, this is not really the case. In reality, some component/machine configurations will not fall into these neat clusters. When this is the case, it may be necessary to buy additional machines, so that they can be integrated into several production cells. Alternatively, work could be partially completed in one cell and then sent over to another cell where the required machines are located; doing so requires more complex routings, and so is a less than ideal solution.

## Summary

The layout of people and equipment within a facility is driven by the expected transaction volume, as well as the variety of outputs expected from it. Depending on the mix of these determining factors, a business may choose to use the fixed location, functional, cell, or line layouts, each of which offers different capabilities. It is also possible to develop a hybrid approach that combines the attributes of any of the standard layout models. The final design chosen may require adjustments over time, as management gains a better understanding of the volume and variety of outputs that are actually being experienced.

# Chapter 8
# Process Technology

## Introduction

Process technology is being integrated into most parts of a company's operations, including artificial intelligence, industrial robots, computer numerical control machines, and 3D printing. These technologies can make a company far more profitable, but managers need to be careful to understand both the risks and rewards associated with them. In this chapter, we focus on the advantages conferred by process technology and the associated risks of using them, including the constraints they impose on an organization.

## The Nature of Process Technology

*Technology* is the practical application of knowledge to a particular discipline – in this case, the operations of a business. It may involve a variety of techniques and processes used in the production of goods or services. It may also be embedded in machines to allow for their operation without a worker having any detailed knowledge of their inner workings.

*Process technology* is the knowledge used to create and deliver a product or service. The use of process technology has driven major changes in the speed with which products can be produced and delivered to customers, while also shortening product cycles and increasing the variety of options available to customers. These advances are so significant that a business would become hopelessly uncompetitive if it did not embrace them.

Process technology does not always take a direct hand in the production of goods or services. Instead, it may simply be involved in the organization of a process. For example, a bar code scanning system may be used to keep track of inventory levels in the warehouse, which has a direct impact on the ability of the production department to manufacture goods in a timely manner. Similarly, the use of a just-in-time production system can be used to organize the flow of jobs through the production area in an orderly manner.

Managers are sometimes forced to use process technology to avoid becoming uncompetitive, or they may be proactive and take on new technology in order to gain a competitive advantage over the rest of the industry. In either case, the performance objective of cost tends to play a key role. If a business is unable to produce goods and services within the general cost range of its competitors, then it will probably go out of business, no matter how well it measures up in the other four performance objectives of quality, speed, dependability and flexibility.

Process technology is especially useful for higher-volume processes. In these areas, a technology that may be able to only shave a few cents off a single unit of production can yield massive cost reductions when these savings are multiplied over thousands or millions of units produced.

## Examples of Process Technology

There are hundreds of examples of process technology. In the following bullet points, we provide a sampling of them that are intended to show the range of possibilities:

- 3D printing machines to create nearly any product from a digital file.
- A bar code scanning checkout system at a supermarket, where customers can pay for their own orders.
- A heads-up display used in the warehouse to show workers which items to pick from stock to fulfill a customer order.
- A heat sensor installed on a machine, which warns of an increased risk of equipment failure.
- A predictive algorithm to identify when customer queues will increase in a cafeteria, so that additional staff can be scheduled for those times.
- A Six Sigma quality system that is designed to eradicate errors from a process.
- A touch screen used at a fast food restaurant for customers to place orders.
- A voice response system that asks call-in customers simple questions, so that their calls can be routed to the correct operator.
- A warehouse management system that tracks the flow of inventory through a warehouse.
- An artificial intelligence system that can spot tumors on x-ray scans.
- An augmented reality system integrated into glasses and used to show a maintenance worker how to repair a machine.
- An automated conveyor belt that starts when a unit is placed on it, and which stops when the unit reaches the other end.
- An automated guided vehicle that can move work-in-process from one work station to another.
- An automated passport scanner in an airport.
- An industrial robot that is used to assemble trucks on an assembly line.
- An on-line ordering system, so that customers can place orders without any human intervention.

## The Process Technology Selection Process

What is the selection process that an operations manager should go through to acquire process technology? The first step is to obtain a general understanding of what the technology does, and how it can potentially impact operations. This does *not* mean acquiring a detailed understanding of the underlying fundamentals, which would require more time than most managers have available. The second step is to compare the targeted technology to alternatives, to see if there are any other options that would do a better job of enhancing company operations. And finally, they must be able to properly manage its installation, so that it dovetails into the processes that it is intended to improve. We deal with each of these three steps in the following sub-sections.

### Understanding Process Technology

Gaining an understanding of process technology means learning about the principles underlying it, so that one can ask pertinent questions and have a reasonable feel for whether it will work within the company. A busy manager may shift this task off onto someone more deeply involved with the technology, or perhaps someone from the IT department. When gaining an understanding of a technology, it is useful for one to clarify the answers to the following questions:

- Are there any risks associated with its use?
- How does it achieve the outcomes it claims?
- How is it different from other technologies in the same general area?
- What benefits will it confer on the company?
- What is the incremental change from the technology it will replace?
- Will it create a new bottleneck within the targeted operations process?

### Evaluating Process Technology

A central concern with any new technology is its track record. When the technology is new and relatively unproven, management needs to evaluate whether it wants to take a chance on having the system fail, or of having the supplier fail. These risks decline over time as the technology gains a foothold in the market and the supplier works out the kinks in its products, but by then a new risk emerges – that the company is behind other competitors who have already adopted the technology. Thus, there tends to be a window within which managers are most likely to acquire new technologies, which is bounded by when it has been proven and when the competitive situation dictates that it must be acquired.

Assuming that a prospective technology acquisition falls into this purchasing window, the manager then needs to evaluate it based on the following three criteria:

- Does the technology mesh with the volume and variety characteristics of the process within which it will be installed? When the technology can work with high process volumes, then it is probably dedicated to a tightly-restricted range of activities for which it has been specifically designed. Conversely, if the technology is able to deal with a wider variety of activities, it is probably more general purpose, and so is less efficient that a high-volume technology. In addition to these capabilities, the manager will need to be concerned with the following issues:

- *Automation.* A technology that deals with high process volumes is more likely to use automation, so that little (if any) human intervention is required. Automation can be expensive, and so increases the fixed cost of a process, requiring a business to generate more sales in order to break even. Conversely, minimal automation introduces the need for more human labor, which keeps fixed costs low but increases variable costs; this results in a lower breakeven point, but also lower margins.
- *Capacity.* A technology may be designed to process large volumes, which usually means that it is more expensive and designed for a limited range of functionality. Conversely, it might be designed for low volume, which carries with it a lower cost. Either option may fit into a company's operations, depending on the situation. For example, if a company elects to have a single, centralized high-speed printer for every computer in a department, it may be able to print at a very low cost per page, but there is a risk that no one will be able to print if this one device fails. Alternatively, a business might equip each computer with its own printer, which probably increases the cost per page, but also makes the departmental printing capability more robust, since it is spread throughout the department.
- *Integration.* A technology should be able to link seamlessly with the other activities within a process. This can be a major problem when a technology has a closed architecture that is not designed to interface easily with the products of other providers, making it necessary for management to develop expensive or awkward workarounds or custom interfaces. When workarounds are needed, this tends to interfere with process throughput times, which negatively impacts the amount of volume that can be run through a process. This is less of a concern when the variety of output demanded is high, since activities may need to be mixed and matched to achieve the desired output – which requires minimal integration between activities.

- What specific parts of the intended process will the technology improve? The technology being evaluated needs to enhance one or more of the operating performance objectives, which are quality, speed, dependability, flexibility, and cost. This investigation should cover a number of possibilities, including the following:
    - Can the technology improve the safety experience for workers?
    - Can the technology reduce the error rates currently being experienced?
    - Can the technology reduce the failure rate of the process?
    - Can the technology shorten the current processing speed?
    - Does the technology provide an entirely new capability for the company?

- Does the technology switch more easily between tasks than is currently the case?

A technology being evaluated may do some of the preceding items *worse* than the technology currently being used; when this is the case, its other performance characteristics need to be much better than the current technology in order to make it a winning choice for the company.

- What is the technology's net present value? Technology investments usually involve making a significant investment up-front, along with a series of maintenance costs over an extended period of time. Offsetting this investment is a (hopefully) long-term series of cash inflows generated by the investment, either from revenue increases or cost reductions. These cash flows can be adjusted to their present values (since money spent or received now has greater value than such transactions at a later date). This information can be summarized in a spreadsheet to show all expected cash flows over the useful life of the technology investment, with a discount rate applied that reduces the cash flows to what they would be worth at the present date. This calculation is known as *net present value analysis*. If the outcome presents a positive net present value, then the investment can proceed.

---

**EXAMPLE**

The Hail Correction Institute is exploring whether it should buy a 3-D printer to create body panels for damaged cars and trucks. The firm's cost of capital is 10%, which it uses as the discount rate to construct the net present value of the acquisition. The following table shows the related net present value calculation, assuming that the purchase price of the 3-D printer is $120,000:

| Year | Cash Flow | Discount Factor | Present Value |
|---|---|---|---|
| 0 | -$120,000 | 1.0000 | -$120,000 |
| 1 | +35,000 | 0.9259 | +32,407 |
| 2 | +35,000 | 0.8573 | +30,006 |
| 3 | +35,000 | 0.7938 | +27,783 |
| 4 | +25,000 | 0.7350 | +18,375 |
| 5 | +25,000 | 0.6806 | +17,015 |
| | | Net present value | +$5,586 |

The analysis reveals that the purchase is projected to have a positive net present value, so there is no financial reason to block the purchase.

The discount factor in the table has a greater impact on cash flows occurring further in the future, since the Institute will have to wait longer to receive them.

---

## Implementing Process Technology

In many cases, successful implementation of new technologies is the lynchpin of a competitive and profitable operation. It can be quite difficult to fully implement a new process technology, with many factors coming into play. In the following bullet points, we note a number of issues that should be addressed in order to improve the odds of success:

- *Technology strategy.* Process technology should only be acquired after a complete technology roadmap has been devised, so that there is a clear understanding of what operations will look like in a few years after a whole set of technology upgrades have been installed. It makes little sense to install something without this roadmap, since the company may end up making a purchase and then pulling it out shortly thereafter because it does not fit with another technology acquisition made at a later date. In addition, this roadmap states the sequence in which technology investments should be made, so that each successive investment builds on what has come before.
- *Senior level support.* Every technology initiative must have a strong supporter on the senior management team. This person must be willing to find the support needed to continue an implementation through to completion. Otherwise, it is quite possible that the "latest and greatest" project will take funding away from it.
- *Process changes.* A technology is more likely to function properly when it is close to the current technology base of the company. When this is the case, employees can draw upon their knowledge of similar systems to analyze problem areas and find solutions. Conversely, a technology solution is that quite different from the current technology base is at much greater risk of failure.
- *Customer interaction.* When customers are expected to interact with a new technology, it should be extensively pilot tested to ensure that customers are comfortable with it. If not, and especially when this is a major process touch point for them, it is possible that sales will decline as customers take their business elsewhere. Customer-facing technology tends to work best when it is simple to use and offers a low range of options from which to make selections.
- *Conversion.* It can be exceedingly difficult to switch over to a new technology, especially when the "cold turkey" approach is used to shut down the old system and immediately switch to the new one. This can cause problems if the new system has not been adequately tested, employees are not thoroughly trained in its functions, or applicable records have not been properly ported over to the new system. Consequently, all of these issues should be addressed in the conversion plan.
- *Implementation staffing.* A number of problems may arise immediately after the implementation date, due to unforeseen issues. To counter these problems, there should be an excess number of the most qualified staff assigned to the project in the days following the system conversion, to ensure that all issues

are dealt with as quickly as possible. This over-staffing period may need to continue for several weeks or months after the conversion date.

- *Internal support capabilities*. Does the company have sufficient people trained to support the technology? If not, any failure may involve extensive downtime while the supplier sends out staff to evaluate and correct the problem – which increases frustration with the system and reduces the level of support for it.
- *Training*. Users need to be fully trained in how a new technology works, including how it fits into a process, what to do when errors occur, and possible variations that can arise during its operation.

## The Future of Process Technology

The operations areas that have seemed most immune to the encroachments of process technologies have been those requiring decision-making based on judgment and insight. However, even these areas are likely to see the onset of process technologies, now that artificial intelligence engines can be trained with large data sets to arrive at the best outcomes without human intervention. Most likely, portions of employee jobs throughout the operations area will be replaced by technology, leaving a scattering of other areas that are not so amenable to technology intrusions that will form the basis for future jobs.

## Summary

There are many types of process technologies from which to choose. To make the right choices, one must first develop a technology roadmap that details how each technology will fit into the organization's overall strategy for the development of competitive operations, and then examine the stability of the underlying technology, how well it meshes with existing systems, its ability to handle various levels of volume and variety, and whether it will generate a positive cash flow return for the business. Once selected, management needs to avoid any implementation pitfalls by investigating how well it will be accepted by employees and customers, ensuring that it has senior management support, and that personnel are properly trained in its use. Working through these steps is essential, given the high cost of many process technologies and the significant downside associated with an implementation failure.

# Chapter 9
# Personnel in Operations

## Introduction

People play a major role in operations, even though most discussions center on other topics, such as layout, technology, and process flows. This is unfortunate, since the proper management of personnel has a profound impact on the effectiveness and efficiency of operations. In this chapter, we discuss those aspects of human resources that most closely pertain to operations.

## The Importance of Personnel to Operations

The bulk of the employees in the typical organization are located within the operations function, so logically they have a tremendous influence on its work products. There are several ways to influence employee productivity, but one of the most important is the *company culture*; this refers to the beliefs and behaviors that determine how a company's employees and management interact and handle outside business transactions. Stated differently, company culture describes how an organization behaves.

The beliefs and behaviors that make up a company's culture may not be the same throughout the organization. It is entirely possible that these cultural components will differ by department, which can make it difficult to manage operations as a whole – which is made up of several departments. The effect is worsened when there are functional silos within the organization, since it tends to group employees within departments, not allowing them much freedom to mix with other departments. In order to standardize behavior within operations, managers need to understand the root causes of culture, which are as follows:

- *What are accepted as self-evident facts*. A group of people tends to develop a shared belief in what the group should be doing. For example, a police department might develop a shared belief that they exist to protect the local community. Though that may seem self-evident, it is possible that a grossly underpaid police department will develop an entirely different view, which is that the local community is a source of income for them, which is to be milked in order to increase police income. The latter approach is unfortunately common in a few third-world countries where police are paid very low wages.
- *What is known about objectives and processes*. Employees should have a strong understanding of *why* they do what they do, as well as how the operations in their area work. This is essential for gaining the full cooperation of employees. Conversely, when this knowledge is not shared with employees,

there is more likely to be strife between employees and management, and significantly less motivation within the department.

- *What are accepted as behavioral norms*. Any department will operate under a set of behavioral norms that involve what is and is not acceptable. This may involve the acceptability of arriving late for work, or whether to shout at someone, or whether it is possible to get away with varying amounts of theft. For example, a behavioral norm in a department where everyone knows the manager is stealing from petty cash is for everyone else to pilfer cash, too. Or, when the manager works extremely late to ensure that customer orders are shipped on time, employees are likely to copy this behavior, which becomes a behavioral norm.

For example, a new operations manager wants to improve the coherence between the procurement and materials management departments. She finds that the procurement staff has a firm belief in the benefits of buying in large quantities in order to obtain robust volume discounts, while the materials management staff has just as strong a belief in buying in small quantities, in order to reduce the burden of tracking inventory in the warehouse. These opposite views are accepted as self-evident facts by the two departments, and so will have to be reconciled in order to create a more coherent culture.

## The Nature of Organizations

Before delving deeper into how to maximize the use of personnel in operations, we will diverge briefly to address the nature of the organizations that employ them. An *organization* is a group of people who have been structured and managed to meet a need or pursue a goal. There are several general types of organizations, but a specific entity rarely exactly matches one of them. Instead, it is more likely to be an amalgamation of several types, based on what management is trying to do and how the organization incrementally changed over time to reach its current state.

*Organizational structure* is the set of rules used to delineate how tasks are controlled within an organization. These rules state the reporting relationships between positions, as well as how work is delegated and controlled. These rules are needed to allow for specialization, so that decisions can be made by those with the most expertise to do so. The type of structure adopted by an organization can be stated graphically in an organization chart. The two general classifications of organizational structure are:

- *Centralized.* Decision-making is concentrated at the top of the organization, with lower levels of the organization being told how to implement those decisions. This approach is more common in large organizations operating in industries that do not experience much change.
- *Decentralized.* Decision-making is diffused throughout the organization, which results in fewer levels within the organizational structure. This

approach works best when the organization needs to be more agile in its decision-making.

More specifically, a business might adopt one of the following organizational structures that is tailored to operate best within its specific business environment:

- *Functional.* This approach breaks up a company into departments, so that each area of specialization is under the control of a different manager. For example, there may be separate departments for accounting, engineering, purchasing, production, and distribution. This is the most common organizational structure.
- *Organic.* This approach has an extremely flat reporting structure, where the span of control of the typical manager encompasses a large number of employees. Interactions among employees tend to be horizontally across the organization, rather than vertically between layers of managers and their direct reports.
- *Divisional.* This approach creates separate organizational structures to service different geographic regions or product lines. For example, one division may be structured to service the Africa region, while another division is targeted at the South America market. It is used in larger organizations. There can be functional or organic structures within a division.
- *Matrix.* This approach allows employees to have multiple responsibilities across multiple functional areas. When implemented correctly, it can result in an effective organization. However, it is confusing for employees and so is rarely used.

## Line and Staff

Line and staff are the two broadest categories within which employees are organized in a business. Line personnel are directly involved in the operations of a business. Line functions include sales, marketing, production, and distribution. The line functions also generate revenue for the organization.

Staff personnel facilitate the activities of line personnel. For example, a human resources employee is ranked within the staff classification, as is an internal auditor, an accountant, a public relations person, and a risk manager. Since staff personnel have more of a planning role, they tend to be primarily responsible for building the strategic capabilities of the operations area.

Line personnel are directly involved in attaining the goals of an organization. They do so by allocating resources, modifying processes, improving outputs, and so forth. Their focus tends to be only on the immediate plan, which usually extends anywhere from the next few weeks to the end of the planning year. Staff personnel are only indirectly involved, since they are facilitating the work of the line personnel. However, staff personnel are more effective when they have a detailed knowledge of the work being conducted by line personnel, so it makes sense for the two groups to work closely together.

There can be conflict between the two types of positions. Line personnel tend to resent staff personnel for interfering with their job functions, while staff personnel complain that they are being ignored by line personnel. The situation can be exacerbated when staff personnel become too involved in line work in order to give the appearance that they are justifying their positions. Ideally, there should be just enough staff personnel to create a net gain in the performance of the organization as a whole. Too many staff personnel will increase costs while reducing the efficiency of the line personnel.

During economic downturns, staff personnel tend to be laid off first, since doing so reduces costs without interfering with the productive capacity of the business.

## Job Analysis

*Job analysis* is the process of assembling activities into specific job descriptions and describing how each job relates to the other defined jobs in an organization. Job analysis also involves the determination of the qualifications needed to succeed in a job, as well as the work environment in which the job is performed.

A significant concept that is considered infrequently is clustering together work that matches a certain type of personality. If the bulk of a job involves detailed work, the ideal person for the job is likely to be an introverted, detail-oriented person. If so, remove from the description other tasks that such a person might find jarring, such as giving presentations to management. Conversely, if a job description is customer-focused, keep detail-level clerical tasks out of the job description. For example, minimize the amount of report writing that a salesperson is required to complete. By paying attention to this important detail, employees are more likely to fit into their assigned positions.

Once a job analysis has been constructed for a position, the result should include the following information:

- *Purpose.* This is the overriding reason for the position.
- *Reporting relationships.* The positions reporting to this job, as well as the position to which this job reports.
- *Responsibilities.* The specific tasks assigned to this job.
- *Work environment.* The surroundings in which the job is to be performed.
- *Requirements.* The knowledge level, skills, and capabilities required of a person in order to adequately fulfill the responsibilities of the job. This may include a certain type of college degree, years of experience, use of certain software, language skills, and so forth. Also note any physical demands on someone working in this position.
- *Performance criteria.* The criteria on which a person holding the position will be judged.

A sample job description that incorporates these criteria follows.

**Procurement Manager Job Description**

Position description: Procurement Manager

Purpose: This position is accountable for sourcing required goods and services to meet the needs of the business.

Reporting relationships: Reports to the operations manager

Responsibilities:

- Develops and executes procurement strategies
- Crafts negotiation strategies with targeted optimal terms
- Forecasts market trends to identify changes in purchase price points
- Monitors and forecasts demand levels
- Assesses and manages procurement risks
- Identifies and partners with reliable suppliers
- Monitors key procurement metrics and acts upon unfavorable variances as needed

Work environment: Normal working hours in an office environment. Will need to travel to supplier sites at least 20% of the time.

Requirements: 10+ years of procurement experience in increasingly responsible positions. Must have managed a staff of at least __ people. Master's degree in supply chain management preferred. Must have strong leadership capabilities.

Performance Criteria: Based on the ability to source materials and services to meet the needs of the organization.

---

In the sample job description, the level of detail is quite specific. This level of detail is warranted, since the job is a recurring one that is unlikely to change, and for which the company must recruit for people capable of engaging in the specific activities noted in the description. A variation on the description layout is to number the responsibilities and list them in declining order of importance. Doing so reveals which tasks call for the most recruiting emphasis.

To obtain a greater understanding of a job, it can be useful to include estimates of the time required per week for each stated task. Doing so can pinpoint those more long-running tasks in which job candidates must be competent.

A considerable amount of analysis is needed to construct a job description that accurately reflects the actual functions that a person is performing. One of the more accurate analysis methods is an iterative series of interviews. In the first interview, the goal is for the interviewer to compile the interviewee's impression of a job. This compilation is then reviewed by the interviewee in subsequent interviews to ensure that the details of the position have been correctly identified. It may also be necessary to observe a person while doing a job, or to have a person maintain a work journal, in order to uncover additional tasks that might not have been recorded in the initial description.

## Scientific Management

*Scientific management* involves the careful study of a job to determine the best possible procedures for conducting it. The emphasis is on finding the best combination of movements, coupled with equipment, to achieve the highest possible amount of output. It involves the following activities:

- Develop a standardized approach for performing a task.
- Select workers who have the correct skills to follow the new standardized approach.
- Train these workers in the use of the standardized approach.
- Eliminate work disruptions so that workers can focus on their assigned tasks.
- Provide wage inducements to incentivize higher output levels.

Despite its contributions to corporate efficiency, scientific management suffers from several flaws. Most critically, it does not provide for inputs from workers, assuming instead that an expert is in the best position to create optimal work processes. This makes workers feel unimportant. In addition, the system makes no provision for the higher needs of workers, who might want to advance beyond their current positions. These issues fueled the rise of organized labor. Consequently, scientific management is no longer followed as a discrete discipline, though some aspects of its teachings have continued to the present day, mostly in regard to devising work standards and holding employees to them with variance measurements.

---

**EXAMPLE**

An example of the origins of scientific management is the work of Frederick Winslow Taylor at the Bethlehem Steel Company in the late 19th and early 20th centuries. Taylor, often called the "father of scientific management," developed his theories by conducting time and motion studies on industrial tasks.

In the 1890s, Bethlehem Steel faced inefficiencies in its production processes, particularly in handling and moving steel and pig iron. Workers used inconsistent methods, leading to wasted time and lower productivity. Taylor closely observed workers' methods and measured how long it took to complete tasks. For example, he studied the process of loading pig iron onto railcars. He found that workers moved only about 12.5 tons per day.

Taylor identified the most efficient way to perform each task. He designed a standardized approach, including the ideal weight of pig iron a worker should move at a time and the best motion patterns to minimize fatigue. He advocated for selecting workers suited for specific tasks based on their physical abilities and provided them with specialized training. He then trained selected workers to use his methods. Taylor also introduced a piece-rate pay system to motivate workers to adopt the new methods, offering higher wages for meeting productivity targets

By applying these principles, Taylor increased the average output per worker from 12.5 tons to 47 tons per day — nearly a 400% improvement. This success demonstrated the potential of scientific management to enhance efficiency and set the stage for broader adoption in manufacturing.

---

## Ergonomic Workplace Design

Given the hands-on nature of operations, it should be no surprise that the design of jobs should encompass the concept of ergonomics. The term *ergonomic* refers to the design of an efficient and comfortable working environment. This means that there must be a fit between people and the jobs they perform, where the job is adjusted to fit the individual. Ergonomic adjustments are usually made to fine-tune the workplace to the size, shape, and other physical aspects of an employee. For example, the height of a position on an assembly line may be adjusted to account for an unusually tall or short person. Or, the expected distance required to reach a part can be shortened to keep a person from having to stretch too far to reach it – which could cause problems if repeated many times. Typically, a work area is configured so that tasks are comfortably concentrated within the range of 95% of the population. There are many ways to make ergonomic adjustments to a workplace, including the following:

- Adequate foot support
- Adjustable computer screens
- Adjustable keyboards
- Adjustable lighting
- Adjustable seat backs
- Adjustable work surfaces

## Job Design to Motivate Employees

A job may be created based on the principals of scientific management, or in order to create an ergonomically-correct workplace. However, the problem with both approaches is that they do not design for the motivation of the person performing the work, who does not want to spend the rest of his days on endlessly repetitive tasks. In addition, one must consider how to motivate employees, so that they actually have an interest in the work. Doing so has numerous positive effects, such as employees being more interested in quality work, making improvement suggestions, and producing a higher volume of output. The following approaches can all be used to motivate employees:

- Introduce a greater variety of tasks into the job to make it more interesting
- Combine work activities so that a coherent unit of output is produced
- Include significant tasks that have a major bearing on the outcome of the work
- Allow employees to modify their own jobs to some extent
- Assign responsibility for the outcome of the work
- Provide them with measurements of the results of their work

---

**EXAMPLE**

An engine manufacturer has been producing the engines on an assembly line, where each worker performs one task. However, the company is experiencing an unacceptably high error rate. To correct it, the assembly line is replaced by small teams that jointly assemble each engine. Each person on a team is responsible for many tasks, and must work with the others on the team to ensure that an engine is completed properly. The team name is then stamped on each completed engine. As a result, error rates decline precipitously.

---

Several additional options for employee motivation appear in the following sub-sections.

### Job Rotations

A possibility for improving employee motivation is periodic job rotations. A *job rotation* is designed to expose employees to multiple aspects of an organization, so that they will eventually have a more well-rounded view of how the entity operates when they are running it. For example, a person initially employed in the engineering department to create new products may work for several years in the marketing department, to see how products are positioned and advertised in the marketplace, and then move on to the sales department to experience the selling process flow. Other rotations might send the individual through the production and accounting departments, to gain a more complete understanding of the remaining key functional areas.

### Job Enlargement

Another way to enhance employee motivation is through *job enlargement,* which involves increasing the number of tasks associated with a job in order to expand the variety of work. This approach is most successful when the added tasks require an employee to increase her knowledge level. For example, a worker on a production line can also be tasked with conducting a quality review on her work. The outcome of job enlargement can be a workforce that is capable of engaging in a broad variety of tasks, including filling in for each other. At a minimum, job enlargement entails not performing the same tasks quite so much, which reduces job monotony.

### Job Enrichment

Yet another way to enhance motivation is *job enrichment,* which expands the amount of responsibility built into an employee's job. By giving the employee more control over his or her work, the intent is to improve the motivation of employees lower down in the organizational structure, who do not normally have much say over their roles. This approach is based on the theory that not having control over your job leads to minimal effort to improve. Job enrichment results in better-trained employees, enhanced morale, and a greater effort to achieve a more effective and efficient workplace. However, it can also result in a heavier workload, especially when employees do not have the right skills or experience to take on an expanded role within the organization. A side-effect of job enrichment is that the role of managers changes, reducing the amount of direct oversight and increasing the amount of coaching.

### Empowerment

Another option is to empower employees to a greater extent. *Empowerment* is the practice of giving employees an increased level of information and decision-making responsibility, so that they can take action to improve the performance of a business. The core concept is to allow those closest to a problem to solve it, rather than deferring judgment until a senior management person can address it. Empowerment allows an organization to make better decisions more quickly, so that the firm is more responsive to changes in the market, and especially in making responses to customers. It can be a significant competitive advantage, especially when competitors do not use the same empowerment practices. Empowerment can also improve employee satisfaction, since employees have a significantly greater amount of control over their jobs.

### Teamwork

Lurking behind many of the preceding employee motivation topics is the need to work in teams. Doing so allows a group with complementary skills to complete a specific task with a great deal of control over how the work is to be done. The team controls such matters as who does which tasks, when the work is to be done, how results are to be measured, and when to add or subtract staff from the team. When done properly, working in teams can be highly motivational, resulting in increased productivity. Teams also tend to generate more innovative ideas, and generate higher-quality outputs. However, they may disintegrate when team members cannot get along with each other. See the author's *Developing and Managing Teams* manual for more information.

## Flexible Hours

Employees may be more productive if they can adjust the hours during which they work, rather than being locked into a regimented set of working hours. Here are several examples:

- *Long commute*. An employee may live many miles from the office, and is stuck in commuter traffic each day. If she can start work an hour later and leave the office an hour later, she can skip much of this traffic.
- *Productive hours*. A software developer finds that he works best late at night, and is nearly non-functional during the morning hours. If his working hours can be shifted well outside of the normal first-shift hours, the company will experience much higher productivity from him.
- *Parents*. A parent needs to be at home to prepare his children for school, after which he can head for the office. This calls for a delayed start to the work day.

In these common situations, it can be difficult to force employees into the straitjacket of the 9-to-5 work day. Instead, consider allowing them to shift their working hours. At a minimum, this can mean allowing the staff to shift their hours slightly around a core set of working hours. For example, all employees are expected to be in the office from the hours of 10 a.m. to 3 p.m. in order to be available for meetings, and can shift their remaining hours as needed. At a more permissive level, employees can work whenever they want, as long as their work products are completed on time.

The concept of flexible work hours is only possible in certain situations. For example, production line operators must work within a specific set of hours, or else there will be no one to operate the equipment. Similarly, a support person such as a receptionist must be available to answer the phones during a company's stated work hours. However, if there is no time-specific responsibility, as is the case for a software developer, industrial engineer, marketing person or accountant, the concept of flexible work hours may be applicable.

## Compressed Work Weeks

For some types of jobs, such as nursing, it is relatively common to have employees work long hours for a smaller number of days per week. Typically, this means working four days, followed by three days off. At a more extreme level, some organizations allow three consecutive 12-hour shifts, followed by four days off. Despite the long hours, this compressed work week is sought after by employees, since they have significantly larger blocks of free time.

The compressed work week is not applicable to most jobs, for several reasons. First, a company can be severely understaffed on the last day of the normal work week, when there is a reduced level of staffing to deal with any issues that may arise. Second, employee productivity tends to decline when the number of work hours increases; there can also be an increase in employee injuries. And third, longer work hours per day can trigger state laws that require overtime to be paid. For example, a state may require that overtime be paid on any day when the number of hours worked exceeds eight hours.

**Working from Home**

The concept of working from home has gradually spread, to the point where a large number of companies will at least consider implementing the concept. The concern with this approach is that employees will be distracted by at-home activities and not focus on their assigned tasks. However, several studies have shown the reverse, with the following effects consistently noted:

- *Greater job satisfaction*. This is no surprise, since employees do not have to waste time commuting to the office, do not need to dress up in office attire, and can set their own schedules (within reason). And, greater job satisfaction means that turnover among those who work from home is reduced.
- *Greater productivity*. This is more of a surprise to those accustomed to working in the office, who assume that close interaction with their fellows is crucial to a high level of productivity. Instead, the inherent distractions of the office are eliminated when employees work from home, resulting in a significant boost in productivity. In addition, people who work from home tend to work longer hours. Also, people tend to continue working even when they are sick.
- *Lower costs*. The employer can save a significant amount on office space that it no longer needs. This cost savings is much higher than the cost of setting an employee up to work at home.
- *Larger candidate pool*. When employees can work remotely, a business can look much further afield for employees. It is possible to profitably employ people who live in entirely different time zones. In addition, this approach allows access to a new group of people who cannot leave the home – those involved with child care and elder care.

Working from home appears to work especially well for those people who are introverted and who either work in clerical positions (such as call center representatives) or are highly skilled experts (such as software developers). The following are all functions to which the work-at-home concept is most applicable:

| | | |
|---|---|---|
| Analysis | Data entry | Software development |
| Budgeting | On-line customer support | Writing |

Nonetheless, there are situations in which working from home may not be the answer. Consider the following situations:

- *Career advancement*. There may be a concern among employees that they will not be considered for promotion if they work from home, on the grounds

that they are not routinely meeting with the rest of their teams or their managers, and so cannot be properly evaluated. This can be a valid concern, depending on the processes used to target employees for advancement.
- *Data security*. An employee may have access to sensitive company information from their home computer, which can now be accessed by anyone who can enter that person's home. Strong password protection that must be reset regularly is probably the best way to guard against this issue.
- *Disaster recovery*. What if an employee is storing information locally and loses the data, either from a system crash or by theft of the equipment? This scenario can be ameliorated by employing on-line data backup services.
- *Equipment retrieval*. The company may have installed expensive computer equipment at a person's home. How difficult will it be to retrieve this equipment if the person's employment is terminated?
- *Low morale*. If employee morale is exceedingly low, it is possible that those people working from home will spend a large part of their time looking for new jobs.
- *Minimal training*. If employees are not well-trained, it is difficult to obtain that training when there is no trainer present, which results in prolonged inefficiency and high error rates. This issue can be overcome by certifying the skill levels of employees before allowing them to work from home.
- *Socialites*. More extroverted employees enjoy the office environment and prefer to be with other people on a regular basis. Their turnover might increase if they were forced to work from home.
- *Technical support*. The computer systems used by employees must be operational for as close to 100% of the time as possible. This is a particular concern when the home computer must be constantly networked into the company's computer system. For example, a travel agent who works from home cannot perform the job unless she can constantly access travel booking sites.
- *Virus protection*. It is possible that an employee could inadvertently download a virus through his home computer and then upload it to the company through the corporate network.

If there is resistance from management about allowing employees to work from home, conduct a pilot project that examines the output of a small group, and continue the test for a number of months. Then compare both the output and turnover rate of this group to the results of a control group that worked from the office during the same time period. If the results are notably better for the work-at-home group, this may present a sufficiently convincing case to trigger a larger rollout of the concept. Part of a pilot project can include the development of guidelines regarding how much equipment the company is to provide, who to call for equipment repair issues, the security of the equipment, personal use of the equipment, reimbursement for home office supplies, ergonomic considerations, and so forth.

One way to select employees for the work-from-home option is to only allow it after a probationary period, during which they are fully trained and evaluated for their organizational and time-management skills. This probationary period may be as short as a few weeks, to ensure that new employees are capable of operating on their own.

One valid concern with working from home is the need to have occasional meetings. There are several ways to do so. One is to use an on-line video chat service, such as Skype. For in-person meetings, schedule certain employees to be in the office on specific days, and schedule meetings around those dates. Another option is to have everyone meet at the office on the same date, though this approach requires a larger investment in office space to accommodate the extra personnel.

## Working Environment Issues

Thus far, we have discussed the design of jobs, but what about the design of the job environment? This is a combination of the noise level, lighting, temperature, and so forth where employees are expected to work. For example, it is not that easy to determine the most appropriate temperature, since it involves a combination of the humidity level, the impact of incoming sunlight, the presence of fans, and the amount of physical work being performed. Generally, clerical work requires a higher temperature, due to the relative level of staff inactivity, while the reverse is the case for someone working in the warehouse.

Another concern in the work environment is lighting, which can vary radically, depending on the work being performed. For example, lighting in storage areas can be quite low, since there is little to no work going on, while lighting in a clerical area needs to be quite bright, so that employees can properly review paperwork.

Yet another environmental issue is the amount of noise in the work area. In addition to the permanent loss of hearing that can accompany persistently high noise levels, it is also much harder to communicate and concentrate in a high-noise environment. Consequently, noise abatement should be a strong consideration in any area where employees are expected to work for extended periods of time.

## Method Study

Thus far, we have talked in generalities about how to create a well-designed job. But how is it actually done? *Method study* is the process of subjecting work to systematic, critical scrutiny to make it more effective and efficient. This involves the following sequence of steps:

1. Identify the work to be studied. This means finding the jobs that are most likely to yield a high return on investment from having studied them. High-frequency jobs are a good option, since any incremental gains found will be repeated many times, generating high returns for the company. Also focus on jobs that present bottlenecks in a process, or which generate large numbers of errors.

2. Identify the relevant facts for the work as it is currently performed. This involves recording the sequence of activities performed and the time required to complete them. It may also involve studying the travel path used by the person in the job. This analysis provides a baseline for a critical analysis.
3. Critically review these facts, answering such questions as why specific tasks are being done, what else could be done instead, can the work be done elsewhere, can it be done at a different time, could someone else do the work, and whether there are alternative ways to complete the work.
4. Develop the most practical and effective alternative. This may involve eliminating activities, merging them, changing the sequence of events, or reducing the work content in order to simplify the job.
5. Install the alternative method and periodically review it. This involves laying out the new sequence of work, with detailed work instructions, providing training for those who will be performing the work, and watching how the new sequence is conducted in practice. This may be an iterative process, where the need for changes becomes evident, once the proposed revisions have been put into practice. In addition, one should review the process periodically, to see if the revised job layout is still being followed.

---

**EXAMPLE**

It has become evident over time that the work of the warehouse staff needs to be improved. They are taking longer and longer to log in received items, put away inventory items and retrieve them, and assemble kits of component parts for delivery to the shop floor. An analysis of the situation reveals that receiving volumes have increased by 20% in the past year, while there are now 18% more inventory items being kept in stock and 16% more jobs being kitted. Meanwhile, the warehouse staff has only increased by one person. Rather than simply adding more staff, the industrial engineering department conducts a method study, where they find that the warehouse staff is spending half of their time walking around the warehouse. The obvious solution is to cut down on travel time by more specifically defining their jobs. The result is a change from one generic warehouse job position to three separate roles. One group only receives goods, so that they are confined to the receiving dock area. Another group only moves goods, which they do from forklifts and with the assistance of heads-up displays that show them where to go next to drop off and pick up inventory items. And the third group is solely responsible for assembling components into kits for delivery to the shop floor. This segregation of duties cuts travel time for the warehouse staff as a whole by 30%, allowing them to be much more efficient in their duties.

---

## Summary

The essential resource in operations is the personnel working within it. Their effectiveness is determined by the culture of the business, its organizational structure, and how jobs have been designed. Ideally, a job should be laid out for maximum efficiency, while being ergonomically planned for the comfort of the employee and intended to enhance employee motivation. Motivation can be enhanced through the use of job rotations, job enlargement, job enrichment, the use of teams, working from home, an enhanced working environment, and several related actions. Jobs will need to be revisited from time to time and adjusted, possibly with method study, to deal with bottlenecks, high error rates, and anything else that might interfere with operations.

# Chapter 10
# Planning and Control

## Introduction

An operation is designed to deliver goods and services at a specific quality and quantity level, and at a predefined cost. A system of planning and control is needed to ensure that these performance criteria are met. In this chapter, we discuss the nature of a system of planning and control, how it is impacted by outside variables, and the activities involved in planning and control.

## The Nature of Planning and Control

A system of planning and control is a combination of software, policies, procedures, and related decision-making that is intended to meet customer demand through the existing resources of a business. For example, the production of something as simple as a wooden sled requires an extensive planning process, including reserving a slot in the production schedule, allocating the time of a properly-trained craftsman to assemble it, assembling a kit of the needed parts in the warehouse and delivering it to the proper place on the shop floor at the correct time, and then moving the completed sled to the paint shed for painting – after which it needs to be properly boxed and sent to finished goods storage. In addition, controls will need to be imposed, such as checking to see that the parts kit contains the correct items, that the customer-requested paint scheme is actually applied, and that the sled is of the correct size. If any aspect of these arrangements is incorrect, then the job will need to be rescheduled, which means that the resources allocated for it must now be re-directed to a different job. All of these planning and control activities are needed to ensure that the sled is produced correctly.

There are distinct differences between the concepts of planning and control. *Planning* involves the creation and updating of a plan that is targeted at achieving a specific goal. However, it is by no means clear that the plan will come to fruition as expected; there may be any number of planning shortfalls that result in an inadequate outcome. For example, parts may not arrive when they are needed, a key production worker calls in sick, or a customer changes an order. This is where control comes in. *Control* is the ability to make changes. This can involve making alterations to any part of a plan, such as swapping out a missing part for a close substitute, calling on the services of a cross-trained employee to take the place of another one, or changing the priorities on a production plan to accommodate a changed customer order. Thus, both planning and control are needed in order to conduct operations as efficiently as possible.

The nature of planning and control varies, depending on the duration of the planning horizon. Over the long-term, the emphasis tends to be much more focused on planning, where the operations manager itemizes such matters as investments in new fixed assets, alterations to process flows, and changes to the product offerings being made to customers. For this time frame, there is little specificity. Instead, the focus is on high-level volume estimates and desired financial outcomes, such as achieving a 30% boost in profits by adding a new product line that will sell 45,000 units per year into the North American market. Given the minimal level of specificity, there is little need for control.

Over the middle-term, the level of planning detail increases, where some additional detail is put into the types of expected demand, typically for specific product lines or functional areas. Thus, the level of demand for the green widget line might be laid out in terms of a monthly forecast, for which the associated production line staffing will have been estimated, as well as the expected raw materials, equipment capacity levels, and working capital. Middle-term planning will include some planning for contingencies, usually in the form of reserves for raw materials, capacity, and staff in order to handle unexpected variations in demand. Again, there is not much need for control, since the primary focus in the middle-term is on planning.

Sales and operations planning (S&OP) is commonly used for middle-term planning. It involves having the sales department collaborate with operations to create a single production plan. The broader goal is to align daily operations with corporate strategy. This may involve such matters as ensuring that product quality improves alongside targeted increases in sales in certain geographic regions, while also drawing down finished goods inventory levels in order to minimize the company's working capital financing needs. S&OP is especially useful for locating unachievable goals, such as drawing down finished goods inventory levels to such an extent that it is impossible to maintain adequate response times to customer orders, thereby driving down sales. S&OP meetings are typically conducted on a monthly basis, when monthly operations planning goals are updated. When these meetings find a misalignment in the various goals being pursued, one or more of the goals is updated to arrive at a more reasonable mixture of goals.

In the short-term, planning is much more precise, where the intent is to specify the exact requirements of operations, not just aggregated estimates. Planning now encompasses specific customer orders or demand from downstream in-house workstations, with capacity on specific machines blocked out for jobs. At this point, planners are trying to balance demand with all aspects of the supply capabilities of the business, which are continually changing on a minute-by-minute basis. At this point, control activities have taken over from the initial planning activities, with many modifications likely having been made to what was originally planned for operations.

## Items Impacting Planning and Control

A number of items can have an impact on the planning and control function. We provide overviews of them in the following sub-sections.

### Volume and Variety

A business that operates at high volume and a low variety of outputs has significantly different planning and control activities from one that operates at low volume and a high variety of outputs. For example, a water desalinization facility can engage in extensive long-term planning, based on expected water usage levels years in the future. In this case, planning is entirely about the amount of water volume that can be delivered to customers – there is no other significant consideration. Controls are usually targeted at ensuring the continual flow of water to customers, with an emphasis on reducing down time. Conversely, an industrial artist sells a highly customized product for which it is difficult to engage in any prior planning. The requirements for each job will only begin to emerge after consultations involving specific requirements, the locations for the art, customer budget sizes, and so forth. Controls are typically targeted at micro-adjustments to plans on a daily basis, as customer requirements and resources change.

### Uncertainty

One of the key items impacting planning and control is the general level of uncertainty impacting the availability of resources, as well as customer demand. For example, in an operation that relies on part-time translators to translate Chinese scientific papers into English, it may be quite difficult to locate the right translator who has the necessary knowledge of the scientific concepts that need to be translated. Or, for an example from the perspective of customer demand, it can be quite difficult to predict demand for hurricane emergency supplies (such as portable power generators) when there is no way to predict the arrival of a hurricane for periods beyond five days. As another example, a hospital has no way of knowing when the next virus will break out, and so has a difficult time estimating how many hazmat suits to keep in stock.

### Demand

One might think that the core source of planning and control uncertainty is the demand for a firm's goods and services, but this is not necessarily the case. Some portions of the production load are based on *dependent demand*, which is easier to forecast. Dependent demand is the demand for component parts or sub-assemblies. For example, when a manufacturing company is producing electric golf carts, dependent demand consists of the production processes to construct the tires, motor, seats, steering wheel, controls, and chassis of however many golf carts are scheduled for production. Thus, if 100 golf carts are scheduled for production, the associated dependent demand includes 400 tires and 100 motors. In this case, the dependent demand for electric motors is based on a known factor, which is the number of golf carts to be manufactured. This allows the procurement department to reliably place orders with suppliers for 400 tires and 100 motors.

Conversely, *independent demand* is the demand for a finished product, which is being ordered by an outside party. It is much more difficult to predict independent demand, since it is subject to the vagaries of customer needs, which in turn may be influenced by such factors as general economic conditions, changes in fashion, and even the weather. Thus, the predicted arrival of thunderstorms may trigger a spike in the demand for umbrellas, while a decline in economic conditions might drive people to buy low-cost ramen noodles in higher volume.

The concepts of dependent and independent demand will vary, depending on the circumstances. For example, a producer of electric motors for golf carts has independent demand for those motors, since it is relying on orders from a number of customers. However, a golf cart manufacturer then buys the company in a bid to become vertically integrated. Now, the acquirer is buying half of the motor company's output, which means that half of the company's sales are now based on dependent demand (coming from the acquirer), while the remainder is independent demand (where orders come from all other customers).

When independent demand is present, operations personnel must continually make decisions about how much demand is likely to occur, which is then inserted into the company's production schedule. When there is a reasonable degree of certainty about independent demand (usually based on historical experience), the company will maintain a certain amount of inventory in stock to deal with this expected demand. The inventory maintained may be in the form of completed units ready for sale, or it may be in the form of sub-assemblies or raw materials, if the firm can readily convert them into finished goods on short notice. Keeping goods on hand to meet independent demand is most likely when there is a high volume of demand but low variety, so that there is a reliable baseline level of demand, and only a few product variations need to be stocked. Conversely, when there is a low volume of demand but high product variety, it is too risky to maintain much inventory; in these situations, the safer approach is to wait for firm orders before scheduling production. There are a few variations available to the seller in these low-volume situations, which are:

- *Make to order.* The lowest-risk approach is to wait for each customer order and then produce it. This is safest for the manufacturer, since there is no risky investment in working capital, but it also represents a slow response to the customer, who will have to wait for the entire production cycle to be completed before an order can be shipped.
- *Assemble to order.* Some products can be easily assembled from a few standard component parts. For example, a microwave oven is comprised of just a few items, which include a power source, a high-voltage capacitor, a cavity magnetron to produce microwave radiation, a metal cooking chamber, a

turntable, and a control panel. Orders may come in from customers that specify various shapes and sizes, but this only impacts the size of the metal cooking chamber – the other parts remain the same. Given the simplicity of this configuration, manufacturers can easily assemble microwave ovens to order within a short period of time.

- *Make to stock*. The company can create its best estimate of what customers will want, and produce those items. This approach presents the risk that finished goods will never be sold, but is a tenable option when the production period is relatively long and customers want short delivery times. For example, a builder could construct a medical office tower on spec, without any tenants, because it believes that population increases in the area will drive the need for doctors, who will eventually lease space in the building.

We will deal with this topic in more detail in the later *Inventory Management* chapter.

**Note:** The delivery of electronic products over the Internet makes these demand issues irrelevant, since products can now be stored on servers and delivered to customers instantly, on demand. There is no concern with dependent or independent demand. Instead, the main focus for the producer is whether it makes sense to develop a product at all, based on the expected demand level for it. Thus, the producer of an app for the iPhone will need to spend $50,000 to develop it, and needs to sell 25,000 units at $2 each to break even on the proposition. Whether this kind of demand will develop is the main risk consideration for the producer, and not whether to produce on demand or make to stock.

### Order Processing Time

When deciding whether to make to order, assemble to order, or make to stock, a major consideration is the amount of time required to process the order. The processing of an order includes the time required to design the product, obtain the associated resources, produce it, and deliver it to the customer. A long processing period can easily turn away customers, especially those who need the product or service in a hurry.

When the order processing time is quite short, it makes more sense from a planning and control perspective to make to order, since customers can be serviced quickly and there is little need to tie up valuable working capital in finished goods inventory. Conversely, when the order processing time is quite long, it makes more sense to use either the assemble to order or make to stock options, in order to reduce the risk of losing sales to customers who are looking for a quick purchase.

## Planning and Control Activities

There are four activities in which the planning and control function engages in order to reconcile the resource supply and customer demand issues being experienced by operations. In the following sub-sections, we delve into the nature of each one.

### Loading Activities

*Loading* is the volume of work assigned to a work center. This is generally a smaller amount than the theoretical maximum capacity of a work center. For example, if a stamping machine were to be run for three shifts, seven days a week, then it is theoretically capable of operating for 168 hours per week. However, it is always down for four hours per week for scheduled preventive maintenance, as well as two hours for equipment changeovers, and two more hours during shift changes, so that its maximum theoretical capacity is really 160 hours. In addition, its productivity level may be reduced due to an inexperienced machine operator, unscheduled equipment failures, missing raw materials or components, power failures, employee strikes, holidays, and so forth. In addition, some of its output may be thrown away due to quality concerns, which means that some jobs may need to be run for longer periods of time to create replacement parts, which takes up more of its available capacity.

In a well-tuned operation, processes are in place to minimize these disruptions, so that schedulers have a good idea of how much loading can be applied to any given work center. In a less-regulated environment, schedulers have a much more difficult job, having to constantly adjust the production schedule as the actual equipment capacity conflicts with the expectations built into the schedule.

Schedulers must employ *finite loading* with most work centers, where only a set amount of work is allocated to each one, which is capped at its estimated capacity level. For example, the work assigned to an insurance claim analyst is capped at an estimated capacity level somewhere below 40 hours per week, depending on any number of limiting factors such as meeting time, bathroom breaks, and so forth. Or, only a certain number of passengers are allowed on a cruise ship, after which additional prospective passengers are shifted over to a different ship in a later period.

Another possibility is to use *infinite loading*, where no attempt is made to limit the amount of work impacting a work center. Instead, the business either accepts a long queue time or increases its capacity to meet increased demand levels. This situation arises when the costs of turning away business are prohibitive. For example, a hospital emergency room cannot realistically turn away someone in need of immediate care; it may be able to call in additional doctors on short notice, but will otherwise have to accept a longer queue of patients until the period of high demand is over.

## Sequencing Activities

Sequencing involves setting the order in which tasks will be completed. This is a prioritization decision that is typically based on a set of operating rules. Examples of these rules are:

- *First in, first out priority.* Most work is dealt with as it arrives, so that the first tasks are given higher priority than tasks arriving later. This is generally considered the baseline prioritization rule, after which any of the following prioritization rules may be imposed. For example, customers arriving at a hotel check-in counter are handled in the order in which they arrive.
- *Customer priority.* A business may give priority to the needs of its most important customers, and then schedule everyone else behind them. This approach works best when there are many small customers and a small number of very large customers. For example, when a small manufacturer sells half of its products to a single large retail chain, it realizes that keeping the retail chain happy is key to its survival, and so will prioritize calls from the retailer before all other customers. This decision rule has to be used with care, since it may result in a major reduction in service to all customers who have not been prioritized.
- *Due date priority.* When a company promises customers that their orders will ship by a certain date, it will likely give priority attention to any orders that are in danger of not being shipped by their promise dates. Many orders will flow through the system normally and be shipped on time without any prioritization, so this rule is targeted at only those orders that are in danger of not shipping on time.
- *Product characteristics priority.* Specific characteristics of process inputs or outputs may impose a constraint on the order in which work is scheduled. For example, the configuration of a production cell may be optimized to only work with a particular product family; if an incoming order belongs to that product family, it is scheduled ahead of work that will require reconfiguring the production cell – which takes time.
- *Last in, first out priority.* There are a few instances in which the most recent work assignments are dealt with first, while older assignments wait. For example, when products are loaded several rows deep in a warehouse lane, the items most recently deposited there must be extracted first, since they are in front and so are most easily accessible.

The following two sequencing rules are commonly used but can be counterproductive, since they do not necessarily result in the best customer service:

- *Longest operation time.* A business may want to enhance the utilization of its work centers, and so gives priority to those jobs that will result in the longest continuous run times. These jobs involve relatively few machine setups in relation to the quantity produced, and so tend to keep operations humming. However, the tradeoff for reporting high work center utilization numbers is the lower priorities accorded to all other jobs, which may annoy some customers.

- *Shortest operation time.* When a business is short on cash, one solution is to give priority to those jobs that have the shortest operation times, so that it can bill customers as soon as possible. While this rule can accelerate cash flow, it may delay shipments to those customers whose orders require longer operation times, and also reduces the reported productivity of operations (since the shorter jobs result in more downtime for machine setups).

The choice of which sequencing rules to use will depend on the objectives of the company. For example, if a business wants to earn a reputation for dependability, it should use the due date priority rule to ensure that all customer orders are shipped on time. Or, a food distributor that wants to maintain a reputation for shipping fresh products is more inclined to use the first in, first out priority rule. As another example, a wealth management firm is quite likely to use the customer priority rule, so that its wealthiest customers receive the most attentive service.

**Scheduling Activities**

The next step after determining the sequencing for inbound jobs is to schedule them into a detailed timetable for exactly when the associated work is to be conducted. For example, a set of customer orders for different types of widgets are itemized in a production schedule that notes when each job is scheduled to begin and end, and the nature of the resources required to complete all associated work. As a different example, a railroad compiles a train schedule that states which equipment is to be assembled into a train, what will be loaded onto it, and when trains will depart and arrive. Scheduling is not possible at a detailed level when customer orders arrive in a random manner, such as in any fast food restaurant; in these cases, scheduling is limited to having sufficient capacity on hand to deal with sudden changes in demand.

The scheduling task can be monumentally complex, especially when work must be routed through a large number of work centers. This can result in millions of possible scheduling combinations. Given the level of complexity, schedulers rarely try to achieve the most exquisitely optimal solution. Instead, given the limited amount of time available for scheduling, they usually settle for a reasonably acceptable schedule that requires only a modest amount of effort. Given the complexity of the scheduling task, employees may take advantage of several methods that can simplify it. Examples of these methods are:

- *Forward scheduling.* This approach involves planning tasks from the date when resources become available in order to determine the due date or shipping date. By beginning work as soon as possible, employees are well-utilized in the short-term, with any open periods being pushed off into the future. However, it is more exposed to risk if a sudden scheduling change arises in the short term, since the schedule is full during this period.

- *Backward scheduling.* This approach involves planning tasks backwards in time from the due date or required-by date to determine the start date and/or any changes in required capacity. This approach is heavily focused on meeting the dates promised to customers, and leaves time in the schedule to accommodate immediate customer demands. A just-in-time scheduling system employs backward scheduling.
- *Staff rostering.* When the main resource of a business is its employees, then the schedule of their work times determines the capacity of the overall operation. In this case, the main scheduling task is to ensure that enough people are working to provide sufficient capacity to meet expected demand levels. For example, the call center for a consumer electronics company develops its staff roster based on inbound call volumes that have historically spiked at certain times of the day, such as during the 8-10 a.m. time slot and immediately after customer work hours, from 6-9 p.m. The staff roster is configured to maximize staffing levels to meet customer demand, and to shift training, vacation, and other downtime slots to periods of less active customer demand. It also involves scheduling around any number of company policies, such as minimizing work on weekends and third shift, as well as limiting the number of overtime hours worked.

Schedules are devised using either a push or pull approach. A common example of a push system is material requirements planning (MRP), which is a computer-driven production scheduling and inventory management system. It uses bills of material, inventory records, and a production schedule to forecast and order materials, so that those materials needed for scheduled production are available in the correct quantities and on the correct dates. However, the data integrity of the data inputs must be high, or else the outputs from the system will be incorrect. Also, conditions at the level of individual work centers may vary substantially from what is built into the MRP modeling system, so the push approach tends to result in excess inventory queueing up in front of some work centers, while other centers are unexpectedly idle. Also, if the customer demand expectations built into the production schedule are wrong, the company can end up with a substantial amount of unneeded finished goods inventory on hand.

Pull-through production is a just-in-time manufacturing method that releases a production order into the manufacturing process when a customer order is received. It uses a Kanban notification system to authorize the production of goods in the immediately preceding work center, so that the receipt of a customer order triggers a ripple effect backwards through the production facility, pulling the related order through it. This approach minimizes any excess investment in inventory, since it should result in very little raw materials or finished goods inventory. With less inventory on hand, it also means that warehouse space can be minimized, which reduces factory overhead costs. The primary downside of pull-through production is that job lots may be as small as a single unit, which requires more overhead to set up equipment within the production process, as well as to place orders for small amounts of raw materials.

## Monitoring and Control Activities

Once a schedule is in place, operations have to be closely monitored to ensure that planned activities are taking place as expected. When an unfavorable event occurs, management can intervene to pull the actual outcome back into alignment with the plan, or alter the plan to accommodate the problem.

A production process may be both widespread and complex, which makes it difficult to decide where to focus one's monitoring and control activities. A good technique for specifying the best location to manage is the *theory of constraints*, which holds that any system contains a choke point that prevents it from achieving its goals. This choke point, which is known as a bottleneck or constraint, must be carefully managed to ensure that it is operational at all times. When the bottleneck is not operating, the firm's profits are reduced.

The theory of constraints completely contravenes the more traditional view of running a business, where all operations are optimized to the greatest extent possible. Under the constraints view, optimizing *all* operations only means that it is easier to generate more inventory that will pile up in front of the bottleneck operation, without profits increasing. Thus, widespread optimization merely leads to the creation of more inventory, rather than more profits.

As noted earlier, it is critical to ensure that the constrained operation is running at maximum capacity, all the time. An excellent tool for achieving this goal is to build up an inventory buffer directly in front of the bottleneck operation. This buffer ensures that any shortfall in the flow of parts from anywhere upstream of the bottleneck will not impede the process flow through the constraint. Instead, the inventory buffer will merely fluctuate in size as it is used and then replenished. The existence of upstream production problems can also be mitigated by installing extra sprint capacity in the upstream production areas, as discussed next.

*Sprint capacity* is an excess amount of production capacity that is assembled in the work stations positioned upstream from the constraint operation. Sprint capacity is needed when the inevitable production failure occurs, and the flow of parts to the bottleneck is halted. During this period, the bottleneck instead uses parts from its inventory buffer, which is therefore depleted. The extra sprint capacity is then used to produce an extra-large quantity of parts to rebuild the inventory buffer, in preparation for the next period of production downtime.

If there is a large amount of sprint capacity incorporated into a production system, then there is less need to invest in a large inventory buffer, since the extra capacity can rebuild the buffer in short order. If there is less sprint capacity, then a larger inventory buffer is needed.

> **Note:** A key point in regard to sprint capacity is that a business should maintain excess capacity in its upstream work areas, rather than paring down its production capacity to a level that just meets its ongoing needs. This means that selling off what may appear to be excess equipment is not always a good idea.

## The Ambiguous Impact of Interventions

As a final thought on the concept of planning and control, it is not always possible to estimate the ripple effect of making a change to one's plans. For example, a decision to call in more staff on a weekend to complete an important customer order is that those employees may then call in sick on Monday in order to give themselves some time off, which in turn interferes with the completion of those orders scheduled for completion on Monday. Or, the decision to defer preventive maintenance on a machine in order to complete an order increases the risk of a catastrophic equipment failure in the near future. As another example, management decides to skip a routine quality check in order to ship an order to a customer by the promised ship date – but doing so also increases the risk that the goods shipped will fail, which in turn increases the risk of losing the customer. In short, there can be unintended consequences associated with making alterations to the plan that may result in problems in future periods. Only the most experienced operations managers are in a position to understand these side effects, and even these people will probably not spot every one of them.

A business is in the best position to learn about the effects of interventions when those interventions occur on a fairly regular basis, such as periodically requiring staff overtime to deal with extra work. In these cases, management is in a good position to learn more about the effects of these interventions, which may alter their decisions in the future. For example, they may find that requiring overtime of not more than two hours will have no effect on the amount of sick time being claimed the following day, while any larger amount of overtime will cause sick time to spike by 50%. This knowledge can then be used to set up an operating rule that limits all overtime to no more than two hours per day.

The reverse of the preceding scenario is that it is difficult to learn about the effects of interventions when they rarely occur. This is a particular problem when starting up a new business, since management has no idea how the various parts of operations interact with each other. It may not know, for example, that a particular supplier is extremely touchy about demands for overnight deliveries of components, and is likely to cut off the company entirely if these demands are made too frequently. Consequently, it is difficult to learn from rare interventions, so they tend to result in a larger number of unintended consequences.

There are several ways to make control decisions that minimize the bad effects of unintended consequences. Consider the following options:

- *Use experts.* When interventions are rare, have an expert make the decision about what to do. These people do not have to wait for a number of recurrences in order to make a good decision, because they have built up enough knowledge over the years from their other jobs, as well as through their training and outside readings, to understand the correct decision to make.
- *Use trial and error.* When it appears that a new process will be repeated on a continuing basis, it can make sense to engage in trial and error solutions to out-of-specification outcomes. For example, the operator of a newly-installed paint booth can experiment with the cleaning intervals for paint nozzles to better understand the amount of time that can pass before the nozzles become too clogged to be of further use.

Some situations occur so infrequently that it is not possible to call upon an expert for assistance with a decision, and the infrequency of occurrence makes it impossible to rely upon the trial and error approach. In this case, the only remaining alternative is intuition, which is essentially reliance upon one's prior experience to reach a less-than-scientific conclusion regarding what to do. When there is no better approach than intuition when making an intervention decision, it is better to consult with others who also have experience in the area, thereby expanding the base of knowledge on which the decision is being made.

## Summary

The reality of operations is that the flow of customer orders and resources into and through a business can be quite messy. Operations of all types are subject to so many problems that the normal state of affairs may look like only slightly-controlled chaos, as issues continually arise relating to staffing, equipment breakdowns, irate customers, missing supplier deliveries, and so forth. The approach to planning and control that was outlined in this chapter can certainly assist with achieving order from chaos, but it is by no means an easy path. Once a complete set of planning and control activities have been installed, they must be continually tweaked to adjust to ongoing changes in the company's operating environment, product line, suppliers, customers, and so forth. In short, planning and control is an ongoing challenge to any business, and so requires constant and intensive oversight.

# Chapter 11
# Capacity Management

## Introduction

Capacity management is the ongoing adjustment of an organization's resources so that the business can better meet customer demand. Those resources may include the machine or labor capacity of the business, as well as its on-hand inventory balances. Capacity levels can be altered by adding equipment, outsourcing work to suppliers, altering work schedules, changing staffing levels, authorizing overtime, and so forth. The main focus of an effective capacity management program is the bottlenecks in an organization; all other operations typically function with excess capacity, and so require little ongoing management. In this chapter, we discuss the nature of capacity management and demand forecasting.

## The Nature of Capacity Management

Capacity management requires one to balance customer demand and the internal need to use company resources as efficiently as possible. If customer demand were the only item of concern, then a business would maintain inordinate levels of capacity in order to gain a strong reputation for responsiveness. However, capacity in any form – human or machine – is expensive, so demand must be balanced against capacity costs. The ideal balance between demand and capacity is the point at which profits are maximized. Though this balancing point might initially appear to require some sacrifices by the customer in terms of longer wait times, this does not necessarily have to be the case, as long as capacity levels are cleverly managed. Here are several examples of such management, as spread out over the short, medium, and long term:

- *Short-term capacity adjustments*. Staffing levels at the checkout counters in a supermarket can be doubled during the lunch and dinner hours, when customer demand spikes. Employee staffing levels remain the same during this period; the extra checkout clerks are taken from other parts of the store during the peak period.
- *Medium-term capacity adjustments*. The human resources department hires additional staff for a consulting firm, based on a medium-term assessment of the rate at which the company is acquiring additional consulting contracts. This results in a relatively smooth ramp-up in total company headcount to provide staffing for the new contracts.
- *Long-term capacity adjustments*. The facilities department manages the construction of new facilities to house the additional staffing estimated to be needed by a call center outsourcing company, based on its projections over

the next five years for the headcount needed to service the call center requirements of its customers. This may initially result in some excess facility space, which will be gradually filled as more people are hired.

Long-term and medium-term capacity planning requires one to aggregate demand and capacity into a small number of general categories. The intent is only, for example, to estimate the total number of dish washers that customers may order within the next few years, not their orders of the 14 specific models produced by a company. This level of aggregation is needed to focus attention on the key capacity concerns, which include such matters as the general headcount level needed, the amount of facility square footage needed, and the locations of production facilities in order to optimize deliveries from suppliers and to customers. For example, a hotel chain evaluates aggregate customer demand levels in Denver, Colorado in order to decide whether projected demand warrants building a hotel near the airport. At this stage, the company is not excessively concerned with estimates of exactly how to configure each room, but rather with whether the facility should be constructed at all. Or, an art gallery chain must decide whether to open a gallery in Aspen; it is not overly concerned at this point with which artists to feature or what the mix of paintings to sculptures will be, only whether it makes economic sense to open the gallery.

When making decisions about capacity – no matter what the timeline may be – the operations manager has to consider a number of issues, some of which conflict with each other. For example:

- *Profits*. Minimizing new capital additions to maximize the use of existing capacity saves money internally, but may cost the company new sales, as annoyed customers take their business elsewhere. Also, if capacity does not increase to match sales, the company is simply incapable of fulfilling orders, resulting in lost sales.
- *Working capital*. If the decision is made to build more product during slow periods to counteract any possible demand spikes, this will increase the required investment in working capital during the inventory build period. The offset to this financial requirement is an increase in sales, since the company is now in a better position to meet customer demand.
- *Quality*. Product quality tends to be higher when the company conducts its operations with a core group of long-term, well-trained staff. If management chooses to cover demand spikes with temporary workers, it will be able to meet demand, but at the cost of lower product quality, since the new workers will not be as well-trained.
- *Speed*. The company can respond more quickly to customer demand when it has a solid capacity surplus or has built up a reserve of finished goods inventory, though this comes at the cost of extra personnel, machinery, and/or inventory.
- *Dependability*. The company will be in a better position to deal with unexpected demand spikes if it has excess capacity, while this will not be the case

when capacity levels are nearly maxed out. Management needs to decide whether to emphasize dependability, or to ignore it and possibly lose out on some customer sales as a result.

## Demand Measurement

The first task when managing capacity is to analyze the patterns of customer demand, with a particular emphasis on the rate of change being experienced in the demand for various goods and services. The rate of change is important, because it indicates when additional capacity must be added to a business (or subtracted, in the case of declining sales). When it takes a long time to add capacity (as is the case when building new hospital facilities), management needs a firm understanding of when to initiate its capacity-addition activities.

There are a number of forecasting methods that can be used to develop a financial forecast. These methods fall into two general categories, which are quantitative and qualitative. A quantitative approach relies upon quantifiable data, which can then be statistically manipulated. A qualitative approach relies upon information that cannot actually be measured. Examples of quantitative methods are:

- *Causal methods.* These methods assume that the item being forecasted has a cause-and-effect relationship with one or more other variables. For example, the existence of a movie theater can drive sales at a nearby restaurant, so the presence of a blockbuster movie can be expected to increase meal sales in the restaurant. The primary causal analysis method is regression analysis.
- *Time series methods.* These methods derive forecasts based on historical patterns in the data that are observed over equally spaced time intervals. The assumption is that there is a recurring pattern in the data that will repeat in the future. Three examples of time series methods are:
    - *Rule of thumb.* This is based on a simplified analysis rule, such as copying forward the historical data without alteration. For example, sales for the current month are expected to be the same as the sales generated in the immediately preceding month.
    - *Smoothing.* This approach uses averages of past results, possibly including weightings for more recent data, thereby smoothing out irregularities in the historical data.
    - *Decomposition.* This analysis breaks down the historical data into its trend, seasonal, and cyclical components, and forecasts each one.

**EXAMPLE**

Celsius Corporate has recently introduced a new line of remote temperature sensors that use the principles of quantum entanglement to monitor temperature levels thousands of miles away. The company is selling these units at an increasing rate. The sales manager is using a moving average of the last three months of sales to estimate the minimum likely sales level for the next month. Her calculation appears in the following table.

| Month | Actual Sales | 3-Month Moving Average |
|---|---|---|
| January | $300,000 | -- |
| February | 320,000 | -- |
| March | 340,000 | $320,000 |
| April | 342,000 | 334,000 |
| May | 350,000 | 344,000 |
| June | 354,000 | 349,000 |
| July | 360,000 | 355,000 |

Since sales are continuing to increase, the moving average is more useful as an indicator of minimum sales levels than of the actual amount of sales that will be encountered.

**EXAMPLE**

Gatekeeper Corporation runs a toll road. The amount of traffic on the toll road is fairly consistent, though there are random effects that cause toll revenues to bounce around in an irregular manner. The chief financial officer decides to average the results for the immediately preceding six months to forecast an approximate toll revenue figure for the following month. The longer six-month smoothing period is used to minimize the effects of random variations. The analysis appears in the following table.

| Month | Actual Sales | 6-Month Moving Average |
|---|---|---|
| January | $174,000 | -- |
| February | 168,000 | -- |
| March | 175,000 | -- |
| April | 163,000 | -- |
| May | 171,000 | -- |
| June | 167,000 | $170,000 |
| July | 176,000 | 170,000 |

**EXAMPLE**

Nautilus Tours owns several submarines, which it uses to conduct shallow-water tours of coral reefs near major tourist locations. Nautilus has an on-line reservation system that tracks the number of prepaid reserved seats, which are derived from both on-line and telephone sales. This system is the primary source of forecasting information, since it represents "hard" sales for the forecasting period. In addition, the company adds an estimate of additional sales for walk-ins, which is based on a moving average of the number of actual walk-ins that the company has experienced for the past few weeks.

---

Examples of qualitative methods are:

- *Market research.* This is based on discussions with current and potential customers regarding their need for goods and services. Information must be gathered and analyzed in a systematic manner in order to minimize biases caused by small data sets, inconsistent customer questioning, excessive summarization of data, and so forth. This is an expensive and time-consuming research method. It can be useful for detecting changes in consumer sentiment, which will later be reflected in their buying habits.
- *Opinions of knowledgeable personnel.* This is based on the opinions of those having the greatest and most in-depth knowledge of the information being forecasted. For example, the senior management team may derive forecasts based on their knowledge of the industry. Or, the sales staff may prepare sales forecasts that are based on their knowledge of specific customers. An advantage of using the sales staff for forecasting is that they can provide detailed forecasts, possibly at the level of the individual customer. There is a tendency for the sales staff to create overly optimistic forecasts.
- *Delphi method.* This is a structured methodology for deriving a forecast from a group of experts, using a facilitator and multiple iterations of analysis to arrive at a consensus opinion. The results from each successive questionnaire are used as the basis for the next questionnaire in each iteration; doing so spreads information among the group if certain information was initially not available to everyone. Given the significant time and effort required, this method is best used for the derivation of longer-term forecasts.

Qualitative methods are especially necessary during the early stages of a company or product, where there is little historical information that can be used as the basis for a quantitative analysis.

## Moving Average Quantitative Forecasting

Moving averages can be used to create a forecast. Their best application is when the historical data does not indicate any cyclical or seasonal component to sales. In addition, there should not be an expectation that the forecast will change significantly. When these conditions are present, a moving average is useful for averaging out the irregular components of historical data over a number of periods. The result is a fairly stable forecast.

A variation on the concept is the weighted moving average. In this case, the most recent data is considered to be more valuable than older data, so a weighting is assigned to the newer data. An example appears in the following exhibit, where much heavier weightings are given to the immediately preceding two time periods. In the example, a simple average of the three historical periods would have yielded a forecast of $1,000,000. Instead, given the stronger weighting of the final period, the forecast is reduced to $985,000.

**Weighted Moving Average Calculation**

| (000s) | Historical Period 1 | Historical Period 2 | Historical Period 3 | Forecast Period 1 |
|---|---|---|---|---|
| Sales | $1,000 | $1,050 | $950 | --- |
| Weighting points | 10 | 30 | 60 | --- |
| Weighted result | $100 | $315 | $570 | $985 |

The problem with a weighted moving average is that the weighting is entirely subjective. By comparing the results of a weighted moving average forecast to actual results, one can adjust the weighting to improve the accuracy of the forecast.

An implicit weighted moving average occurs when the number of periods over which an average is calculated is shortened. When this happens, the entire weighting is focused on only the few most recent periods, rather than being spread out over a number of periods. The concept is best explained with the following example. A company is forecasting unit sales using a moving average for the past six weeks. Its calculation for the past six weeks is:

$$\frac{500 + 480 + 540 + 535 + 570 + 585}{6} = 535$$

In this calculation, the weighting is spread evenly over each of the past six weeks. The formula is then changed, so that it only encompasses the past three weeks of unit sales. The formula now changes to:

$$\frac{535 + 570 + 585}{3} = 563$$

In effect, the final three weeks have cumulatively been awarded a 100% weighting, while the preceding three weeks were given a 0% weighting. Consequently, altering the number of periods used in a moving average calculation effectively results in a weighting of the model.

A problem with any type of moving average forecasting system is that detailed records must be kept of the relevant financial information from which forecasts are being calculated.

**Exponential Smoothing**

Exponential smoothing is a forecasting method that is based on historical patterns in the data. It is a time series method, as defined earlier in the chapter. This method employs a smoothing constant in combination with recent and actual forecasted activity to derive a forecast. A smoothing constant determines the level at which actual experience influences a forecast. Thus, if a prior forecast was too high, the smoothing constant is used to reduce the forecast in the next period. Conversely, if a prior forecast was too low, the smoothing constant increases the forecast in the next period. The smoothing constant should be low if the pattern of sales has been relatively stable in the past. The smoothing constant increases in size if there have been large changes in sales. The smoothing constant is inserted into the following formula to derive a forecast:

$$\text{New Forecast} = \text{Past Forecast} + \text{Smoothing Constant} \times (\text{Actual Demand} - \text{Past Forecast})$$

The information requirements for exponential smoothing are quite limited. It is only necessary to employ the data from the prior two periods in order to derive the smoothing constant. The calculation of the smoothing constant is as follows:

$$\frac{\text{Period 2 forecast} - \text{Period 1 forecast}}{\text{Period 1 actual demand} - \text{Period 1 forecast}}$$

---

**EXAMPLE**

Grizzly Golf Carts uses exponential smoothing in its financial forecasting. In January, Grizzly forecasted that customers would order 300 of its golf carts. Actual demand was 330 carts. The February forecast is that 315 carts will be ordered. The company's forecaster uses this information to derive the smoothing constant, which is calculated as follows:

$$\frac{\text{315 Carts forecasted in February} - \text{300 Carts forecasted in January}}{\text{330 Carts ordered in January} - \text{300 Carts forecasted in January}}$$

$$= \text{0.5 Smoothing constant}$$

**EXAMPLE**

Green Lawn Care forecasted customer orders of 500 electric lawn mowers in the past week, and actual demand for that week was 490 mowers. The company's smoothing constant is 0.2. The company uses the following exponential smoothing calculation to derive the following forecast for the next week:

| New Forecast | = | 500 Units Past Forecast | + | 0.2 Smoothing Constant | × | ( | 490 Units Actual Demand | - | 500 Units Past Forecast | ) |
|---|---|---|---|---|---|---|---|---|---|---|

= 498 Mowers

In essence, the company is using a modest smoothing constant to slightly reduce its forecast for the next period, since the actual demand in the past week was lower than expected.

---

**Regression Analysis**

Regression analysis is a forecasting method that is based on a cause-and-effect relationship between a dependent and independent variable. The two factors involved in this analysis are:

- *Independent variable.* This is a variable that is not impacted by any other variables being measured.
- *Dependent variable.* This variable is impacted by other variables. An independent variable can cause changes in a dependent variable, but a dependent variable cannot cause changes in an independent variable.

As examples of independent and dependent variables, a person's income (the independent variable) impacts the amount of the individual's spending (the dependent variable). Or, the price of a product (the independent variable) impacts the number of units sold (the dependent variable).

This type of analysis only yields accurate results when the variables used are reliable indicators of an activity. The level of this reliability can be measured using the correlation coefficient, for which the formula is:

$$r = \frac{n(\sum xy) - (\sum x)(\sum y)}{\sqrt{[n(\sum x^2) - (\sum x)^2]\,[n(\sum y^2) - (\sum y)^2]}}$$

The symbols in the preceding formula are explained as follows:

x = Independent variable
y = Dependent variable
n = Number of observations

The result of the formula ("r") is a value between negative one and positive one, where a value closer to positive one represents a tight relationship between the dependent and independent variables. The following table illustrates how the output of the correlation coefficient calculation can be interpreted.

**Strength of Correlation Coefficient**

| R Value | Level of Relationship |
|---|---|
| Positive 0.70 or higher | Very strong positive relationship |
| Positive 0.40 – 0.69 | Strong positive relationship |
| Positive 0.30 – 0.39 | Moderate positive relationship |
| Positive 0.20 – 0.29 | Weak positive relationship |
| Positive 0.01 – 0.19 | Minimal positive relationship |
| Zero | No relationship |
| Negative 0.01 – 0.19 | Minimal negative relationship |
| Negative 0.20 – 0.29 | Weak negative relationship |
| Negative 0.30 – 0.39 | Moderate negative relationship |
| Negative 0.40 – 0.69 | Strong negative relationship |
| Negative 0.70 or lower | Very strong negative relationship |

Once an independent variable has been found that closely correlates with the dependent variable, a line can be plotted through the data using the following formula for a straight line:

$$Y = a + bx$$

The symbols in the preceding formula are explained as follows:

Y = Dependent variable
a = Intercept point of the regression line and the y axis
b = Slope of the regression line
x = Independent variable

---

**EXAMPLE**

The Sojourn Hotel and Spa has established a strong positive relationship between the number of room guests and the number of spa treatments in the adjacent spa. An analysis of the data results in the following equation that graphs the regression analysis:

$$Y = 100 + 1.55(x)$$

For example, if there are 1,000 room guests in a given period, then the number of spa treatments is estimated to be as follows:

$$Y = 100 + 1.55(1{,}000)$$

$$= 1{,}650 \text{ Spa treatments}$$

The calculation indicates that 100 spa treatments are conducted that are not related to room guests, and that each guest pays for an average of 1.55 spa treatments.

---

An examination of a regression calculation may find that the earlier or later data points used to plot a line result in a closer fit with the line. If so, it can make sense to assign a weighting to the data points, so that those points assigned a higher weighting are factored more heavily into the regression calculation, and those weighted less have a lesser impact on the outcome. For example, a weighting of 1.0 has no impact, while a weighting of 0.7 reduces the impact of a data point, and a weighting of 1.3 increases the impact. The most common application of this concept is to assign a reduced weighting to the oldest data points, so that more recent data is given more weight in the calculation of a fitted line.

A more advanced form of regression analysis is multiple regression analysis, where the impact of two or more independent variables on a dependent variable is analyzed. For example, forecasts could be derived for:

- Sales of Hawaiian helicopter tours that are based on the impact of an advertising campaign *and* the number of visitors to the islands.
- Sales of consumer goods that are based on the impact of advertising frequency *and* the type of media used.
- Sales of freemium products that are based on the price at which the premium product is offered *and* the features offered in the free product.

A multiple regression analysis should be used when a simple regression does not result in a sufficiently high R value to show a strong relationship between a single independent variable and the dependent variable.

## Simple Forecasting Methods

We have already described several relatively advanced quantitative forecasting methods. Given the level of complexity involved, many organizations do not use them. Instead, they employ a variety of simplified techniques that require little analysis work and minimal forecasting knowledge. Examples of these methods are noted in the following table.

**Simple Forecasting Methods**

| Method | Commentary |
|---|---|
| Prior year actuals × Adjustment factor | Likely the most common forecasting method, where the prior period actual results are expected to repeat in the current period, possibly adjusted for any number of factors such as expectations of an industry downturn or the introduction of a new product line. |
| Prior year budget × Adjustment factor | Only yields useful results if the prior year budget closely predicted actual results. This is most likely to be the case in a low-growth industry where long-term results are highly predictable. |
| Average of multiple prior periods | Works well when there is no significant trend in sales, but rather a sales level that moves up and down moderate amounts from period to period. Should not be used when there is a clear upward, downward, or seasonal trend in the historical data. |
| Expected unit sales basis | The sales department creates a detailed unit forecast at the level of the individual product, and calculates sales dollars based on the expected selling price. This approach works well in a stable market where product life cycles are long and there is little pricing pressure. |
| Spending per customer | Works well when each customer buys a consistent average amount per forecasting period. However, it can yield inaccurate results when the business switches to a new market segment in which customer spending habits are different. |
| Change in advance bookings or orders | Useful when advance bookings or orders are considered a strong indicator of future sales. Works well in seasonal businesses such as hotels and resorts, or for consumer products for which there is significant marketing support. |

Some of the methods listed in the preceding table are described further in the following subsections.

**Prior Year Actuals × Adjustment Factor**

The use of the prior year's actual results as the basis for a forecast is probably the most common forecasting method, for the following two reasons:

- The forecast is based on an aggregate figure that is derived from all types of sales, which requires little effort to compile (as opposed to the later sub-section describing the expected unit sales basis).
- The entity has already achieved the prior year sales figure, so there is no question that the required market share exists and that the organization has the capacity to meet the indicated sales level.

The management team can then add to or subtract from the prior year actual results for any number of factors that are expected to take place during the forecast period, such as:

- Product price changes
- Additions to production capacity
- Certain customers will be added or dropped
- New sales regions will be added
- New product lines will be added
- New distribution channels will be added

The adjustments to the prior year actuals may be the most difficult to predict, especially if the organization is making changes for which there is no history, such as an entirely new product line.

This forecasting method does not work well when a business' products are subject to short life cycles, and especially when there is little corporate or product branding that will attract and retain customers over the long term. In this situation, sales levels may spike and drop at irregular intervals, with no consistent sales level that can be predicted forward into the next year.

---

**EXAMPLE**

Rubens Trailers specializes in the production of double-wide trailers. Sales of these trailers have proven to be remarkably consistent over the past decade, featuring a modest 2% average growth rate, though demand in the past year came close to maxing out the company's production capacity. For the upcoming year, Rubens has invested in an oversized new production facility that can handle a weighty increase in production.

In the past year, the company had $40 million of sales. The capacity problem will no longer be an issue, so there is an expectation of an additional 2% increase in sales to match the long-term trend, which is $800,000. In addition, the company is launching a standard-width trailer that it hopes will achieve $5 million in sales. Since this is a new product for which there are many competing products, there is considerable uncertainty about the $5 million figure. Thus,

Rubens has a $40.8 million component to its forecast that it considers to be solid, and a $5 million component from which actual results may vary a great deal.

---

## Average of Multiple Prior Periods

A business that is locked into a relatively flat revenue pattern can consider using an average of several prior periods as its forecasting method. This method may work well for governments, which typically service relatively flat population levels for long periods of time (in the absence of new residential construction). The same can be said for businesses that have monopolies or near-monopolies, but which are restricted from operating outside of their core areas, such as regulated utilities.

---

**EXAMPLE**

The Waiakea Botanical Gardens are located in Hawaii. The gardens are famous for their outrageously large plant life, which is fed by an ideal mix of morning sun and afternoon rain. The gardens serve a consistent client base of gardening devotees who come from all over the world. There is no upward or downward trend in the number of customers in any given year, so the garden's bookkeeper uses the following simple method to average sales for the past three years in order to forecast the most likely sales level for the coming year:

| | 2 Years Ago | 1 Year Ago | Current Year | Next Year |
|---|---|---|---|---|
| Sales | $450,000 | $462,000 | $440,000 | $451,000 |

---

## Expected Unit Sales Basis

A unit-based sales forecast contains an itemization of a company's sales expectations for the forecast period, which may be in both units and dollars. If a company has a large number of products, it usually aggregates its expected sales into a smaller number of product categories; otherwise, the forecasting process becomes too unwieldy.

The basic calculation in the revenue forecast is to itemize the number of unit sales expected in one row of the forecast, and then list the average expected unit price in the next row, with the total revenues appearing in the third row. If any sales discounts or returns are anticipated, these items are also listed in the forecast.

**EXAMPLE**

Quest Adventure Gear is a maker of rugged travel gear. One of its equipment lines is a propane-powered camp stove. Its revenue forecast is as follows:

| | Quarter 1 | Quarter 2 | Quarter 3 | Quarter 4 | Total |
|---|---|---|---|---|---|
| Forecasted unit sales | 5,500 | 6,000 | 7,000 | 8,000 | 26,500 |
| × Price per unit | $35 | $35 | $38 | $38 | -- |
| = Total gross sales | $192,500 | $210,000 | $266,000 | $304,000 | $972,500 |
| - Sales discounts and allowances | -3,850 | -$4,200 | -$5,320 | -6,080 | -19,450 |
| = Total net sales | $188,650 | $205,800 | $260,680 | $297,920 | $953,050 |

Quest's sales manager expects that increased demand in the second half of the year will allow it to increase its wholesale unit price from $35 to $38. Also, the sales manager expects that the company's historical sales discounts and allowances percentage of two percent of gross sales will continue through the forecast period.

This revenue forecast example only incorporates a single product, which results in a very simplistic forecast. Realistically, most companies sell many products and services, and must find a way to aggregate them into a forecast that strikes a balance between revealing a reasonable level of detail and not overwhelming the reader with a massive list of line-item projections. There are several ways to aggregate information to meet this goal.

One approach is to summarize revenue information by sales territory, as shown in the following exhibit. This approach is most useful when the primary source of information for the revenue forecast is the sales managers of the various territories, and is particularly important if the company is planning to close down or open up new sales territories; changes at the territory level may be the primary drivers of changes in sales. In the example, the Central Plains sales territory is expected to be launched midway through the forecast year and to contribute modestly to total sales volume by year end.

**Sample Revenue Forecast by Territory**

| Territory | Quarter 1 | Quarter 2 | Quarter 3 | Quarter 4 | Total |
|---|---|---|---|---|---|
| Northeast | $135,000 | $141,000 | $145,000 | $132,000 | $553,000 |
| Mid-Atlantic | 200,000 | 210,000 | 208,000 | 195,000 | 813,000 |
| Southeast | 400,000 | 425,000 | 425,000 | 395,000 | $1,645,000 |
| Central Plains | 0 | 0 | 100,000 | 175,000 | 275,000 |
| Rocky Mountain | 225,000 | 235,000 | 242,000 | 230,000 | 932,000 |
| West Coast | 500,000 | 560,000 | 585,000 | 525,000 | 2,170,000 |
| Totals | $1,460,000 | $1,571,000 | $1,705,000 | $1,652,000 | $6,388,000 |

Another approach is to summarize revenue information by contract, as shown in the next exhibit. This is realistically the only viable way to structure the revenue forecast in situations where a company is heavily dependent upon a set of contracts that have definite ending dates. In this situation, divide the forecast into existing and projected contracts, with subtotals for each type of contract, in order to separately show firm revenues and less-likely revenues. This type of forecast is commonly used when a company is engaged in services or government work.

**Sample Revenue Forecast by Contract**

| Contract | Quarter 1 | Quarter 2 | Quarter 3 | Quarter 4 | Total |
|---|---|---|---|---|---|
| **Existing Contracts:** | | | | | |
| Air Force #01327 | $175,000 | $175,000 | $25,000 | $-- | $375,000 |
| Coast Guard #AC124 | 460,000 | 460,000 | 460,000 | 25,000 | 1,405,000 |
| Marines #BG0047 | 260,000 | 280,000 | 280,000 | 260,000 | 1,080,000 |
| Subtotal | $895,000 | $915,000 | $765,000 | $285,000 | $2,860,000 |
| | | | | | |
| **Projected Contracts:** | | | | | |
| Air Force resupply | $-- | $-- | $150,000 | $300,000 | $450,000 |
| Army training | -- | 210,000 | 600,000 | 550,000 | 1,360,000 |
| Marines software | 10,000 | 80,000 | 80,000 | 100,000 | 270,000 |
| Subtotal | $10,000 | $290,000 | $830,000 | $950,000 | $2,080,000 |
| | | | | | |
| Totals | $905,000 | $1,205,000 | $1,595,000 | $1,235,000 | $4,940,000 |

Yet another approach for a company having a large number of products is to aggregate them into product lines, and then create a summary-level forecast at the product line level. This approach is shown in the next exhibit. However, if a revenue forecast is created for product lines, also consider creating a supporting schedule of projected sales for each of the products within that product line, in order to properly account for the timing and revenue volumes associated with the ongoing introduction of new products and cancellation of old ones. An example of such a supporting schedule is also shown in the following exhibit, itemizing the "Alpha" line item in the product line revenue forecast. Note that this schedule provides detail about the launch of a new product (the Alpha Windmill) and the termination of another product (the Alpha Methane Converter) that are crucial to the formulation of the total revenue figure for the product line.

**Sample Revenue Forecast by Product Line**

| Product Line | Quarter 1 | Quarter 2 | Quarter 3 | Quarter 4 | Total |
|---|---|---|---|---|---|
| Product line alpha | $450,000 | $500,000 | $625,000 | $525,000 | $2,100,000 |
| Product line beta | 100,000 | 110,000 | 150,000 | 125,000 | 485,000 |
| Product line charlie | 250,000 | 250,000 | 300,000 | 300,000 | 1,100,000 |
| Product line delta | 80,000 | 60,000 | 40,000 | 20,000 | 200,000 |
| Totals | $880,000 | $920,000 | $1,115,000 | $970,000 | $3,885,000 |

**Sample Supporting Schedule for the Revenue Forecast by Product Line**

| | Quarter 1 | Quarter 2 | Quarter 3 | Quarter 4 | Total |
|---|---|---|---|---|---|
| **Alpha product line detail:** | | | | | |
| Alpha Flywheel | $25,000 | $35,000 | $40,000 | $20,000 | $120,000 |
| Alpha Generator | 175,000 | 225,000 | 210,000 | 180,000 | 790,000 |
| Alpha Windmill | -- | -- | 200,000 | 250,000 | 450,000 |
| Alpha Methane Converter | 150,000 | 140,000 | 25,000 | -- | 315,000 |
| Alpha Nuclear Converter | 100,000 | 100,000 | 150,000 | 75,000 | 425,000 |
| Totals | $450,000 | $500,000 | $625,000 | $525,000 | $2,100,000 |

A danger in constructing a supporting schedule for a product line forecast is that one can delve too deeply into all of the various manifestations of a product, resulting in an inordinately large and detailed schedule. This situation might arise when a product comes in many colors or options. In such cases, engage in as much aggregation at the individual product level as necessary to yield a schedule that is not *excessively* detailed. It is nearly impossible to forecast revenue at the level of the color or specific option mix associated with a product, so it makes little sense to create a schedule at that level of detail.

## Spending per Customer

Forecasting based on the average spend per customer works well when customers buy a consistent amount per forecasting period. This approach can yield the most consistent results when essential goods are being sold on a repetitive basis, such as food sales by a grocery store. In this scenario, a business probably services customers within a specifically-defined geographic region, who have limited alternative purchasing options. Another example is an agricultural supply store in a farming district where the nearest competing store is 50 miles away.

For more precision in the forecast, it can make sense to stratify customers, since the top and bottom groups of customers may spend substantially different amounts than the median group.

**EXAMPLE**

Lonely Lake Lodge is the only purveyor of foodstuffs within a 20-mile radius in the backwoods of Minnesota. The owner's customers are comprised of two distinct groups, which are the 500 permanent residents of the area, and the 2,000 campers who descend on the area during the summer months. The spending habits of these two groups are entirely different, as outlined by the sales forecast in the following table, which identifies spending by each type of customer for each season of the upcoming year.

| | Winter | Spring | Summer | Fall |
|---|---|---|---|---|
| Full-time residents | 480 | 500 | 500 | 480 |
| × Spending/each | $1,200 | $1,000 | $1,000 | $1,200 |
| Full-timer spending | $576,000 | $500,000 | $500,000 | $576,000 |
| | | | | |
| Seasonal residents | 50 | 750 | 2,000 | 200 |
| × Spending/each | $200 | $150 | $150 | $200 |
| Seasonal spending | $10,000 | $112,500 | $300,000 | $40,000 |
| | | | | |
| Grand total spending | $586,000 | $612,500 | $800,000 | $616,000 |

## Change in Advance Bookings or Orders

Forecasting based on changes in advance bookings or orders is an essential tool in the tourism industry, especially in those areas where travel plans are made months in advance. If advance bookings are down, this likely means that a resort will need to offer cut-rate deals to bring in vacationers at the last minute, which reduces overall revenues. Conversely, an increase in advance bookings may allow a business to increase its last-minute rates for any residual capacity, thereby boosting revenues.

**EXAMPLE**

The Saba Dive Resort caters entirely to scuba divers, who enjoy the pristine underwater views off the southwest coast of the island. It is now July, and the Caribbean has already been hit by four hurricanes, with additional storms queued up off the coast of Africa and headed towards the Caribbean – and the Saba Dive Resort.

The resort's bookkeeper is attempting to forecast sales for September, when hurricane season will be at its peak. To do so, she reviews the changes in advance bookings for September, and notes that 20% of these bookings have been cancelled, likely due to the nervousness of divers regarding how the hurricane season is trending.

The resort also earns revenue from day-trippers who fly in from St. Maarten with little advance warning. She assumes that the September numbers for this group will drop by an equivalent amount, for the same reason. Her forecast is based on the resort's actual results for the preceding September, which results in the following forecast detail:

| | September Actual Preceding Year | September Forecast Current Year |
|---|---|---|
| Revenue from advance bookings | $380,000 | $304,000 |
| Revenue from day trippers | 50,000 | 40,000 |
| Total Revenue | $430,000 | $344,000 |

## Additional Points Regarding Demand

There are several other considerations regarding the calculation of demand, which are covered in the following bullet points:

- *Translation to units.* A key point when using forecasts to plan for capacity requirements is to express the forecasts in units that can be applied to capacity planning. Thus, a sales forecast expressed in dollars will need to be shifted into machine hours of usage, square footage required, number of staff hours, and so forth.
- *Inherent uncertainty.* Some forecasts include a large proportion of highly uncertain sales. When there is this much uncertainty in a forecast, it can make sense to not worry so much about developing a detailed forecast; instead, it may make more sense to design operations to be as responsive to changes in demand as possible. This may mean using comparatively more people and less equipment, since staffing levels are easier to ramp up and down to meet variations in demand levels.
- *High capacity usage.* A high degree of forecast variability is a particular concern when a company is operating near the upper end of its available capacity. When this is the case, management wants to be quite certain about its demand

forecasts, since any forecasted increase in demand will require a substantial additional investment in capacity.

- *High cost of lost sales*. When customers are likely to take their business elsewhere if goods are not in stock, and especially when profit margins are quite high, it makes more sense to invest in extra capacity, even when the demand forecast indicates that sales will probably be lower than the highest sales level that the new capacity can meet. In this case, the lifetime value of a customer comfortably offsets the need to exactly match capacity with demand.

## Demand Management Techniques

There are several techniques available for adjusting demand levels in order to more closely align them with available capacity. These techniques involve either dampening peak demand or increasing off-peak demand. Here are several demand management tools:

- *Alternative products*. When a company has facilities that are not being used during certain times, it can offer alternative products to maximize usage levels. For example, a winery can rent out its tasting room for weddings or other events, while a ski resort can host business conferences during the summer months.
- *Commitment fees*. When a business has a fixed amount of capacity, it cannot afford to have customers pull out at the last moment, since it is then losing the revenue that had been associated with those specific customers. To keep customers from leaving on short notice, a common revenue management tactic is to charge them a commitment fee. For example, someone attempting to change a seat reservation on a plane is charged a fee for doing so; this is not just a way to increase revenue – it is also designed to deter customers from making changes.
- *Coupons*. Coupons encourage customers to take discounts during specific date ranges when there is expected to be an excess amount of available capacity. They are typically only used by more price sensitive customers, which tends to be a small subset of the entire customer group.
- *Demand-based pricing*. Prices can be adjusted upward during periods of high demand and downward when there is little demand. For example, a mountain resort will increase its fees during the summer and winter months in order to limit demand to its available rooms, and then lower prices during the lower-demand shoulder seasons in order to fill up the rooms.
- *Limited access*. A company may allow only limited access to its goods and services during certain time periods, which forces customers to shift to other periods when the available capacity levels are higher. For example, it is difficult to be seated at a restaurant during the peak lunch hours, but customers willing to come early can be seated at once.

## The Measurement of Capacity

*Capacity* is the maximum sustainable rate of output that an operation can achieve. The key word in that definition is "sustainable," since the capacity of an operation will be downgraded at various times to factor in the effects of maintenance operations, employee breaks, labor shortages, missing raw materials, power failures, and so forth. Given the impact of these items, it is useful to define several types of capacity, which (in declining order of capacity level) are:

- *Theoretical capacity*. This is the output that can be attained if a production facility were able to produce at its peak efficiency level with no downtime. It should not be used for planning purposes, since it is nearly impossible to attain in practice.
- *Practical capacity*. This is the highest realistic amount of output that a factory can maintain. It is the maximum theoretical amount of output, minus the downtime needed for ongoing equipment maintenance, machine setup time, scheduled employee time off, and so forth.
- *Normal capacity*. This is the amount of output that can be reasonably expected over the long term. The normal capacity level can decline over time as production equipment ages, since the equipment then requires more maintenance.

---

**EXAMPLE**

A 3-D printing machine is theoretically capable of running for 24 hours per day, seven days per week, which is 168 hours per week. This is its theoretical capacity. Over the long term, the machine will require 10 hours per week of maintenance time, as well as an average of four hours to load new product files into the machine and two hours for employee changeover periods. This results in 152 hours of practical capacity per week. In addition, the machine is likely to experience unscheduled maintenance time that averages two hours per week, plus four hours for raw material shortages and three hours for employee training time. This results in 143 hours of normal capacity per week.

---

Capacity can be designed to attain the theoretical capacity level for short periods of time. For example, the kitchen of a fast food restaurant can be fully staffed during peak meal periods, with all employee time off shifted into other parts of the day. Or, a manufacturing facility can defer all equipment maintenance until after a critical customer order has been processed. Thus, theoretical capacity *can* be attained – just not for a very extended period of time.

In a business that only deals with a simplified product line, it can be relatively easy to measure capacity in terms of the number of hamburgers cooked per hour, or the number of red widgets manufactured per day. However, capacity measurement becomes more difficult when there are many products being offered. For example, a hospital may offer several hundred different procedures, while a college offers hundreds of different classes – in both cases, the offerings may require radically different times to complete, making it difficult to measure capacity. A good way to deal with this issue is to only measure the amount of bottleneck capacity, and assume that there is excess capacity in all non-bottleneck activities. Thus, the bottleneck for a long-term care facility is the number of beds, while the bottleneck for a consulting firm is probably the number of senior staff, and the bottleneck for an electric utility is the peak output of its nuclear reactor.

A further concern with the measurement of capacity is that it may not be fixed. On the contrary, it may be highly variable, depending on the availability of production resources. For example, if the local power utility is having trouble keeping up with demand, it may institute rolling blackouts that will shut down a production facility for a certain period of time every day. Or, a meatpacking plant can only staff its production lines during certain times of the day, because its workers are local farmers who need to tend to their crops, and so are only available for limited periods of time. When this is the case, operations managers need to balance varying levels of demand with varying levels of capacity, which can be a difficult chore.

## Capacity Management Techniques

There are several ways to conceptually deal with the capacity of a company's operations, as described in the following sub-sections. Several caveats to these concepts are noted in the final sub-section, "The Reality of Capacity Management."

### Base Capacity Planning

Every operation should maintain a base level of capacity, which it may then adjust up or down to match expected demand levels. The base level of capacity should be derived from the performance objectives of the business. For example, if the core objective is to keep costs low, then the base capacity level will probably need to also be low, to minimize the investment in capacity. Alternatively, if the key objective is speed, then the base capacity is set higher, because there needs to be sufficient capacity on hand to turn around customer orders as quickly as possible. Some businesses will elect to maintain a low base level for their capacity and use slack periods to build up finished goods inventory, which can then be drawn down during peak demand periods. However, this alternative requires a working capital investment and also increases the risk of inventory obsolescence.

Base capacity will need to be set at a relatively high level when a product is perishable, since it is not possible to build up a buffer of finished goods. Thus, a sandwich shop can only prepare a small number of pre-made sandwiches, since they will become stale within a few hours.

When a business experiences high levels of demand variability, management is more likely to set the base capacity level relatively high. By doing so, operations can meet most customer orders, even when there are unexpected spikes in demand.

### Level Capacity Planning

Once the base capacity level has been set, management may implement level capacity planning, where operations generate the same amount of output, irrespective of actual customer demand. This approach works well when finished goods can be stored for long periods of time. If there are concerns about product obsolescence, then management only authorizes the over-production of products when they have a stable sales history that is expected to remain the same in the future. All other products are only produced to meet immediate customer demand.

There are several benefits to level capacity planning. It allows for stable staffing, the development of procedures for more efficient production, and generally high levels of productivity. On the downside, some investment in working capital will be required to pay for warehoused finished goods.

Level capacity planning can be cost-prohibitive in a services organization, where full staffing is used, irrespective of actual demand levels. If full staffing is used in months when customer demand is quite low, it is likely that the firm will suffer losses. However, when profit margins are high, then even a few sales will still turn a profit. For example, a restaurant (with low margins) in a seasonal resort area will find it difficult to maintain full staffing for the entire year, while an art gallery located in the same area may be able to remain open, because it makes so much money from even a few sales per month.

---

**EXAMPLE**

The Santa Candy Cane Company has a fixed capacity level that can reliably produce 100,000 candy canes in every month of the year. The sales department has just created its final sales forecast for the upcoming year. The operations manager itemizes the planned production level for each month next to the estimated sales for each month; this information appears in the following table.

| Month | Planned Unit Production | Estimated Unit Sales | Cumulative Inventory at Month-End |
|---|---|---|---|
| January | 100,000 | 0 | 100,000 |
| February | 100,000 | 0 | 200,000 |
| March | 100,000 | 0 | 300,000 |
| April | 100,000 | 0 | 400,000 |
| May | 100,000 | 0 | 500,000 |
| June | 100,000 | 0 | 600,000 |
| July | 100,000 | 25,000 | 675,000 |
| August | 100,000 | 75,000 | 700,000 |
| September | 100,000 | 350,000 | 450,000 |
| October | 100,000 | 425,000 | 125,000 |
| November | 100,000 | 225,000 | 0 |
| December | 100,000 | 100,000 | 0 |
| Totals | 1,200,000 | 1,200,000 | 0 |

Based on this comparison, it appears possible for the company to maintain its base capacity level, produce to inventory for most of the year, and still meet all customer requests through the end of the year, after which its finished goods inventory will be entirely eliminated.

---

In the preceding example, a possible issue for the operations manager to consider is the exact timing of customer orders. Since the end-of-month inventory in both November and December is estimated to be zero, there will be little or no buffer stock on hand during those months, depending on exactly when customer orders are received. Therefore, in those two months, it would make sense to refine the sales forecast to the specific day or week in which each customer order is expected, and compare that to the on-hand inventory on those dates. It is quite possible that this analysis will reveal inventory shortages that would not be apparent when the analysis is only conducted on a monthly basis. For example, if the entire 225,000 estimated unit sales for November were to all appear in the first week of the month, the company would have a 100,000-unit shortage that it would not be able to entirely fulfill until the end of the month, which could trigger the loss of the order.

## Chase Capacity Planning

The alternative to level capacity planning is chase capacity planning, where capacity is constantly being adjusted to match forecasted demand as closely as possible. This can be a difficult proposition, since it may involve changes in both equipment and staffing, sometimes on quite short notice. This approach works best for companies that produce perishable goods or which have substantial amounts of customer interaction (such as call centers). In these cases, businesses rely on staff overtime, the use of contract or part-time employees, outsourcing, staff scheduling adjustments, and either layoffs or hiring sprees to match capacity levels to demand. These options can be expensive, since overtime, outsourcing, and layoffs are costly. Also, the use of short-term staff can result in lower quality, since these people have neither the training nor the procedural experience to match the output of full-time employees.

### The Reality of Capacity Management

The preceding alternatives show the *theoretically* correct ways to deal with capacity. However, managers are routinely confronted by a mix of conflicting objectives, such as increasing customer service while reducing the overall investment in inventory. In this situation, a manager is more likely to use a mix of capacity management techniques in order to achieve the stated objectives. For example, in a period of low demand, one might elect to offer discounts to a few clients to entice them into placing orders now, while keeping capacity costs low by outsourcing the work to third parties. In this case, management is adjusting both the demand and capacity sides of the business.

One of the most imposing realities of capacity management is the need to deal with both variable demand and variable capacity. While stable demand in both areas is the ideal scenario, it is a rarity in most industries. More commonly, the situation ranges from moderately variable demand to completely unpredictable variations. When moderate to extreme variability is the norm, senior management needs to decide whether to increase the base capacity level to take on as much demand as possible, or whether to operate more conservatively and refuse some customer orders.

## Incremental Capacity Planning Effects

Over the short term, the operations manager is faced with the options of paying overtime or outsourcing work to third parties, or of investing in more substantial facilities that will boost capacity by a substantially greater amount. When making this decision, the basic rule to be aware of is that the marginal cost of making a capacity change increases with the size of the change. Thus, a modest increase of a few percent of capacity might be achieved by adding a few people to a shift or by paying overtime for a few extra hours. However, a capacity increase of 20 percent or more will likely be more expensive, since it requires a greater investment in equipment, square footage, and long-term staffing to achieve.

Given these differences in cost, management will need to consider the long-term outlook for customer demand. If the long-term outlook is weak, then it makes more sense to pay for overtime and a few additional staff, and wait for demand levels to fall. However, if the long-term outlook for customer demand is strong, then management might want to instead make an immediate investment in base capacity, in anticipation of a strong sales surge.

## The Freelancer Impact on Capacity

The gig economy has exploded; people are available for temporary work in nearly every discipline, and are usually easily found through a website that specializes in their services, providing a platform to connect workers with temporary employers. While the most commonly-known gig jobs relate to driving people from point to point, there are many other jobs available, ranging from artificial intelligence developers to car mechanics. The gig economy allows a business to quickly ramp up its capacity in certain areas, rather than having to increase the size of its core staff. This is a particularly useful option when demand levels spike only occasionally; in this case, the company can reasonably estimate how many people to hire, and outsources all other work.

There are a few concerns relating to the gig economy. One is that legislation in some states is making it easier for gig workers to claim employee status, so that the hiring party must pay payroll taxes and provide certain benefits. Another problem is allowing a gig worker access to the intellectual property of a business, which may then be stolen.

## Summary

Ultimately, capacity management is driven by the anticipated level of customer demand, so correctly forecasting that demand is critical. There are a number of tools available for forecasting, but this can still be a difficult chore in many industries. When demand is difficult to anticipate, the capacity management decision shifts to the supply side, where management needs to decide what level of base capacity to maintain. After that decision is made, the next issue is whether to produce at a standard rate and use excess inventory to meet variations in customer demand, or to continually adjust capacity levels to meet customer demand on the fly. These decisions will vary by individual business, depending on the objectives of the firm and the characteristics of the industry.

# Chapter 12
# Constraint Management

## Introduction

Constraint management involves determining whether a company operation is constraining the entire business from earning a greater profit, and then focuses all decision-making upon how to mitigate the effects of this constraint (or "bottleneck"). This chapter gives an overview of constraint management, and then delves into a number of management decisions where using it can alter one's perception of how to manage a company.

**Related Podcast Episodes:** Episodes 43 through 47 of the Accounting Best Practices Podcast discuss constraint analysis. They are available at: **accountingtools.com/podcasts** or **iTunes**

## Constraint Analysis Operational Terminology

Constraint analysis makes use of several unique terms, so we will begin with a set of definitions before proceeding to an overview of constraint analysis. The key operational terms are:

- *Drum*. This is a third variation of the *constraint* term, along with *bottleneck*. It is the operation, person, or (occasionally) the materials within a company that prevent the business from generating additional sales. Since the ultimate profitability of the company depends on this one item, it sets the pace for how the company operates. Picture the drum beating on a rowed galley, which indicates why it is called a *drum*.
- *Buffer*. The drum operation should operate at as close to 100% of capacity as possible, but this is impossible when the flow of materials from upstream operations is unreliable. The buffer is inventory that is positioned in front of the drum operation, and which protects the drum from any stoppage in materials coming from upstream operations. The buffer may need to be quite large if there is considerable variability in the inflow of materials, or it may be of more modest proportions if the inflow is more stable.
- *Rope*. The rope represents the date and time when jobs must be released into the production process in order to have inventory arrive at the buffer just when it is needed by the drum; thus, it is really the total time duration needed to bring work-in-process to the drum.

These three terms are sometimes strung together in a single phrase, and are called the *drum-buffer-rope* system. As a group, they describe the essential operational components of constraint analysis.

## Overview of Constraint Management

The key points in understanding constraint management are the following two concepts:

1. A company is an integrated set of processes that function together to generate a profit; and
2. There is a chokepoint somewhere in a company that absolutely controls its ability to earn a profit.

The chokepoint is also known as the drum operation (as defined earlier, or the bottleneck, the constrained resource, or the constraint).

The first concept, that of a company being an integrated set of processes, applies very strongly at the product line level, but less so at the corporate parent level. At the product line level, there is almost certainly a bottleneck that restricts the ability to generate more profit. At the corporate parent level, there may be multiple subsidiaries, each with a multitude of product lines. Thus, from the perspective of the corporate parent, there are still bottlenecks, but there may be a number of them scattered throughout the operations of the subsidiaries.

The second concept, that of the bottleneck, is most typically characterized by a machine that can only process a certain number of units per day. To improve profits, a company must focus all of its attention on that machine by taking such steps as:

- Adding supplemental staff to cover any employee breaks or downtime during shift changes
- Reviewing the quality of work-in-process going into the operation, so that it does not waste any time processing items that are already defective
- Positioning extra maintenance personnel near it to ensure that service intervals are short
- Reducing the amount of processing time per unit, so that more units can be run through the machine
- Adding more capacity to the machine
- Outsourcing work to suppliers

It is also possible that the bottleneck is not in the production area at all. It may be caused by a materials shortage, or by a lack of sales staff. In those rare cases where there is simply no bottleneck to be found, then the company has excess capacity, and can choose to either reduce its capacity (and the related cost) or try to sell more volume, possibly at a lower price.

---

**EXAMPLE**

Hammer Industries produces construction equipment. Its products are large, complex, and mostly sold through a request for proposals process. An operations analyst has reviewed all production operations in detail and concluded that there is no bottleneck operation to be found. Instead, the real chokepoint appears to be in the sales department.

Hammer has a multi-tiered sales process, where one group makes initial contacts with prospective customers, another group of technical writers responds to requests for proposal (RFP), yet another group conducts sales presentations, and a final group conducts final contract negotiations. A brief analysis shows that the technical writers are completely overwhelmed with writing RFP responses, and have missed several RFP filing deadlines. The sales staff positioned ahead of them in the process flow, those making contacts with prospective customers, are aware of the problem and have scaled back their activities to meet with new customers, since they know the company is not capable of making timely RFP responses. Thus, it is evident that the sales department is the true company bottleneck.

The analyst reports this issue to management, and recommends a combination of additional technical writer hiring and the purchase of RFP response software to simplify the writing task.

---

One can usually tell where the bottleneck is located, because it has a large amount of work piled up in front of it, while the work operation immediately downstream from it is starved for work.

A major part of the management of the bottleneck operation is the inventory buffer located immediately in front of it. Constraint analysis holds that there will always be flaws in the production process that result in variability in the flow of materials to the bottleneck, so it is necessary to build up a buffer to insulate the bottleneck from these issues. The buffer should be quite large if there are lots of upstream production problems, or much smaller if the production flow is relatively placid.

If production problems start to eat into the size of the inventory buffer, then the bottleneck is in danger of having a stock-out condition, which may cause it to run out of work. To avoid this, have a large *sprint capacity* in selected upstream production operations. Sprint capacity is essentially excess production capacity. There should be sufficient sprint capacity available to rapidly rebuild the inventory buffer. If the company has invested in a significant sprint capacity, there is also less need for a large inventory buffer.

Finally, there is the concept of the *rope* that was mentioned earlier as a key definition. It is very important to only release new jobs into the production queue so that they arrive at the inventory buffer just in time to be used. The natural inclination of a production scheduler would be to release jobs too soon, to ensure that there is always a healthy flow of jobs arriving at the inventory buffer. However, doing so represents an excessive inventory investment, and also confuses the production staff, which does not know which of the plethora of jobs to process next. Thus, the rope concept represents a fine balance between overloading the system and starving it of work.

In summary, the bottleneck operation is the most important operation in a company. The management team needs to know where it is located, and spend a great deal of time figuring out how to maximize its operation so that it hardly ever stops.

## Types of Constraints

Given the importance of the constraint concept, it is of considerable importance to understand the types of bottlenecks to which a business may be subjected. Consider the following types:

- *Physical constraint.* A machine that has a large amount of work-in-process in queue in front of it is obviously being fully used, and so could be a constraint.
- *Paradigm constraint.* When employees hold a belief that causes them to act in a certain way, this is called a paradigm constraint, and can impact a process to such an extent that the belief is considered a constraint. An example is the belief that the only good workstation is one humming along at 100% of capacity, even though there is not enough demand to justify so much work. The result could be a divergence of resources away from the true constraint (perhaps a machine), resulting in suboptimal use of the actual constrained resource. This item is noted again later as a policy constraint. Another paradigm constraint is the overriding belief that costs are to be reduced throughout the business, on the assumption that this will cause an inevitable increase in net profits. In reality, more expenditures must be made if doing so results in better utilization of the constraint. This item appears as several policy constraints, such as the freight cost reduction rule, the minimum production run rule, and the overtime rule.

---

**EXAMPLE**

The owners of Industrial Landscaping perceive their company to be in the business of providing landscaping services solely to corporations. The number of local businesses has been declining for years, so the perceived target market of Industrial is shrinking. If the owners can get past the paradigm constraint of only seeing their market as businesses, they could reorient the company to offer the same services to individuals.

**EXAMPLE**

The constraint faced by High Noon Armaments is in the hiring of armorers for its production staff. The perception of company management is that the only qualified armorers are those with a certification from one of a few armorer programs in the country. This paradigm constraint can be broken by convincing management that people trained through an in-house apprenticeship program can be just as qualified, thereby increasing the number of skilled staff in the production area.

---

- *Policy constraint*. This is a management-imposed guideline for how a process is to be conducted. Unless carefully monitored, these policy constraints can interfere with the orderly flow of work through a business. Policy constraints are difficult to find, since one must track backwards to them by observing their effects on a business. It may be equally difficult to eliminate such a constraint, since it may have been used by employees for years, and they now consider it inviolate. Here are several examples of policy constraints:
    - *Batch sizing rule*. There may be a policy in place that requires a workstation to first fill up an outbound pallet before it will be shifted to a downstream workstation for additional work. This rule is usually implemented in order to keep from overworking the materials handling staff that operates the forklifts that move the pallets. However, this rule also means that the downstream workstations are alternately starved of incoming parts and then flooded with them, given the surging nature of the inventory flow. This rule can be eliminated by using conveyors between workstations or much smaller transport containers.
    - *Break rule*. Employees are allowed a specific amount of rest time away from their workstations, during which time the machines remain idle. These rules are routinely included in the demands of unions, which justifiably claim that workers need to periodically stand down from their work. This issue can be ameliorated by using roving teams of replacement workers who take over during breaks, even though this may increase the total cost of labor.
    - *Cost reduction rule*. Costs are to be reduced in all parts of the production process, which can negatively impact the ability of a company to support its constrained resource. Instead, more cash should be spent to ensure that the constraint is fully supported at all times.
    - *Minimum production run*. All production runs must generate a certain minimum number of units, which supposedly justifies the equipment setup cost by spreading this cost over an increased number of units. In reality, a larger production run just robs the next job in line of valuable machine time, and may also create excess inventory that is in danger of obsolescence and consumes company cash. Also, most workstations (other than the constraint) have more than enough excess capacity, so spending extra time on a larger number of setups does not interfere with throughput.
    - *Overtime rule*. Overtime may not be allowed, in which case there is no one to operate the constraint operation after regular work hours or during breaks, which halts production. On the contrary, overtime should always be allowed at the constraint, to ensure the highest possible level of utilization.
    - *Production line balance rule*. The industrial engineering staff attempts to convert the production process into a production line, where capacity levels are just enough in all areas to match production

requirements. This policy falls apart when there is a production snafu, which reduces the input to the constrained resource and causes total throughput from the entire process to decline. Instead, sprint capacity is to be encouraged upstream from the constraint, thereby maintaining a certain amount of protective capacity.

  - *Resource maximization rule.* All phases of the production facility are to be operated at their maximum capacity levels, which results in excess amounts of inventory being generated, which in turn clogs the production floor. Instead, all workstations should operate at whatever level is needed to support the constrained resource, and no more.

  Many of the preceding policy constraints were originally instituted to optimize a specific issue, but without taking into consideration the impact of the throughput generated by the entire system. Thus, a rule to balance the production line will reduce the amount of capacity needed, but will inevitably result in a throughput reduction when the lack of excess upstream capacity starves the constrained operation of materials to process.

- *Raw material constraint.* When there is not enough of a raw material available to meet all customer orders, the raw material is the constraint. This constraint is most likely to arise when there is excessive industry-wide demand for a particular raw material, and where there are not enough substitutes available to replace the raw material. In essence, this means that the constraint is located at a supplier. Since the supplier is not (usually) under the control of the company, this is one of the more difficult constraints to resolve or manage on an ongoing basis.
- *Sales department constraint.* When the sales process is complex, any step in the process that does not have sufficient resources can result in a reduced level of sales. For example, a shortage in sales engineers can result in too few product demonstrations, and therefore in too few sales being completed.
- *Marketplace constraint.* A company may have worked through all of its constraint issues, in which case obtaining more orders from the market is considered the constraint. This constraint can be overcome by offering better deals to customers in order to spur sales growth.

It would initially appear easy enough to change a policy constraint and experience an immediate increase in throughput. However, these changes can be surprisingly difficult, since employees are accustomed to using the existing policies, and resist change. The management group may be even more difficult to persuade than the line workers, since the managers may have originally mandated the offending rules, and so have a personal emotional investment in them. Consequently, the alteration of a policy constraint can encompass employee relations issues, added training, changes to supporting procedures and bonus plans, and possibly even the replacement of some staff.

Despite the work involved to alter a policy constraint, there can be a considerable monetary payoff associated with doing so. Consequently, there should be an ongoing effort to locate and correct issues related to policy constraints.

Management may choose to have a constraint in a particular place within the company. This happens when the cost of increasing the selected constraint's capacity is so high that managing and working around this constraint is the most cost-effective way to run the business. For example, the cost of adding another paint booth may be so excessive that management would prefer to concentrate on managing every last minute of its time and outsourcing all remaining work.

## Local Optimization

The concept of the constraint is very much at odds with the traditional concept of local optimization, where the target is to improve the efficiency of every operation throughout a company. The operations analyst is involved in many of these decisions, trying to decide whether to invest in any number of efficiency projects. In many cases, these improvements do nothing to increase overall company profits, because the primary driver of profits is still the bottleneck operation. Consequently, if investments are made in local optimization projects, profits do not improve, but the investment in the company increases, so the only logical outcome is that the return on investment declines.

The following exhibit contains several examples of how constraint analysis alters one's view of local optimization.

### Constraint Analysis Scenarios

| Situation | Local Optimization Solution | Constraint Analysis Solution |
|---|---|---|
| Overtime is 10% of payroll | Restrict all overtime | Do not restrict overtime if it is being spent on the bottleneck operation, or on any operations feeding the bottleneck |
| A machine is not being utilized | Sell the machine | Keep the machine if it provides sprint capacity for the bottleneck operation |
| A product can be redesigned | Only do so if the product is at the end of its normal life cycle | Do so if the redesign reduces the product processing time at the bottleneck operation |
| The production staff is not fully utilized | Cut back on operations and lay off staff | If there is no bottleneck operation, lower prices to attract more sales |
| A machine is reaching its maximum utilization | Buy an additional machine | Only buy an additional unit if it will provide more sprint capacity. Do not buy if it is located downstream from the bottleneck operation |
| A supplier is asking us to outsource production | Do so if it passes a cost-benefit analysis | Do so if it reduces the load on the bottleneck operation |

In all of the cases noted in the table, it is necessary to step back from the individual decision and see what the impact will be on the entire company before determining the correct course of action.

In particular, be aware of two problems that are caused by local optimization:

1. *Excess inventory*. If a production operation is optimized that is not the bottleneck operation, all that has been accomplished is give it the ability to churn out even more inventory than was previously the case, and which the bottleneck will be unable to process. Thus, management has not only needlessly invested in the operation, but also needlessly invested in additional inventory that must now wait to be processed.
2. *Overly efficient labor*. When a good manufacturing process was considered to be one with very long production runs, there was an emphasis on highly efficient labor. If the focus is instead on maximizing the amount of production passing through the bottleneck – and nowhere else – the bottleneck operation can be grossly overstaffed to make sure that it is always operating; much less attention is paid to labor efficiencies elsewhere. Employees should only work if inventory is actually needed. In short, it is better to have employees be underutilized and produce less inventory than to be more efficient and produce inventory that is not needed.

In summary, a company does not even have to be especially efficient in production areas located away from the bottleneck operation. Instead, the one and only focus is on maximizing the efficiency of the bottleneck. This change in focus alters most of the decisions that would be reached if one were to only focus on local optimization.

## Constraint Management Financial Terminology

By now it should be apparent that constraint analysis is quite a valuable tool from an operational perspective. But what about from a financial perspective? How does the operations analyst use it to make decisions? There is a model for using constraint analysis in this role, but first we need to define the terms in the model. They are:

- *Throughput*. This is the margin left after totally variable costs have been subtracted from revenue. This tends to be a large proportion of revenues, since all overhead costs are excluded from the calculation.
- *Totally variable costs*. This is usually just the cost of materials, since it is only those costs that vary when one incremental unit of a product is manufactured. This does not normally include the cost of labor, since employees are not usually paid based on one incremental unit of output (unless they are paid under a piece rate plan, where they are paid for the number of units produced). There are a few other possible costs that may be totally variable, such as commissions, subcontractor fees, customs duties, and freight costs.
- *Operating expenses*. This is all company expenses other than totally variable costs. There is no differentiation between overhead costs, administrative costs or financing costs – quite simply, *all* other company expenses are lumped into this category.

- *Investment.* This is the amount invested in assets. "Investment" includes changes in the level of working capital resulting from a management decision.
- *Net profit.* This is throughput, less operating expenses.

## Constraint Management from a Financial Perspective

When a company is looked at from the perspective of constraints, it no longer makes sense to evaluate individual products, because overhead costs do not vary at the individual product level. In reality, most companies spend a great deal of money to maintain a production infrastructure, and that infrastructure is what really generates a profit – the trick is making that infrastructure produce the maximum profit with the best mix of products having the highest possible throughput. Under the constraint analysis model, there are three ways to improve the financial position of the entire production infrastructure. They are:

- *Increase throughput.* This is by either increasing revenues or reducing the amount of totally variable costs.
- *Reduce operating expenses.* This is by reducing some element of overhead expenses.
- *Improve the return on investment.* This is by either improving profits in conjunction with the lowest possible investment, or by reducing profits slightly along with a correspondingly larger decline in investment.

Note that only the increase in throughput is related in any way to decisions made at the product level. The other two improvement methods may be concerned with changes anywhere in the production system.

## Constraint Management

Once the constraint has been found, how is it managed? There are a number of methods available for improving the efficiency and effectiveness of the constraint, which we address in the following sub-sections.

### Additional Staff

The throughput passing through the constraint is extremely valuable, much more so than the cost of the labor required to operate the constraint. Consequently, it nearly always makes sense to overstaff the constraint to ensure that it is always operational. Here are several variations on the concept to consider:

- *Breaks.* Always have experienced backup people available to continue running the constraint when the primary staff takes scheduled breaks, so that the constraint keeps running. There are several implications. First, the breaks must be scheduled, so that the arrival of backup staff can be properly coordinated. Second, the backup staff must be just as experienced as the primary work crew, so that efficiency does not suffer while they are filling in. And finally, consider scheduling routine maintenance for employee breaks. The last option is an especially good one when there are no qualified backup people available to fill in for the primary work crew.

- *Shift changes.* The normal activities for a production workstation are for the current operator to shut it down and clean up the area prior to leaving at the end of the shift, after which another operator arrives for the second shift and starts up the workstation again. This gap between shifts can be quite long, depending on company procedures regarding safety or production scheduling meetings. To avoid this downtime during the shift change, schedule overlapping shifts just for the constraint, so that the incoming work crew can take over immediately from the outgoing work crew. This means that the team assigned to the constraint will work somewhat longer than a standard eight-hour shift, so the company will incur a certain amount of overtime cost.
- *Administration and maintenance.* The employees operating the constraint may have to deal with a number of administrative and/or maintenance activities besides operation of the constraint. For example, they may need to fill out paperwork, clean up around the area, report issues, conduct preliminary machine setup work, and handle routine preventive maintenance tasks. While these issues may be quite acceptable in other parts of the production area, they are a distraction at the constraint, and keep the crew from maintaining a high level of utilization. Instead, assign an extra staff person to deal with these incidental activities.
- *Training.* There must always be a well-trained group operating the constraint. This means that the number of fully-trained personnel exceeds the number of people actually operating the workstation, so that the most efficient personnel are always available to cover for employee breaks or days off. However, training should not be conducted *on* the constraint, since this reduces utilization. Instead, create a practice workstation that is solely dedicated to training.
- *Overload.* In general, overload the constraint with extra staff, just to ensure that any constraint downtime is not caused by a staff shortage. If the work is considered unusually boring or physically demanding, pay a higher hourly rate to ensure that there are enough personnel willing to engage in the work. A high rate of pay also tends to reduce the amount of employee absenteeism.

Of all the types of constraint management discussed in this section, proper staffing of the constraint is the most easily achieved, and has the best results. Consequently, management attention should be squarely focused on this area.

### Constraint Scheduling

The capacity of the constraint operation can be expanded by running the operation for all three shifts, every day of the year. The production manager may be resistant to this concept, since it involves keeping a portion of the production facility open at all times, keeping the facility heated or air conditioned, paying shift premiums, paying for extra supervisors, and so forth. There may also be a justifiable concern that the efficiency of the constrained workstation will decline during later shifts. Nonetheless, this is a necessary step that can greatly ease the burden on the production schedule, as well as increase throughput. The additional cost of running extra shifts is actually minor, when compared to the resulting increase in throughput.

### Processing Quality

The constraint operation needs to achieve the highest possible level of first-pass quality. This concept is defined as the ability to manufacture parts correctly the first time. It is unacceptable to rework parts at the constraint, since doing so requires additional constraint time. There are a number of techniques available for increasing processing quality at the constraint, such as additional staff training, only staffing with the most experienced personnel, paying bonuses for first-pass quality, and engaging in problem analysis to determine the reasons for any rework issues found.

### Maintenance

If machinery is involved in the constraint operation, it will require periodic maintenance in order to operate properly. If the machinery is run flat-out in pursuit of maximum operating hours, it is more likely that the level of maintenance provided will be inadequate, eventually resulting in equipment breakage that completely halts the workstation. This concern can be addressed through the intelligent use of maintenance, which may include the following:

- *Adjacent staffing*. Position a maintenance crew nearby, so they will not have to travel far to address any stoppage issues.
- *Adjacent parts storage*. Maintain a parts locker next to the constraint that contains all replacement parts and maintenance tools needed to conduct repairs.
- *Schedule maintenance*. Create a schedule that states exactly when preventive maintenance is to be conducted. Doing so at regular intervals makes it less likely that a catastrophic failure will occur.
- *Schedule off-hours repairs*. When a major downtime repair is needed, schedule it away from the most productive working hours of the constraint. This may mean that major maintenance is conducted during second or third shift, which may require the company to pay higher hourly rates to the maintenance staff.

### Merged Operations

In an effort to save money on production labor, an upstream or downstream operation may have been combined with the constraint. This means that the group running the constraint is now spreading its time across multiple work activities. These employees may be diverted by maintenance problems, setup work, moving inventory, and so forth in the other operation. Doing so yields less available time to work on the constraint, which will likely result in a lower utilization level and therefore less throughput.

A better approach is to simplify the operation of the constraint as much as possible by removing the additional operation from the responsibility of the work crew dealing with the constraint. With a narrower focus, they are more likely to achieve a higher utilization level on the constraint.

### Off-Load Work

There may be older or less efficient workstations on the premises that can process some of the work scheduled for the constraint. These workstations may be far less efficient, and yet should be considered, since they can still generate throughput that the constraint does not have the capacity to handle. This may mean that some tasks that are normally automated are instead processed manually. Or, the business may have old machinery that is considered outmoded, but which can still process work at a vastly reduced rate. If so, compare the incremental cost of using these alternatives to the amount of throughput they can generate. This comparison might lead to the conclusion that equipment scheduled for disposal should be retained and refurbished.

Another option is to outsource work. Suppliers will charge higher fees in order to generate a profit, but this is acceptable as long as the incremental increase in cost does not exceed the incremental amount of throughput generated by using outsourcing. However, the decision to outsource is not as simple as a comparison of cost to throughput. Designated suppliers must be able to meet the company's requirements for product quality and delivery times, while also having sufficient available capacity to meet the delivery dates demanded by the company's customers.

### Quality Inspection

The amount of constraint time is fixed and cannot be expanded, so do not waste this time by running low-quality parts through the constraint. These items will eventually be rejected somewhere downstream for being out of specification, so the related amount of constraint time will be lost. There are several ways to reduce the risk of low-quality parts entering the constraint:

- *Inspection location.* Set up a quality inspection station immediately in front of the constraint. Those manning the inspection station can remove all flawed parts from the inventory buffer. An additional role is to be proactive in discussing any quality issues found with the operators of the upstream workstations, so that flaws are dealt with promptly.

- *Supplier report card.* If there is a risk of low quality in the parts being delivered by suppliers, create a report card system that tracks the quality of these parts. The information can be shared with suppliers to upgrade their performance, and as justification for replacing suppliers.
- *Supplier certification.* Certify the ability of suppliers to produce goods to specifications; these suppliers are allowed to ship directly to the production area, bypassing incoming inspections.

### Redesign Products

A longer-term solution to constraint management is to redesign company products so that they require less processing time at the constraint, or none at all. This can be a difficult solution, for the current design may be one that is low-cost and trouble-free, while alternative designs may be subject to a higher failure rate. Another concern is that products may have quite long life cycles, in which case the time required to circumvent the constraint will be inordinately long. Still, this may be an option in a few cases.

### Add Capacity

A final management option is to add capacity to the constraint. This option is listed last, because it can be quite difficult to increase capacity in this area. Doing so may be inordinately expensive, require highly skilled employees who are in short supply, and so forth. Accordingly, this is likely to be considered the last possible option after all other constraint management techniques have been used.

---

**EXAMPLE**

Monk Books produces replicas of famous medieval books. Customers are museums, which keep the fakes available for presentation while the originals are stored in secure vaults. The company's constraint is the artwork function in the illustration of medieval book replicas. The amount of backlog at this constraint is 6,200 minutes. The company's throughput per minute is $10.00, so this backlog represents $62,000 of throughput that cannot be processed. The management team investigates the situation to see how this constraint can be properly managed.

The artists who illuminate the books have uniquely individual styles and different color palettes, so it is impossible to have more than one artist work on a single book. However, it *is* possible to hire pencil sketch apprentices to block out the general outlines of the artwork to be added. Pencil work is quite time-consuming, currently taking up 20% of the artists' time. Consequently, the apprentices are hired and commence work. Since the artists must spend time supervising the apprentices, the amount of time saved is not as great as anticipated, at 15%.

Still, this reduces the backlog by 15%, to 5,270 minutes, allowing Monk to recognize an additional $9,300 of throughput.

An additional concern is the quality of the handmade paper used in the book replicas. Approximately 4% of all pages produced prove to have a cracking problem that is usually only noticeable after pages have been completed, which means that these pages must be re-illustrated. Further investigation reveals that this cracking can be found with a $5,000 portable electron microscope that operates as an attachment to a smartphone. Accordingly, the paper refinishing and coating team is required to conduct a microscope scan of each page as it leaves the paper fabrication department. This review eliminates all of the pages that would otherwise have to be re-illustrated at the constraint.

A further issue is that the illustrators use paintbrushes based on medieval designs, which are miniver brushes – made from the fur of the stoat. Stoat hairs tend to separate easily from the brush and stick on the painted pages, which require a considerable amount of time to manually extract from the pages and repaint over the resulting gaps in the illustrations. After some debate regarding the need for medieval paintbrushes, the artists accept modern synthetic brushes instead, which do not have the dropout problem. Making this change completely eliminates the stoat hair removal issue.

These constraint mitigation activities remove work from the constraint, keep bad components from entering the constraint, and eliminate rework. This means that the total amount of throughput generated by Monk will increase, with no capital investment other than the portable electron microscope.

---

We are not yet done with ways to manage the production constraint. The inventory buffer is important enough to deserve separate treatment, and so is addressed in the next section.

## The Inventory Buffer

There will always be flaws in the production process that result in variability in the flow of materials to the constrained resource. This means that there will be periods when there is no inventory to feed into the constraint, so that the constraint will not be used. This issue is dealt with by building up a buffer of inventory in front of the constraint. In the following sub-sections, we deal with several buffer issues.

### Buffer Sizing

If ongoing industrial engineering efforts have succeeded in reducing inconsistencies in the flow of goods to the bottleneck, the constraint buffer can be relatively small. Conversely, if there is still considerable variability in the flow of parts to the bottleneck, it will be necessary to protect the constraint with quite a large inventory buffer.

The existence of a large buffer is particularly important if a company does not have a sufficient amount of excess capacity upstream from the constraint, since these upstream operations will not be able to easily build up a surge of new parts to rebuild the buffer in the event that the buffer is depleted. In this case, a production snafu may clear out most of the buffer, and then put the business at risk of another constraint shutdown during the extended period when the buffer is being slowly rebuilt back to its former size.

A large buffer cannot substitute for the addition of production capacity to upstream workstations, especially since it takes lots of excess capacity to build the buffer in the first place. Ideally, there should be sufficient available capacity to rebuild the buffer in short order, if a production snafu requires that inventory be withdrawn from the buffer.

The amount of upstream capacity needed to initially build and then maintain an inventory buffer does not necessarily require an inordinate investment, if a proper analysis is conducted to determine the exact amounts of additional capacity needed. The correct amount of capacity can be determined over time by gradually increasing the capacity level in response to actual buffer penetrations, or by modeling such penetrations to see where capacity needs to be bolstered. Another option is to increase capacity in those areas where labor is needed, rather than fixed assets, by engaging in a considerable amount of cross-training and then calling in the extra staff when there is a sudden need to increase production volume.

A theoretical alternative to the inventory buffer is to maintain a skimpy buffer, but a large investment in upstream production capacity. This would mean that any inventory shortfalls could be fulfilled quite rapidly. However, the cost to maintain an inventory buffer is not especially large, while the cost of the fixed assets needed to maintain a comprehensive level of upstream capacity can be inordinately large. Consequently, the briefest financial modeling will usually indicate that a larger inventory buffer should be maintained.

---

**EXAMPLE**

Sharper Designs manufactures knives for chefs. The company's facility is located in a flood plain, and the shop floor was recently inundated with flood waters for two days, rendering the facility inoperable. The constraint, a manual knife handle carving operation, continued to run on the second floor of the building, and soon ran out of work when there were no more knife blades arriving from the upstream (no pun intended) operations located on the first floor. The president of Sharper faces the following choices:

- *Continue as before.* The president accepts the fact that floods will interrupt operations from time to time, and does nothing new to guard against it. This approach is a reasonable one if floods are a rare occurrence.
- *Install levees.* The company can build levees around its perimeter, so that floodwater up to a certain depth cannot enter the facility. This approach is feasible if there is a

reasonable probability of recurring floods, and the amount of lost throughput offsets the cost of the levees.

- *Create inventory buffer*. The company can invest in a sufficient amount of knife blade inventory buffer to protect against the expected amount of downtime caused by a flooding event. This assumes that the flooding will not be so bad that constraint operations cannot continue on the second floor.
- *Build upstream capacity*. Invest in more metal fabrication equipment, so that the flow of knife blades to the knife handle carving operation is not significantly interrupted. This could work if combined with a sufficient inventory buffer to last through the expected duration of a flood. However, an additional concern is that the extra equipment could be damaged by floodwaters.

If the probability of additional flooding is high, another consideration for the president is to move the entire facility away from the flood plain, to higher ground.

---

The preceding example shows that there are many viable alternatives for management to sort through, each of which optimizes the situation under different circumstances.

## The Expedite Zone

A portion of the inventory buffer may be designated as an expedite zone. This is the final tranche of inventory that is accessed before the buffer is emptied. As soon as inventory is accessed from this part of the buffer, the management team is notified to expedite an accelerated rate of production in the upstream workstations, so that the buffer can be refilled. If there is no expedite zone, management has to continually monitor the entire buffer to see if there will be any incipient shortages.

## The Assembly Buffer

Thus far, our assumption has been that the inventory is only positioned in front of the constraint. However, if there is a final assembly function where materials arrive from several sources and are assembled into a final product, it will also be necessary to place a buffer in front of that area. The issue is not a shortfall of parts arriving from the constraint – after all, this is the most heavily monitored operation in the company, and the constraint does not have sufficient capacity to provide a buffer of constraint-originating parts. Instead, the buffer is used to guard against shortages of all *other* types of parts.

The assembly buffer operates under the same principles used for the constraint buffer – that it provides sufficient unit quantities to guard against shortages caused by upstream workstations. This may involve the use of an expedite zone to warn management of impending shipment delays.

By having an assembly area buffer, it is easier to establish a rapid flow of parts from the constraint, into the final assembly area, and out through the shipping dock to customers. In short, this additional buffer is needed to ensure that there is no final hitch in the production process that can interfere with the realization of revenue.

Oddly enough, the sales manager may have a greater interest in this buffer than in the constraint buffer, since the assembly buffer is more closely associated with any shipment delays occurring in the immediate future.

### Buffer Holes

When there is a sudden decline in the unit count in the inventory buffer, this is called a hole in the buffer. Such a hole is caused by a production failure at an upstream workstation that delays the arrival of parts. Every buffer hole should be investigated in detail to ascertain the reason for its existence, which is then documented in a buffer penetration report. A sample report follows.

### Sample Buffer Penetration Report

| Date | Delay Duration | Source Work Station | Problem |
|---|---|---|---|
| Feb. 13 | 8 hours | Splitting | Cutter saw blade broke; no replacement on site |
| Feb. 14 | 6 hours | Sanding | Staff reduction due to injury |
| Feb. 15 | 4 hours | Bleach bath | Incorrect bleach concentration |
| Feb. 18 | 2 hours | Drilling | Drilling template damaged |

The information in the report is used to locate and correct the problems causing buffer holes. If the occurrence of these items can be contained, the number and severity of buffer holes will drop, allowing a company to reduce its investment in the inventory buffer.

### Dynamic Buffering

A more time-consuming way to manage the buffer than the expedite zone is dynamic buffering. Under this approach, the production planning staff attempts to strike a balance between the amount of extra upstream capacity needed and the smallest possible investment in the inventory buffer. Doing so requires constant oversight of the level of buffer inventory. This approach is usually only necessary when the cost of upgrades in upstream capacity is considerable, and there is a large monetary investment in inventory. The amount of monitoring work required may mean that a full-time staff person is needed, which is described next.

### The Buffer Manager

If it is unusually critical to maintain a large stock of inventory in the buffer, especially when there is dynamic buffering, it may be cost-effective to hire a buffer manager. This person's sole responsibility is the buffer – to monitor current usage patterns, predict which items will be depleted, and work with the upstream workstations to refill the buffer as expeditiously as possible. This should not be considered an entry-level clerk position, but rather a person with significant experience in inventory management and production control.

## Sprint Capacity

Sprint capacity is an excess amount of production capacity located upstream from the constrained resource, possibly in several different workstations. The intent of having sprint capacity is to ensure that any inventory shortages at the constraint can be rapidly refilled.

Sprint capacity can be expensive to incorporate into a production process, especially when it involves acquiring production equipment. In other cases where additional capacity mostly involves adding additional staff to a work area for a short period of time, additions are less of an issue. In either case, the best way to add sprint capacity is based on an analysis of inventory shortfalls in the past, and determining the amount of extra capacity that would have been needed to overcome those prior shortages.

Sprint capacity cannot involve outsourced capacity, unless suppliers have remarkably fast reaction speeds. In most cases, the usual delay of several days in receiving ordered parts from suppliers makes this alternative impractical.

---

**EXAMPLE**

To continue with the preceding Monk Books example, the illustration group obtains the gold paint used in its illustrations from a specialist firm in France that has been compounding gold paint for the past 300 years. The paint contains a high (20%) proportion of real yellow gold, and so requires oppressively expensive security procedures that include only shipping the paint by boat. Given the vagaries of the weather at sea and the random nature of the boat itinerary (to foil thieves), the paint may arrive up to a week late, which essentially shuts down the illustration department after it runs out of paint. The procurement manager faces the following choices to deal with this issue:

- *Continue as before*. The constraint is entirely shut down for at least 2,000 minutes per year because of delayed paint shipments, which represents a reduction of $20,000 of throughput per year.
- *Purchase more frequently*. Monk could place more frequent orders of a smaller individual size, so that the size of each stockout is smaller. The procurement manager estimates that this option will reduce the total stockout time by half, to 1,000 minutes per year, but at an increased transportation cost of $9,000. This is an improvement over the "as is" option, but still leaves a substantial amount of constraint downtime.
- *Create a buffer*. A close examination of prior stockout conditions clarifies that an extra investment in $8,000 of gold paint will offset 98% of all stockout conditions, resulting in a paltry 40 minutes of projected constraint downtime. This choice increases throughput by $19,600 at an investment cost of $8,000. This is the best option; if it appears that the paint will go bad if held too long, an additional step is to ensure that the paint in the buffer is used up and replaced by new deliveries.

---

## Production Scheduling

It is very important to only release new jobs into the production queue so that they arrive at the inventory buffer just in time to be used. By doing so, the production staff can focus all of its attention on a limited number of jobs, so that each one is completed within the minimum possible period of time.

The natural inclination of a production scheduler would be to release jobs too soon, to ensure that there is always a healthy flow of jobs arriving at the inventory buffer. However, doing so represents an excessive inventory investment, and also confuses the production staff, which does not know which of the plethora of incoming jobs to process next. A typical outcome of having too many jobs being processed at once is that workstation operators have to choose between jobs for which there is no priority designation, resulting in all jobs being delayed from their scheduled due dates.

The following sub-sections deal with the demands on the production scheduler and the different facets of scheduling where the focus is on the constraint.

### Scheduling Demands

The general concept of a limited release of jobs sounds easy enough in theory, but is more difficult in practice. The production scheduler faces demands every day from numerous parties to release production jobs onto the shop floor. These demands come from the following parties:

- *Customers*. Customers in immediate need of products will demand through the sales department or order entry staff that their orders be released to the shop floor at once, under the mistaken impression that an order release will result in an earlier completion of their order.
- *Managers (ethical issue)*. A cannier manager with a reduced ethical sense may demand that jobs be released, solely because doing so means that the jobs can begin to accumulate factory overhead, which defers the recognition of that overhead to a later period, resulting in increased profits.
- *Managers (utilization)*. One of the most damaging policy constraints is that management likes to see all workstations in the production area fully utilized. If the production scheduler is forced to accede to this requirement, it will be necessary to load additional jobs onto the shop floor, though the eventual result will only be an increased pile of unneeded inventory in front of the constraint.
- *Managers (filled process flow)*. A manager not experienced in constraint management might associate having a large number of released jobs with a busy manufacturing operation, not realizing that doing so slows down the production process.

In addition, the production scheduler is held at least partially responsible for some of the key metrics used in the production area. The key measurement from the perspective of the sales department is the on-time delivery percentage, while the controller will also be interested in several cost containment measurements, such as a minimal level of overtime expenditures and a reduced investment in inventory.

One issue that the production scheduler does *not* try to maximize is throughput. Throughput is more of a strategic issue that is addressed by management when it sets product prices and decides which products to actively market to customers. From the perspective of the scheduler, there are simply a number of orders that have been promised to customers with varying due dates, and those orders must be completed. It is possible that the scheduler is not even aware of the amount of throughput associated with each order.

**Scheduling Priorities**

The order of priority that a scheduler assigns to jobs will vary by company, but typically follows this path:

1. *Late deliveries*. If a delivery will be late, this job is typically given the highest priority. If a business were to accord these jobs a normal priority ranking, they would be delivered even later. If the organization were to establish a reputation for late deliveries, it would lose customers or at least be forced to lower its prices in order to attract customers.
2. *Regular deliveries*. Normal customer orders are to be scheduled in the order in which they were received, subject to any raw material or subassembly shortages that might cause a delay. However, if there are situations where the constraint is about to run out of work and an order can be run through it immediately, that order can jump the queue. Doing so ensures that constraint usage is maximized.
3. *Inventory replenishment*. If there is room left in the schedule and management wants to bolster the amount of finished goods deliberately kept on hand, these replenishment orders are scheduled last. This may be the dominant production activity in a seasonal business, where sales only occur during a few months of the year.

An additional work priority that is usually addressed separately is goods requiring rework. These items tend to pile up in the production area and interfere with the flow of goods. However, they are usually of lower priority, since customers have already been shipped new replacement goods. Also, it can be difficult to determine the extent of rework required, with some jobs calling for much more work than initially expected. Consequently, there is a risk that these goods can interfere with the normal flow of production. Given these issues, the production scheduler tends to view rework as a separate scheduling activity that is inserted into the schedule as room becomes available, or when the volume of units scheduled for rework becomes too large.

No matter what the scheduling priority may be, the total number of jobs released to the shop floor is essentially driven by the available time at the constraint, which we address next.

**Reasonable Constraint Time**

A major issue for the production scheduler is the estimate of how many minutes of constraint time are actually available each week. The theoretical number of minutes per week is easy enough to calculate, assuming three shifts that run every day. The calculation is:

$$7 \text{ days} \times 24 \text{ hours} \times 60 \text{ minutes/hour} = 10{,}080 \text{ minutes}$$

However, a respectable proportion of this time is not really available. There may be constraint downtime for a number of reasons, including the following:

- Scheduled maintenance
- Unscheduled maintenance
- Power outages
- Parts shortages
- Staff shortages
- Strikes

Some of these items can be built into the production schedule as certainties, such as scheduled downtime for preventive maintenance. However, there is simply no way to determine exactly when or for how long some of the other items on the list will impact the constraint. This means that the scheduler is constantly revising the schedule of job releases based on the latest information arriving from the constraint crew.

A reasonable basis for initial scheduling purposes is to use an estimate of available constraint time that incorporates scheduled maintenance, plus the average amount of unscheduled downtime that has occurred over the past few weeks.

**Raw Materials Release**

One of the worst things that a production scheduler can do is to release a vast amount of raw materials onto the shop floor when only a small proportion of it can be immediately used. Doing so creates a great deal of clutter on the shop floor (especially when workstations are grouped close together), which presents the following problems:

- Raw materials left out in the open are more likely to be damaged by passing forklifts
- There is less room to move parts between workstations, which increases the time required to shift parts from one workstation to another, which in turn increases the period required to produce goods

- There is a greater risk of using parts from one job on another job
- There is a greater risk of theft
- Employees are not sure which jobs to process next

Instead, raw materials should only be released at the rate at which they can be consumed at the constraint. This may mean that the raw materials associated with quite a large job are parceled out for processing via a number of smaller releases. Doing so results in a greatly reduced amount of raw materials on the shop floor.

Ideally, the timing of a raw materials release is based on the time required to attain a fully-loaded inventory buffer, plus the aggregate amount of processing time needed by all of the workstations upstream from the constraint. This concept is illustrated in the following example.

---

**EXAMPLE**

To return to the Monk Books scenario from previous examples, the Monk Books production process involves releasing new replica projects into the production area (actually more similar to a well-lit library than a production floor) when there is time available in the artwork area, which is the constraint. The problem is that the sales department is constantly being asked by museum customers whether their book projects are in production yet, so there is pressure to release additional jobs to production. If additional jobs were to be released to production, there could be confusion in the scribing and artwork groups regarding which jobs to work on next, which could result in some earlier customer orders being delayed behind later orders.

The correct approach to releasing jobs is to base it on the need to keep the inventory buffer full, plus the processing time needed by the upstream workstations. There are two work groups ahead of artwork, which are paper refinishing and coating, and scribing. Barring any changes in the inventory buffer, the release of jobs should be based on the time required to create the paper for a job and then manually write the associated text on the pages.

There are several general types of medieval books, each having a significantly different number of pages and text. These types, and their associated upstream production time, are as follows:

| Book Type | Description | Upstream Production Time |
|---|---|---|
| Girdle books | Small portable books with a tail that is tucked into one's girdle or belt. Typically less than 100 pages, with small page dimensions and few illustrations | 40 days |
| Bibles | Comes in different versions, but all have massive page counts and are liberally illustrated | 120 days |
| Scientific | Generally smaller page count but larger pages, with detailed illustrations | 60 days |

The scribes are accustomed to working on particular types of books. For example, girdle books are typically written in the smallest font, while scientific texts include excerpts in Greek, Latin, or Arabic. Consequently, it is easiest from a scheduling perspective to release a job for a new girdle book to the paper refinishing and coating group when the scribe on an in-process girdle book indicates that there are 10 days remaining before the book is released to the artwork group. The 10 day lead time is used, because the paper refinishing and coating group requires 10 days to prepare the requisite number of pages for the next job. This is essentially a kanban process, where the completion of one job triggers the release of the next job. The same approach is used to schedule the release of the bible jobs and scientific text jobs.

---

## Labor Considerations

The production process may involve a mix of different staff positions, each one uniquely qualified to perform certain tasks. Ideally, the production area is already staffed with a sufficient number of each position to deal with any reasonable mix of products within a certain volume range. However, the reality is that some positions may be in short supply or temporarily overworked, which means that the scheduler may need to delay the release of certain jobs if the required skill sets are not available. Conversely, this could mean that some jobs that do not require skilled processing can be jumped ahead of the queue and released before other jobs.

Proper consideration of the use of certain positions can be enhanced with the use of labor routings. A labor routing is a listing of the quantity and types of labor required to manufacture a product. The production scheduler combines labor routings with the prospective production schedule to see if any labor shortages are flagged, and alters the schedule accordingly.

## Batch Sizes

A potentially significant issue for the scheduler is the number and duration of the batches that are scheduled to run, both upstream from the constraint and at the constraint. The issues are:

- *Proportion of setup time.* If there are a large number of small jobs, and those jobs require a significant amount of setup time, this reduces the number of minutes in the period that are available for actual processing work. This is more of an issue at the constraint (with its limited availability) than at the upstream workstations, which have more time available to accommodate numerous setups.
- *Delivery speed.* The speed with which batches of parts are delivered to the next downstream workstation is increased when the size of each batch decreases. The reason is that it takes less time for a workstation operator to complete a batch when a smaller number of units must be placed in the shipping container. The concept is explained in the following sample batch sizing exhibit, where there is an inventory buffer for which the unit quantity is

mandated to be 50 units. If the unit count in the buffer declines to 25 units, the expedite zone will be accessed, which will trigger a notification to the production manager that there is a problem. In Situation 1, the batch size being delivered is 25 units, which will be drawn down to zero before the expedite zone is accessed, due to the longer periods required to complete a batch of 25 units. In Situation 2, the batch size is cut to 15 units, which means that batch deliveries are made about twice as fast. Because the replenishments occur so much more frequently, there are less drastic declines in the buffer inventory between deliveries. In short, smaller batch sizes allow for a smaller investment in work-in-process inventory, while still maintaining an adequate buffer stock.

**Sample Batch Sizing Scenarios**

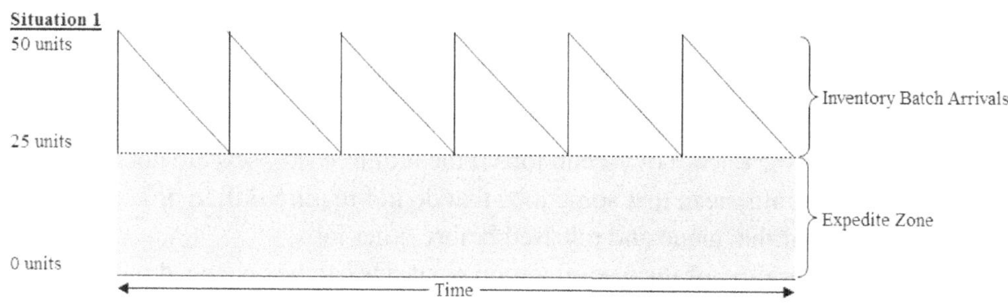


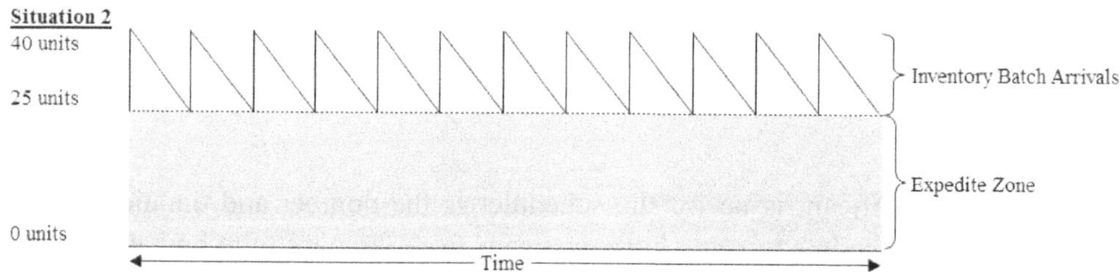


There are two production scheduling issues to take away from this discussion of batch sizes, which are:

- It is acceptable to have small batch sizes upstream from the constraint, since these workstations have excess capacity that can absorb the extra time required for the many machine setups associated with small batch sizes. These small batch sizes are useful for reducing the size of the inventory buffer. The production scheduler could consider an ongoing program of scheduling ever-smaller batch sizes until the burden of the additional setups begins to cut into the excess amount of sprint capacity available upstream from the constraint.
- It is substantially less acceptable to follow the same philosophy for the constraint, where there is no excess time to waste on additional setups. If there

are many setups and the setups are time-consuming, the total amount of throughput generated will decline. Instead, if setups at the constraint are lengthy, focus on larger batch sizes just in this one area. A larger batch size that still produces throughput can be created when several customer orders are combined for production purposes. If a larger batch is authorized that cannot be immediately sold, the scheduler must balance the saved setup time against the cost of holding the inventory.

**Tip:** The ultimate solution to the problem of long setups at the constraint is to constantly refine the amount of time that it takes to complete a setup, such as by prepositioning dies, tools, and inventory at the constraint. Shorter setups make it economically viable for the constraint to process short-duration jobs. Conversely, it makes less sense to achieve shorter setups on other workstations, since these other areas already have excess capacity (though such improvements can increase sprint capacity).

**Tip:** An option for creating instant sprint capacity is to increase the size of batches at upstream workstations just while additional inventory is needed to replenish the buffer, after which batch sizes can be reduced to their normal level.

### Expediting

*Expediting* involves assigning an expediter to a specific high-priority job, who then walks it through the entire production process, shifting other jobs out of the way to make room for the designated job. Expediting can destroy the efficiency of a production area and also delay other customer orders, since the bulk of all orders are given a lower priority and must also contend with the removal of assigned materials in favor of higher-priority jobs.

In general, there is no room for expediting in an environment where the constraint is being properly managed, since expediting jumbles the flow of jobs into the constraint. However, there can be a tightly-defined use for expediters when certain jobs are likely to be delivered late. In these situations, an expediter closely monitors the progress of each late job and works with the scheduler and production staff to make sure that delays are minimized. The expediter is not allowed to override existing production priorities; he can only represent the interests of the customer in ensuring that additional delays are minimized.

### Summary of Scheduling Activities

The production scheduler is routinely assailed from multiple directions with demands to release jobs to the shop floor as soon as possible, for a number of reasons. The correct way to manage the constraint via production scheduling is to keep as many jobs away from the shop floor as possible, so that the workstation operators have a clear view of the priority of jobs and can work within an uncluttered production area. Doing so requires the use of scheduling rules, estimating with reasonable constraint times, only releasing a prudent amount of raw materials, and taking into consideration the availability of skilled labor for certain tasks.

## The Constraint Analysis Model

There is an excellent constraint analysis model that was developed by Thomas Corbett, and which is outlined here. The basic thrust of the model is to give priority in the bottleneck operation to those products that generate the highest throughput per minute of bottleneck time. After these products are manufactured, priority is then given to the product having the next highest throughput per minute, and so on. Eventually, the production queue is filled, and the operation can accept no additional work.

The key element in the model is the use of throughput per minute, because the key limiting factor in a bottleneck operation is time – hence, maximizing throughput within the shortest possible time frame is paramount. Note that throughput *per minute* is much more important than total throughput *per unit*. The following example illustrates the point.

**EXAMPLE**

Mole Industries manufactures trench digging equipment. It has two products with different amounts of throughput and processing times at the bottleneck operation. The key information about these products is:

| Product | Total Throughput | Bottleneck Processing Time | Throughput per Minute |
|---|---|---|---|
| Mole Hole Digger | $400 | 2 minutes | $200 |
| Mole Driver Deluxe | 800 | 8 minutes | 100 |

Of the two products, the Mole Driver Deluxe creates the most overall throughput, but the Mole Hole Digger creates more throughput per minute of bottleneck processing time. To determine which one is more valuable to Mole Industries, consider what would happen if the company had an unlimited order quantity of each product, and could run the bottleneck operation non-stop, all day (which equates to 1,440 minutes). The operating results would be:

| Product | Throughput per Minute | | Total Processing Time Available | | Total Throughput |
|---|---|---|---|---|---|
| Mole Hole Digger | $200 | × | 1,440 minutes | = | $288,000 |
| Mole Driver Deluxe | 100 | × | 1,440 minutes | = | 144,000 |

Clearly, the Mole Hole Digger, with its higher throughput per minute, is much more valuable to Mole Industries than its Mole Driver Deluxe product. Consequently, the company should push sales of the Mole Hole Digger product whenever possible.

---

The constraint analysis model is essentially a production plan that itemizes the amount of throughput that can be generated, as well as the total amount of operating expenses and investment. In the model, we use four different products, each requiring some processing time in the bottleneck operation. The columns in the model are as follows:

- *Throughput per minute.* This is the total amount of throughput that a product generates, divided by the amount of processing time at the bottleneck operation.
- *Bottleneck usage.* This is the number of minutes of processing time required by a product at the bottleneck operation.
- *Units scheduled.* This is the number of units scheduled to be processed at the bottleneck operation.
- *Total bottleneck time.* This is the total number of minutes of processing time required by a product, multiplied by the number of units to be processed.
- *Total throughput.* This is the throughput per minute multiplied by the number of units processed at the bottleneck operation.

This grid produces a total amount of throughput to be generated if production proceeds according to plan. Below the grid of planned production, there is a subtotal of the total amount of throughput, from which the total amount of operating expenses are subtracted to arrive at the amount of profit. Finally, the total amount of investment in assets is divided into the profit to calculate the return on investment. Thus, the model provides a complete analysis of all three ways in which the results of a company can be improved – increase throughput, decrease operating expenses, or increase the return on investment. An example of the model follows.

**Sample Constraint Analysis Model**

| Product | Throughput per Minute | Bottleneck Usage (minutes) | Units Scheduled | Total Bottleneck Time | Total Throughput |
|---|---|---|---|---|---|
| 1. Hedgehog Deluxe | $80 | 14 | 1,000 | 14,000 | $1,120,000 |
| 2. Hedgehog Mini | 70 | 20 | 500 | 10,000 | 700,000 |
| 3. Hedgehog Classic | 65 | 40 | 200 | 8,000 | 520,000 |
| 4. Hedgehog Digger | 42 | 10 | 688 | 6,880 | 288,960 |
| | | Total bottleneck scheduled time | | 38,880 | |
| | | Total bottleneck time available* | | 38,880 | |
| | | | | Total throughput | $2,628,960 |
| | | | | Total operating expenses | 2,400,000 |
| | | | | Profit | $228,960 |
| | | | | Profit percentage | 8.7% |
| | | | | Investment | $23,000,000 |
| | | | | Annualized return on investment | 11.9% |

* Minutes per month (30 days × 24 hours × 60 minutes × (1 – 0.10 maintenance time)

In the example, the Hedgehog Deluxe product has the largest throughput per minute, and so is scheduled to be the first priority for production. The Hedgehog Digger has the lowest throughput per minute, so it is given last priority in the production schedule. If there is less time available on the bottleneck operation, the company should reduce the number of the Hedgehog Digger product manufactured in order to maximize overall profits.

In the middle of the model, the "Total bottleneck scheduled time" row contains the total number of minutes of scheduled production. The row below it, labeled "Total bottleneck time available," represents the total estimate of time that the bottleneck should have available for production purposes during the scheduling period. Since the time scheduled and available are identical, this means that the production schedule has completely maximized the availability of the bottleneck operation.

One calculation anomaly in the model is that the profit percentage is normally calculated as profit divided by revenues. However, since revenues are not included in the model, we instead use profits divided by throughput. Since throughput is less than revenue, we are overstating the profit percentage as compared to the traditional profit percentage calculation.

Use the constraint analysis model in a before-and-after mode, to see what effect a proposed change will have on profitability or the return on investment. If the model improves as a result of a change, then implement the change. In the next few sections, we will examine how the constraint analysis model is used to arrive at several management decisions.

## The Decision to Sell at a Lower Price

A common scenario is for a customer to promise a large order, but only if the company agrees to a substantial price drop. The sales department may favor such deals, because they bolster the company backlog, earn commissions, and increase market share. The trouble is that these deals also elbow out other jobs that may have higher throughput per minute. If so, the special deal drops overall throughput and may lead to a loss. The following example, which uses the basic constraint model as a baseline, illustrates the problem.

---

**EXAMPLE**

Mole Industries has received an offer from a customer to buy 2,000 units of its highly profitable Hedgehog Deluxe, but only if the company reduces the price. The new price will shrink the Deluxe's throughput per minute to $60. The analysis is:

| Product | Throughput per Minute | Bottleneck Usage (minutes) | Units Scheduled | Total Bottleneck Time | Total Throughput |
|---|---|---|---|---|---|
| 1. Hedgehog Deluxe | $60 | 14 | 2,000 | 28,000 | $1,680,000 |
| 2. Hedgehog Mini | 70 | 20 | 500 | 10,000 | 700,000 |
| 3. Hedgehog Classic | 65 | 40 | 22 | 880 | 57,200 |
| 4. Hedgehog Digger | 42 | 10 | 0 | 0 | 0 |
| | | Total bottleneck scheduled time | | 38,880 | |
| | | Total bottleneck time available* | | 38,880 | |
| | | | | Total throughput | $2,437,200 |
| | | | | Total operating expenses | 2,400,000 |
| | | | | Profit | $37,200 |
| | | | | Profit percentage | 1.5% |
| | | | | Investment | $23,000,000 |
| | | | | Annualized return on investment | 1.9% |

* Minutes per month (30 days × 24 hours × 60 minutes × (1 – 0.10 maintenance time)

The baseline production configuration generated a profit of $228,960, while this new situation creates a profit of only $37,200. The profit decline was caused by a combination of lower throughput per minute for the Hedgehog Deluxe and the increased production capacity assigned to this lower-throughput product, which displaced other, more profitable products. Note that there was no production capacity available at all for the Hedgehog Digger product. Clearly, the company should reject the customer's offer.

---

## The Decision to Outsource Production

One way to manage the bottleneck operation is to outsource work to keep some of the production burden away from the bottleneck. This option is always acceptable if the throughput generated by the outsourced products exceed the price charged to the company by the supplier, *and* the company can replace the throughput per minute that was taken away from the bottleneck operation. The following example, which uses the basic constraint model as a baseline, illustrates the concept.

---

**EXAMPLE**

Mole Industries receives an offer from a supplier to outsource the Hedgehog Classic to it. The supplier will even drop ship the product to customers, so the product would no longer impact Mole's production process in any way. The downside of the offer is that the supplier's price is higher than the cost at which Mole can produce the Classic internally, so the total monthly throughput attributable to the Classic would decline by $300,000, from $520,000 to $220,000. However, there is a large customer order backlog for the Hedgehog Digger, so Mole could give increased production priority to the Digger instead. The analysis is:

| Product | Throughput per Minute | Bottleneck Usage (minutes) | Units Scheduled | Total Bottleneck Time | Total Throughput |
|---|---|---|---|---|---|
| 1. Hedgehog Deluxe | $80 | 14 | 1,000 | 14,000 | $1,120,000 |
| 2. Hedgehog Mini | 70 | 20 | 500 | 10,000 | 700,000 |
| 3. Hedgehog Classic | 65 | 40 | 200 | N/A | 220,000 |
| 4. Hedgehog Digger | 42 | 10 | 1,488 | 14,880 | 624,960 |
| | | Total bottleneck scheduled time | | 38,880 | |
| | | Total bottleneck time available* | | 38,880 | |
| | | | | | |
| | | | | Total throughput | $2,664,960 |
| | | | | Total operating expenses | 2,400,000 |
| | | | | Profit | $264,960 |
| | | | | Profit percentage | 9.9% |
| | | | | Investment | $23,000,000 |
| | | | | Annualized return on investment | 13.8% |

* Minutes per month (30 days × 24 hours × 60 minutes × (1 – 0.10 maintenance time)

Despite a large decline in throughput caused by the outsourcing deal, the company actually earns $36,000 more profit overall, because the Hedgehog Classic uses more of the bottleneck time per unit (40 minutes) than any other product; this allows the company to fill the available bottleneck time with 800 more Hedgehog Digger products, which require the smallest amount of bottleneck time per unit (10 minutes), and which generate sufficient additional throughput to easily offset the throughput decline caused by outsourcing. Mole Industries should accept the supplier's offer to outsource.

---

## The Capital Investment Decision

In a large production environment, there are constant requests to invest more funds in various areas in order to increase efficiencies. However, it rarely makes sense to invest in areas that do not favorably impact the bottleneck operation in some way. In particular, investments in the capacity of operations located downstream from the bottleneck operation rarely yield a return, since improving them does nothing for the overall profitability of the entire system. The issue is addressed in the following example, which uses the basic constraint model as a baseline.

---

**EXAMPLE**

The industrial engineering manager of Mole Industries examines the entire production line, and concludes that he can double the speed of the paint shop for an investment of $250,000. This operation is located at the very end of the production line, and so is located downstream from the bottleneck operation. The analysis is:

| Product | Throughput per Minute | Bottleneck Usage (minutes) | Units Scheduled | Total Bottleneck Time | Total Throughput |
|---|---|---|---|---|---|
| 1. Hedgehog Deluxe | $80 | 14 | 1,000 | 14,000 | $1,120,000 |
| 2. Hedgehog Mini | 70 | 20 | 500 | 10,000 | 700,000 |
| 3. Hedgehog Classic | 65 | 40 | 200 | 8,000 | 520,000 |
| 4. Hedgehog Digger | 42 | 10 | 688 | 6,880 | 288,960 |
| | | Total bottleneck scheduled time | | 38,880 | |
| | | Total bottleneck time available* | | 38,880 | |
| | | | | Total throughput | $2,628,960 |
| | | | | Total operating expenses | 2,400,000 |
| | | | | Profit | $228,960 |
| | | | | Profit percentage | 8.7% |
| | | | | Investment | $23,250,000 |
| | | | | Annualized return on investment | 11.8% |

* Minutes per month (30 days × 24 hours × 60 minutes × (1 – 0.10 maintenance time)

The only item that changes in the analysis is the amount of the investment, which increases by $250,000 and results in a reduced return on investment. Improving the capacity of the paint shop has no effect on throughput, since the entire production line can still only run at the maximum pace of the bottleneck operation.

---

There are some types of investment that can make sense, even if they are not associated with the bottleneck operation. In particular, if an investment can reduce the cost of an operation, the investment is acceptable, as long as the return on investment percentage increases as a result of the change. The concept is illustrated in the following example.

---

**EXAMPLE**

Rather than proposing a capacity increase in the paint shop (as was the case in the last example), the industrial engineering manager of Mole Industries proposes to invest $250,000 in the paint shop, but only to add sufficient automation to reduce operating expenses by $5,000 per month. The analysis is:

| Product | Throughput per Minute | Bottleneck Usage (minutes) | Units Scheduled | Total Bottleneck Time | Total Throughput |
|---|---|---|---|---|---|
| 1. Hedgehog Deluxe | $80 | 14 | 1,000 | 14,000 | $1,120,000 |
| 2. Hedgehog Mini | 70 | 20 | 500 | 10,000 | 700,000 |
| 3. Hedgehog Classic | 65 | 40 | 200 | 8,000 | 520,000 |
| 4. Hedgehog Digger | 42 | 10 | 688 | 6,880 | 288,960 |
| | | Total bottleneck scheduled time | | 38,880 | |
| | | Total bottleneck time available* | | 38,880 | |
| | | | | Total throughput | $2,628,960 |
| | | | | Total operating expenses | 2,395,000 |
| | | | | Profit | $233,960 |
| | | | | Profit percentage | 8.7% |
| | | | | Investment | $23,250,000 |
| | | | | Annualized return on investment | 12.1% |

* Minutes per month (30 days × 24 hours × 60 minutes × (1 – 0.10 maintenance time)

The investment creates a sufficient decline in total operating expenses to yield an increase in the annualized rate of return, to 12.1%. Consequently, this is a worthwhile investment opportunity.

---

## The Raw Material Availability Decision

How can throughput be maximized when there is not a sufficient quantity of raw materials on hand to process all orders? In this case, the model is changed to focus on the amount of throughput that can be generated for each unit of the raw material. After this initial pass is conducted, the proposed production plan is run through the standard model to see how many units can be produced, given the usual amount of available constraint time within the company. The concept appears in the following example.

## EXAMPLE

The rare earth element neodymium is used in the ceramic capacitors in Mole Industries' products. The supply of neodymium has become severely restricted due to local protests in Brazil, where the company's main supplier is located. Until arrangements can be made to shift to an Australian supplier, Mole will have to work through a raw materials restriction. The operations analyst alters the standard throughput scheduling model to account for the effects of this change. In the model, she changes the priority to be throughput per ounce of neodymium, so that the throughput associated with the new constraint can be maximized. Doing so swaps the positions of the Hedgehog Deluxe (formerly first priority) and the Hedgehog Digger (formerly fourth priority). The revised model follows:

| Product | Throughput per Ounce of Neodymium | Constraint Usage (Ounces) | Units Scheduled | Total Constraint Ounces | Total Throughput |
|---|---|---|---|---|---|
| 1. Hedgehog Digger | $100 | 10 | 700 | 7,000 | $700,000 |
| 2. Hedgehog Mini | 80 | 20 | 500 | 1,000 | 80,000 |
| 3. Hedgehog Classic | 65 | 30 | 200 | 6,000 | 390,000 |
| 4. Hedgehog Deluxe | 60 | 40 | 275 | 11,000 | 660,000 |
| | | Total ounces scheduled for use | | 25,000 | |
| | | Total ounces available | | 25,000 | |
| | | | | Total throughput | $1,830,000 |
| | | | | Total operating expenses | 2,400,000 |
| | | | | Profit | -$570,000 |
| | | | | Profit percentage | -31.1% |
| | | | | Investment | $23,000,000 |
| | | | | Annualized return on investment | -29.7% |

The model shows how maximizing use of the neodymium yields a severe decline in throughput. In addition, the accountant is not sure if the indicated production levels can be processed through the company's own constraint. Accordingly, she runs the indicated units of production through the standard throughput model, which yields the following outcome:

| Product | Throughput per Minute | Constraint Usage (minutes) | Units Scheduled | Total Constraint Time |
|---|---|---|---|---|
| 1. Hedgehog Digger | $42 | 10 | 700 | 7,000 |
| 2. Hedgehog Mini | 70 | 20 | 500 | 10,000 |
| 3. Hedgehog Classic | 65 | 40 | 200 | 8,000 |
| 4. Hedgehog Deluxe | 80 | 14 | 275 | 3,850 |
| | | Total constraint scheduled time | | **28,850** |
| | | Total constraint time available* | | **38,880** |

* Minutes per month = 30 days × 24 hours × 60 minutes × (1 – 0.10 maintenance time)

The throughput model shows that the revised production schedule can easily be processed through the constraint, since only 28,850 minutes of processing are needed, and 38,880 minutes are available. The main issue for the company at this point is to find a new source of neodymium as soon as possible, since the restriction is causing Mole to lose money every day, based on the amount of its operating expenses.

---

The example shows a common outcome of a raw materials constraint, which is that the ability to generate throughput is severely impacted. The outcome shows the need for risk management, where raw material restrictions can be modeled in advance to highlight which raw materials should be sourced with multiple suppliers.

## Designing the Organization around the Constraint

Proper management of a company's constraint requires that *all* aspects of the business be designed to support the operation of the constraint. If the organization is not carefully designed in all respects to ensure maximum constraint use, the optimum amount of throughput will not be achieved. Here are examples of elements of an entity that must be tailored to support the constraint:

- *Bonus plans*. All bonus plans must be configured to either maximize use of the constraint or at least have a neutral effect. For example, offering a bonus for achieving an inventory reduction target can trigger a deliberate cutback in the size of the inventory buffer, which can reduce throughput.
- *Policies*. Policies should be designed to not impose false constraints on the business, such as a requirement to only move parts between workstations in large batches. When in doubt, do not impose policies at all.
- *Procedures*. The use of a procedure implies that an activity must be conducted in a certain way, which tends to lock in older work rules that are not overly efficient. A better approach is to give the manager of the constraint and any upstream workstations a higher degree of flexibility, perhaps by using more general procedures.
- *Quality assurance*. Quality review stations should be placed immediately in front of the constraint resource, to ensure that no faulty parts are processed through the constraint. Do not allow review stations to be set up in areas that do not support this goal.
- *Performance metrics*. Management tends to do whatever it takes to improve the official performance metrics of the organization, so be sure to only report metrics that are supportive of the constraint. For example, reporting on the utilization of production workstations can trigger a drive to increase utilization, even though the result will only be an increased investment in unneeded inventory.

Given the number of issues noted here, it should be no surprise that changing the constraint to a different location within a company may create a major problem; doing so means that all of the supporting bonus plans, policies and procedures, metrics, reports, and so on must be altered to maximize the use of the new constraint. In many cases, it is easier to keep the constraint where it is, and design the organization around that location.

There may come a time when the organization has greatly increased the capacity of the constrained resource, to the point where there is no longer any constraint within the company. There are a sufficient number of employees in all departments to handle the current volume of customer orders, and there is a sufficient amount of raw materials available from suppliers to ensure that the constraint will not shift back to them. If so, the constraint is said to be in the marketplace, which means that only the use of a different price point or other incentive is needed to obtain additional business.

In this latter situation, it is to be expected that sales will eventually increase again, at which point the constraint will shift back into the organization. If so, watch for where the constraint will arise, using the criteria noted in the Production Basis of Constraint Management chapter to determine the location of the constraint. It is entirely possible that the new constraint will be located somewhere else in the company than the old constraint. If so, be prepared to redesign the organization to focus all attention on maximizing the utilization of the new constraint. This can be difficult, if the management team has become hidebound in its use of the old systems that were tailored to the old constraint. If so, the company president must be willing to force the organization to re-orient to the new constraint, which may require the selective alteration of the management team to support the new constraint.

## Summary

Constraint management is one of the primary tools of the operations analyst. It makes quite clear where the bottleneck operation is located, the extreme expense associated with not maximizing it, and how to manage operations to maximize profits. However, it can be a foreign concept to many managers, who have spent their careers working on local optimization issues, allocating overhead, and improving the efficiency of labor – all of which are concepts that constraint analysis teaches do not improve overall profitability.

# Chapter 13
# Supply Chain Management

## Introduction

A company that has a serious interest in managing its inventory levels realizes that it must interact with the chain of suppliers that provide it with goods. If there is a delivery problem or quality issue anywhere in this chain, the issue will impact the company, and therefore its performance with customers. Consequently, the best approach to managing the supply chain is to think of it as an interlinked set of companies that will compete as a group to secure sales. With this viewpoint in mind, we have structured the following sections to focus on how to identify the best suppliers, construct a supply chain, and manage suppliers, as well as what to do when there are disruptions in the chain. The ideal result is a cluster of organizations that can operate with a minimum of inventory, and which can deliver goods right through the chain in the most efficient manner.

## Sole Source Inventory Purchases

A traditional method for reducing the cost of purchased parts is to put them out to bid, thereby forcing suppliers to bid against each other to offer the lowest price. This also gives a company a designated backup supplier, in case there are problems dealing with the primary supplier. However, the primary focus on obtaining the lowest prices also has the following negative effects:

- Products may be of lower quality
- Deliveries may be delayed
- Extra time is needed by the purchasing staff to monitor bidding situations
- There may be lower-volume purchases from each supplier, which tends to drive costs higher

Given the number of problems with having multiple suppliers, it may be better to instead sole source purchases with a smaller number of core suppliers. Doing so has the following advantages:

- Suppliers can be screened in advance to ensure high product quality
- Suppliers will be more amenable to requests for custom packaging and unique order sizes
- Deliveries are more reliable, since suppliers want to preserve a long-term relationship

- There is minimal purchasing paperwork required to place orders, since there are no bids
- Since the same order volume is spread among fewer suppliers, the result should be volume discounts
- Less time is required to monitor suppliers, since there are fewer suppliers
- A supplier may give the company preference when it does not have enough goods to fill all customer orders
- Long-term suppliers are more likely to agree to just-in-time deliveries
- In order to make just-in-time deliveries, the company can set up electronic notifications with its suppliers
- Long-term suppliers are more inclined to participate in joint product development teams

In cases where key components are involved, it may still be necessary to designate a backup supplier, but in most cases the advantages of sole sourcing far outweigh the use of multiple suppliers.

## Supplier Assessment

If the decision is made to sole source, there should be an evaluation process for determining which suppliers to use. The evaluation does not have to be a rigid one, with point scoring for various criteria. It may be better to evaluate based on a range of issues, and then settle upon the best supplier based on the overall mix of results. The following points are worth investigating as part of the evaluation:

High priority items

- *Financial condition.* The supplier must be in good financial condition, based on a review of its financial statements for the past few years. This point should only be overridden when materials cannot be obtained from any other supplier.
- *Capacity.* The supplier must have enough capacity to service the needs of the company on a timely basis. Otherwise, late or partial deliveries could become a serious hindrance.
- *Quality.* The supplier must be able to produce goods to the company's specifications with such reliability that there is no need to inspect the goods upon receipt.
- *Just-in-time capabilities.* If the company demands just-in-time deliveries, then the supplier must be able to deliver on a very frequent basis. This usually calls for a local production facility or distribution warehouse.
- *Number of facilities.* If there is a concern that a production facility could be shut down for any reason, evaluate whether a supplier can also produce needed goods from another facility. The second facility should not be subject

to the same risk as the first facility. For example, if one facility is located in a flood plain, the backup facility should not also be in the same flood plain.

Lesser priority items

- *Engineering capabilities.* Many components are commoditized, so no special supplier engineering capabilities are needed. In other cases, a supplier can provide significant service to a company by assisting in joint development efforts. If the latter is the case, engineering capability becomes a high priority item.
- *Health and safety compliance.* This issue is generally left to suppliers to handle on their own. However, if a company (usually in the consumer goods field) is subject to review by watchdog organizations, it may be necessary to ensure that certain minimum standards are maintained by suppliers. Otherwise, the company may find that its suppliers are a public relations problem.
- *Legal system.* If there is an expectation that the company may have to pursue legal remedies against a supplier, is the legal system where the supplier is located sufficiently developed to allow the company to gain satisfaction? Realistically, if the company must consider this option, it should not be dealing with a prospective supplier at all.

When engaging in sole sourcing, be sure to devise a reporting system for evaluating the quality, prices, delivery times, and other factors for each *existing* supplier, to see if the company is obtaining sufficient service from each one.

## Enhanced Supplier Relations

It is useful to examine the suppliers that a company uses, to determine which ones provide unique and particularly valuable goods and services, and which ones provide more pedestrian products to the company. If a supplier falls into the first category, it behooves the company to go to some lengths to establish deep and long-term relations with it. By doing so, the company may be able to obtain preferred customer status, which gives it delivery priority, best pricing, and cooperation in the development of new products.

However, the establishment of deep relations with a supplier does not mean an occasional lunch between the owners. Instead, all of the following may be needed:

- *Long-term purchase orders.* The company should show its commitment to long-term purchases by negotiating long-term master purchase orders that commit it to make significant purchases over a long period of time.
- *Information sharing.* Allow the supplier to have direct access to the company's production planning system, so the supplier can properly schedule deliveries.

- *Product planning*. Invite the supplier to participate in the company's new product development process, in exchange for sole sourcing the components built into these products.
- *Partnerships*. Create joint product development projects, in which each party has an equity stake.
- *Ownership*. Consider offering to buy a minority stake in the supplier, or even swapping shares in each other for a cross-ownership arrangement.

It is quite difficult to maintain the level of interaction with a supplier that is recommended here. Consequently, it can make sense to limit the number of these close relationships to only those suppliers considered most crucial to the competitive stance and long-term viability of the company.

## Foreign Sourcing Considerations

It is generally better to use suppliers located as close as possible to the company. Doing so presents advantages in terms of responsiveness and short delivery times. Nonetheless, some organizations find the low costs of some foreign suppliers to be an overwhelming argument in favor of foreign sourcing. However, before being swept away by the attractiveness of low prices, consider the following issues:

- *Exchange rate risk*. The company will likely have to pay its foreign suppliers in their home currencies, which presents the risk that the exchange rate will have trended in an unfavorable direction by the time the payment is due. Also, the company may engage in hedging transactions to offset this risk, which presents an additional cost.
- *Intellectual property*. A less-ethical supplier may sell cut-rate knock-offs of the company's products in the local market, which are then spread world-wide and compete with the company's products everywhere.
- *Management*. The company will probably need to maintain a local management presence at the site of each supplier, to make decisions on behalf of the company. This can be expensive, since the local representatives must be housed and provided with an adequate level of security.
- *Shipping distance*. If goods must be shipped a long distance from a foreign supplier, this not only increases the freight cost of deliveries, but also decreases the responsiveness of the supplier. The company must place orders far in advance of when the goods are needed, and will continually have to sell off a large amount of in-transit inventory from the supplier before it can launch new products.
- *Trends in labor costs*. If a country has unusually low labor costs, many other companies will also buy from suppliers in that country. The resulting increased demand for labor will drive up wage rates, especially if there is not an especially large pool of laborers in the country. The result is a relatively

short period of time during which labor rates are unusually low, after which a cost spike can be expected.

Given the concerns noted here, a reasonable position to take is that foreign sourcing is a more attractive option over the short term. As the time line extends, it becomes more apparent that the cost advantages of foreign labor markets will decline.

A better reason to use foreign sourcing is when the supplier in question has such superior products and services that it would be foolish to use any other supplier. In this case, the *supplier* is more likely to be choosy about selecting its customers, in which case the company may not be able to obtain the services of the supplier that it wants.

## The Lead Supplier

A company may have a difficult time coordinating the deliveries of a large number of suppliers. This can be a particular problem when the company's purchasing department is understaffed or does not share its production schedule with suppliers. The result is a continuing series of missed production runs, since manufacturing must be halted when parts do not arrive on time. Or, to counteract late or missing deliveries, the purchasing staff elects to keep much more reserve inventory on hand than would normally be the case.

This state of affairs can be improved upon by designating a small number of suppliers as lead suppliers. These suppliers are responsible for delivering major sub-assemblies to the company, and do so by coordinating the activities of all the suppliers who deliver components for a particular subassembly. The result is a much smaller group of suppliers for the company to deal with on a direct basis.

The lead supplier role is relished by many suppliers, since it gives them a larger share of the company's purchasing dollars. In addition, such a supplier is in an excellent position to increase its profits, either in exchange for the greater administrative task it has taken on, or by controlling the prices charged by the sub-contractors for which it is now responsible.

There are some downsides to the lead supplier concept, which are:

- The company is now sole-sourcing a larger part of its business to a potentially powerful supplier, which could use this position to demand higher prices.
- If a lead supplier gets into financial difficulties or goes bankrupt, this can cause considerable disruption among the sub-contractors for which it was responsible.

Despite these disadvantages, many organizations can profit from the use of lead suppliers, if only to streamline the structure of their supply chains.

## The Stable Production Schedule

Once materials have been sole sourced, the next step in managing the supply chain is to provide suppliers with a stable production schedule. This means that the company commits to locking down its production schedule for a certain period of time. By doing so and providing the production schedule to suppliers, they can reliably determine the amount of goods that must be shipped to the company, and so can use this information to create their own production estimates. Otherwise, if the production schedule is constantly being changed, suppliers will be unable to plan their own production, resulting in a gyrating series of inventory shortages and overages.

For what period of time should the production schedule be locked down? This interval should equate to the amount of lead time that suppliers need in order to deliver goods to the company. Thus, if the supplier with the longest lead time requires at least two weeks of advance notice before it can make a delivery to the company, then the company should freeze its production schedule for the final two weeks before products will enter the manufacturing process.

**Tip:** If customers demand shorter lead times than the company can give, the solution may be to eliminate those suppliers that demand the longest lead times. Doing so compresses the time period over which the production schedule must be frozen, which in turn allows for shorter quoted lead times to customers.

The stable production schedule concept is less applicable in a pull production environment, where the company is only producing to the orders of its customers. In this situation, the production schedule that forms the core of a push production environment does not exist, so suppliers are forced to either maintain significant inventory buffers to deal with the short-term orders of the company, or to shift to their own pull production environments.

## Automatic Supplier Replenishment

What about a situation where a customer is a retailer, and is selling a supplier's goods straight to the end customer? In this case, the purchasing department of the retailer examines the sales data from its point-of-sale terminals and issues a replenishment purchase order to the vendor supplying the goods. The retailer's purchasing department represents a delay in the fulfillment chain, since it may require several days for this group to spot an upcoming shortage and issue a purchase order to correct the issue. A possible solution is to give the supplier direct access to the retailer's point-of-sale information, and allow it to refill stock positions automatically.

Automatic supplier replenishment eliminates the retailer's purchasing department from ongoing reordering activities, possibly cutting several days from the interval normally needed to refill a stockout condition. With a shorter lead time requirement for replenishments, this means it is possible for the retailer to reduce the amount of stock it maintains at its stores. However, the following conditions must be present for automatic supplier replenishment to work:

- *Steady demand.* There should be a reasonable history of consistent customer demand, so the supplier can send a consistent stream of goods to the retailer.
- *Replenishment level.* The retailer will not want to run the risk of being responsible for paying for large amounts of additional inventory that are jammed into its stores by suppliers, and so will put a cap on the amount of goods automatically replenished. This will likely be close to the amount by which customers draw down stocks at retailer locations.
- *Review intervals.* The retailer is relying on the supplier to ascertain when inventory should be replenished, so the supplier must commit to detailed monitoring of the point-of-sale information it is given.

## The Total Inventory Concept

Many of the changes that a company makes to reduce inventory do not actually eliminate inventory – they just move inventory back to a supplier. The supplier is supposed to hold a larger amount of inventory off-site, and deliver it only when called upon. This approach increases the amount of working capital that the supplier must invest, and also shifts all the usual inventory holding costs onto the supplier. The result is a weakening of the finances of a company's supplier base. When suppliers earn a lower profit, they are less interested in working with the company, are at increased risk of bankruptcy, and cannot reinvest in their own operations to improve efficiencies. In short, shifting inventory back onto suppliers is a short-term proposition that does not help a company in the long run.

The only way to maintain a healthy group of suppliers is to strip inventory out of the *entire* supply chain. This approach requires a large amount of effort, working with primary suppliers to improve their systems and practices. One way to detect which suppliers to approach with this assistance is to measure total inventory. Total inventory is the sum of all inventories in all locations, which is calculated as:

| | |
|---|---|
| + | Inventory already located at the company |
| + | Inventory already produced for the company by suppliers |
| = | Total inventory |

This calculation requires that the company ascertain the amount of company-specific inventory at suppliers, which can be difficult to obtain. Consequently, this may be a measurement that is only compiled once every quarter or year. However, the calculation effort can highlight the largest pockets of inventory, which are then targeted for reduction.

**Tip:** The total inventory concept works best when inventory items are sole sourced. In this case, a company's engineers and procurement specialists only have to work with a single supplier to create reductions in total inventory. This work is multiplied if the company must work with several suppliers to reduce the same inventory item.

---

**EXAMPLE**

Mole Industries manufactures a variety of trench-digging machines. The company assembles components produced by five primary suppliers. The president of Mole is deeply interested in reducing the total inventory of the company, and so commissions the following total inventory measurement:

| Inventory Specific to: | Inventory at Mole Industries | Inventory at Supplier | Total Inventory |
|---|---|---|---|
| Supplier A | $2,500,000 | $1,250,000 | $3,750,000 |
| Supplier B | 150,000 | 1,000,000 | 1,150,000 |
| Supplier C | 10,000 | 3,000,000 | 3,010,000 |
| Supplier D | 1,700,000 | 250,000 | 1,950,000 |
| Supplier E | 450,000 | 250,000 | 700,000 |
| Totals | $4,810,000 | $5,750,000 | $10,560,000 |

The initial calculation reveals that there may be significant opportunities for inventory reduction by working with Suppliers A, B, and C. The most egregious case of excessive inventory appears to be related to Supplier C, where the company maintains essentially no inventory on site, having shifted a large inventory burden back onto Supplier C.

---

The concept of total inventory can be applied to several of the following sections, which advocate stripping inventory out of the entire supply chain.

## Supply Chain Buffer Stock Reduction

When a supplier does not have much visibility into the ordering patterns of a major customer, the supplier is much more likely to create a large buffer stock of finished goods to protect it from excessively large orders placed by the customer. Meanwhile, the customer may also be maintaining a safety stock buffer to protect it from shortages if the supplier cannot fulfill an order in a timely manner. If this sort of duplicate inventory buffering is occurring throughout several levels of a supply chain, there can be an inordinate amount of excess inventory. If the level of ordering information can be enhanced down the supply chain, the various members of the chain can agree to reduce some of this inventory.

An improved level of communication can be achieved by sending real time customer sales information as far down the supply chain as possible, along with constant updates to orders being prepared for delivery to the various suppliers. There must also be a formal discussion of the amount of inventory buffers actually needed in the supply chain, with the intent of sparing as many companies as possible from the burden of maintaining an excess investment. This is a difficult process to achieve, and is only a realistic option when the ultimate customer is a large one that places significant orders back through the supply chain. A minor customer will not attract the interest of its suppliers in regard to a joint inventory reduction.

The main concern of customers in reducing supply chain buffers is that a supplier may go out of business or decide to stop selling to the customer. If so, and the customer had already reduced its safety stock, the customer will be faced with immediate stockout conditions while it searches for a replacement supplier, which can cripple its sales. Consequently, this approach should only be followed when there is a healthy operating relationship with a set of financially robust suppliers.

## Reduce Supplier Delivery Times

Suppliers may require a fairly long lead time on orders placed by their customers. If so, customers must estimate the amount of usage they will actually need during the lead time interval, and maintain that amount of inventory on hand to ensure that they do not run out. Further, if there is a sudden spike in usage, customers must maintain additional safety stock to prevent a stock out condition. This issue can be mitigated by switching to suppliers that offer shorter lead times. A shorter lead time allows customers to maintain less inventory on hand, which reduces their working capital investment.

The ideal supplier is one that can deliver goods on a same-day or next-day basis. In this case, the reduced working capital investment can offset any increased price that such a supplier may charge. This type of extremely fast delivery period also means that customers only have to forecast their usage for a few hours or a day, resulting in extremely accurate orders that will closely match actual requirements.

The type of supplier that can be so responsive to customer orders is almost certainly located near its customers, or maintains warehouses near them, thereby reducing delivery times. This has the additional benefit of reducing the risk of interrupted deliveries due to weather events, such as icy roads and traffic accidents that plague longer-distance deliveries. Unfortunately, it can be difficult for a smaller business to persuade a high-grade supplier to relocate to a nearby facility. In this case, a company may be forced to continue using a distant supplier. If so, a possible option is to work with a local supplier to upgrade the quality of its goods and services, and then shift all purchases to it.

A variation on the local supplier concept is to deliberately use local suppliers, even if they are more expensive, for the delivery of goods that have higher usage variability. The company is essentially paying more for the ability to order more frequently and in lesser volumes. By doing so, it can maintain relatively low inventory levels for items that have uncertain demand. For all other goods that have more consistent and predictable demand levels, it is probably still possible to use more distant and lower-cost suppliers that demand larger order sizes.

## Aggregate Deliveries with Freight Forwarders

What if a business has a number of suppliers within a geographic region? Should they be allowed to individually deliver their own goods to the company? Doing so can result in an unreliable mix of delivery times, and many suppliers may not issue advance notice of their deliveries with electronic advance shipping notices (ASNs). An alternative that organizes these deliveries is to use a freight forwarding company.

A freight forwarder sends trucks to each supplier in turn to pick up goods intended for the company, aggregates these goods in a consolidation warehouse, sends a single ASN to the company for each truckload to be delivered, and then ships the goods. This approach is especially valuable if a number of suppliers are located in a foreign country, since a freight forwarder can be responsible for getting all of the goods from that country through customs. Forwarders are especially adept at working with customs officials, and so can eliminate valuable time from the customs clearing process.

Ideally, a freight forwarder can also maintain goods in a nearby warehouse and only ship them to the company's facility when they are needed for a production run.

Though freight forwarders are expensive, they provide a number of valuable services that can improve the reliability of deliveries, speed customs approvals, and improve the flow of information regarding goods in transit. They are particularly useful when a company works with a mix of smaller suppliers located well away from the company's facilities.

## Suppliers Own On-Site Inventory

Have suppliers own their inventory in the company's warehouse until the moment when it is used or sold. This eliminates the holding period for inventory, thereby shifting the cost of the inventory to suppliers until the inventory is needed. Also, the company incurs no risk of inventory obsolescence, since suppliers will take back any unused inventory.

This approach is usually only possible if inventory is sole sourced to certain suppliers, so that they can be assured of more sales in exchange for taking on the inventory holding cost. Also, the goods cannot be customized, so that suppliers can take back their goods if not used by the company and sell them elsewhere.

This approach works best if the company tracks the on-hand unit levels for supplier-owned inventory, and suppliers are given access to this information. Better yet, give suppliers direct access to the company's production schedule, so they can plan for the exact amount of upcoming demand for the items for which they are responsible. Another possible trigger is to send notifications to the supplier when inventory levels reach a predetermined reorder point, which places responsibility for triggering replenishment activities on the company, not the supplier.

While this approach will reduce a company's investment in inventory, there may be an offsetting increase in the prices charged by suppliers. They are taking on an increased funding cost, and may also need to send their staff on-site to review inventory levels. However, a price increase may be avoided if a supplier can be the sole source of an increased number of items. Another concern with supplier-owned inventory is that suppliers may want to overstock goods, in order to keep from making too many replenishment trips to the warehouse. If so, the company may find that it is allocating an excessive amount of warehouse space to the supplier's goods.

## Reserve Supplier Capacity

There may be situations where a company must obtain a certain quantity of parts for its production process, but supplies are constrained. In this case, the company could pay a fee to a supplier to reserve capacity in its production system for a certain number of units. The company then has the choice of activating the option or electing to not have the extra units manufactured. If activated, the company then pays the supplier the usual price for any delivered goods, which is in addition to the fee already paid to reserve capacity. If no additional units are needed, then the supplier retains the fee.

This approach is more likely to be accepted by suppliers when they can activate extra reserve capacity by opening up another production shift. It is not a viable option when there is no reserve capacity available, and the supplier will have to delay deliveries to another customer in exchange for giving priority to the customer paying the fee. Earning a reputation for accepting payments from customers to jump the priority queue is a good way to lose customers.

## Vertical Integration

There may be situations where certain suppliers provide such a valuable service to a company that it makes sense to buy them outright. By engaging in vertical integration, the company is assured of the entire output of the supplier. This can be of critical importance if there are few other suppliers available, and especially if the company has been experiencing restrictions on the amounts of raw materials that it can obtain. Vertical integration is a particularly choice alternative when the purchase of a supplier can be used to prevent raw materials from being sent to a competitor. Another good reason for an acquisition is when a supplier owns intellectual property that keeps other suppliers from providing goods of the same level of quality, price, or innovation.

Despite the advantages of vertical integration, this concept should only be employed at rare intervals. There are several reasons for minimizing its use, including the following:

- *Reduced competitive pressure*. When a supplier is purchased, the sale of its entire output may essentially be guaranteed to the buyer. When this happens, there is less pressure within the supplier to improve its competitive posture, eventually resulting in reduced efficiency and a stale product line.
- *Integration risk*. If there is an intent to combine operations with the supplier, there will likely be disaffection among employees at some of the changes, resulting in the departure of key employees.
- *Cost*. The cost of an acquisition is high, since the owners of a valuable supplier are unlikely to part with their shares unless a stout premium is offered. Consequently, there must be a real need for an acquisition before a company decides to part with a large pile of cash.

## Supply Chain Cooperation

Inventory problems can begin deep in the supply chain, resulting in pockets of unnecessary inventory piling up that a company may not even be aware of. However, suppliers are aware of these issues, and will charge the company for the holding cost of this inventory. Consequently, it makes sense to improve the level of cooperation between suppliers and the company. Here are several ways to do so:

- *Sponsor workshops*. The company can have on-site or off-site meetings with its suppliers, where the company pays for industry experts (or its own engineers) to speak on various subjects. This can spread knowledge down through the primary suppliers, but only if they choose to attend, and implement what they learn.
- *Create joint ventures*. Rather than using entirely new suppliers for certain parts, establish joint ventures with existing suppliers. Doing so provides them with more revenue, builds their expertise, and gives the company more experience in dealing with them.
- *Work together on improvements*. There may be any number of projects that the company and its suppliers can jointly work on to improve processes and/or reduce the amount of inventory in the system. These projects are especially useful for building trust over time.
- *Work together on new products*. Suppliers can provide a considerable amount of input into the components used for new product designs. In exchange, the company provides suppliers with orders for their parts, to be used in new product designs. The outcome should be more robust and lower-cost products that are better able to attain targeted margins.

## Supply Chain Configuration Issues

Theoretically, it should be possible to minimize inventory throughout the supply chain by ordering parts from suppliers only when a customer order is received. In this scenario, the receipt of an order triggers notifications to all primary and secondary suppliers to produce and forward the requisite materials to the company for final assembly. Ideally, such a fully-synchronized supply chain would operate with minimal inventory, while still providing a reasonably high order fill rate. In reality, a fully synchronized supply chain is quite difficult to achieve. Consider the following issues that can interfere with the concept:

- *Deep bill of materials*. The bill of materials for a complex product may require the use of multiple levels of subassemblies, each of which is created by a secondary or primary supplier, and each of which requires a certain amount of lead time.
- *Number of suppliers*. A complex bill of materials may contain hundreds or even thousands of parts, involving a large number of suppliers whose activities must be synchronized.
- *Sole sourcing*. Some parts are only available through one supplier, who may not be amenable to any synchronization efforts.
- *International*. Additional delays are built into shipments coming from international suppliers, where logistical costs are commonly reduced by waiting for several less-than-container load shipments to aggregate into a full container load.

These issues are less severe when products have few components and are produced in high volume, since there are only a few suppliers, and demand is reasonably predictable. Conversely, synchronization is an increasingly elusive target when customer demand is low and products are highly complex.

No matter what the level of product complexity may be, there is still some opportunity for supply chain synchronization. There should be a core group of primary suppliers for which customer orders will trigger inventory deliveries to the company. For these suppliers, goods are produced to order, with no replenishment. The rate and mix of production will match actual customer orders.

However, the use of customer orders to trigger production will break down at the point where additional delays in the supply chain will extend the production time period beyond the time that a customer is willing to wait for an order to be fulfilled. Beyond this point, the supply chain must rely upon forecasts of expected demand, and produce in expectation of customer orders.

At the point in the supply chain where the production triggering mechanism changes from a pull system to a push system, there should be an inventory buffer. This buffer should be of sufficient size to ensure that inventory orders can be fulfilled. It is quite likely that the number of items subject to these orders will be substantially smaller than the number of items further down the supply chain that are controlled by a push system.

**Tip:** The synchronization concept breaks down in the supply chain wherever the maximum output of a bottleneck is less than a spike in customer demand. These hitches will become apparent when there are spikes in demand, or anticipate them by making inquiries of suppliers regarding their bottleneck issues.

A key point in developing a system of supply chain synchronization is to have the company issue a notification as deep in the supply chain as possible, as soon as a customer order is received. Otherwise, it may take days for a primary supplier to issue a notification to a secondary supplier, and so forth down the supply chain. In the latter case, there may be weeks of notification delays built into the supply chain.

In summary, there are limits to the effectiveness of the supply chain synchronization concept, which are set by the nature of the product and the volume of customer demand. The concept is still tenable, but only for a certain distance back into the supply chain, after which a variety of factors water down its effect. If a company wants to synchronize as much of its supply chain as possible, it must weigh the benefits against the cost of creating a customer order notification system, as well as of increasing bottleneck capacities and buffer stocks at key points in the supply chain.

**Tip:** If the company anticipates considerable sales growth, it should communicate this concern back down the supply chain, so that bottleneck capacities and buffer stocks can be increased well in advance of the projected sales increase.

## Supply Chain Risk

The supply chain can be critical to the survival of a business, especially if a large part of the value that a business delivers to its customers actually comes from its suppliers. In these situations, one should evaluate the likelihood of occurrence of each possible supply chain failure, as well as the ability of these failures to disrupt operations. Examples of common supply chain risks to which these analyses can be readily applied are:

- Inadequate supplier performance
- Forecasting errors that lead to shortages or over-investments in purchased goods
- Breakdowns in transportation between suppliers and the company
- Changes in the prices charged by suppliers

The preceding list involves situations that occur with a relatively high degree of frequency, so there is an obvious payback in spending the time to analyze these types of risks. But what about situations in which there could be a major disaster, but only at long intervals? Here are several examples:

- There has been one instance of a river flooding that is adjacent to a supplier's production facility, but the last case was 50 years ago. A 20% increase in the maximum water level would flood the facility.
- A manufacturing facility has been built on an island on the southern fringe of the Caribbean that is well outside of the normal hurricane tracks, but which experienced a Category Two hurricane 15 years ago. During the last occurrence, it took two weeks for the island's government to restore utilities.
- A supplier's headquarters is situated over an earthquake fault that has not shifted in over 100 years. According to historical records, the last earthquake leveled the town in which the building is now situated.
- A major multinational supplier is considering building a production facility in a small country that is currently stable, but which experienced a military take-over two elections ago, followed by a small amount of asset expropriation.

In all of the preceding scenarios, the events are rare enough that it can be difficult to even find detailed historical information about them – and yet there is evidence that a reoccurrence would inflict major damage on the business. A common outcome of these situations is that a proper risk analysis is never completed, since the risk manager is more concerned with events that have much higher frequencies. The result can be epically negative consequences, since there is no contingency in place at all to offset the effects of a major disaster.

A method for dealing with these rare events is to not focus on the probability of occurrence, but rather on the impact of a potential failure in the supply chain. For example, rather than focusing on a minimal probability that a supplier will be shut down due to flood damage, look instead at the impact if that supplier will not be operational for a period of time – irrespective of the cause. A likely outcome is the discovery that the company has planned well for possible shutdowns in deliveries from its high-spend suppliers, but done little to guard against shutdowns elsewhere in its supply chain. For example, a business might maintain large reserve stocks of rare earth minerals for its electronics business because there are so few reliable suppliers, but has completely overlooked its commodity components, which are subject to a different set of risks.

In the market for commodity goods, the main competitive factor is price, which typically leads to rapid industry consolidation as those with the largest and lowest-cost facilities gain market share. The problem with this arrangement from a risk management perspective is that there are very few suppliers remaining, so if a disaster shuts one down, a large part of the total industry capacity has just been eliminated.

## Cross-Firm Effects of Supply Chain Disruptions

When a number of companies all buy from a major supplier or group of suppliers located in the same geographic region, this can amplify the negative effects of a supply chain disruption. For example, a major flood shuts down the largest supplier of a certain computer part; because of its production excellence, many major customers order from this supplier. As a result of the shutdown, any of these customers will find that they are in the midst of a broad scramble for alternative supplies, which can greatly increase the cost of replacement parts, while also making it nearly impossible to obtain replacement supplies in a timely manner.

## Supply Chain Risk Mitigation Techniques

There are a number of ways to reduce the risk of failures in the supply chain, which are only limited by the imagination of the management team. Here are several risk mitigation alternatives:

- *Build inventory reserves.* Maintain additional stocks of inventory that exceed the amounts strictly necessary to maintain the flow of goods through the company's internal production processes, or to ensure that customer stock-out conditions are minimized. This additional safety stock guards against the sudden termination of supplier deliveries. A useful side benefit of a stockpiling program is that it also provides extra stock if there is an unexpected increase in demand.
- *Buy from nearby suppliers.* Shift orders to suppliers located closer to the company or its distribution points, or at least avoid placing orders with the more distant suppliers. Doing so eliminates the risk of in-transit disruptions.
- *Use alternative transport.* It may be possible to arrange for multiple forms of transport, such as by river barge, rail, airplane, and/or truck. By fostering multiple forms of transport, the materials management group gains experience in how to rapidly shift inbound transport when its main form of conveyance is disabled. For example, a truckers' strike may shut down freight hauling on the roads, but still leaves rail transport as a viable alternative.
- *Add suppliers.* Maintain more than one supplier, and consider using a backup supplier that is located in a different geographic location. By doing so, a disaster that impacts one supplier is less likely to also affect the backup. A variation is to pay a backup supplier to reserve a portion of its capacity, rather than actually placing orders with it on an ongoing basis. The company is then entitled to immediately access this capacity as needed.
- *Encourage additional production sites.* Incentivize suppliers to build additional factories in disparate locations, so that work can continue even in the face of a disaster at one of the locations. The incentives could include low-cost loans to build the extra factories, the promise of a larger share of orders, or outright bonuses.

- *Conduct credit monitoring.* Use such credit research firms as Moody's Analytics and Dun & Bradstreet to monitor the financial health of suppliers. If the credit information forwarded by these research firms indicates a problem, the purchasing department can bolster its planning to ramp up production with secondary suppliers, in anticipation of a default by the primary supplier. This approach can also be used to swap out secondary suppliers that appear to be having financial difficulties. This type of overview can become more detailed if the credit research firms detect a significant problem, perhaps involving an on-site team that investigates the condition of a supplier.
- *Shift production in-house.* If the capital investment is not excessive, it might be economical to produce certain components in-house, rather than outsourcing them to a supplier that is evaluated as being high risk.
- *Develop flexible production facilities.* Develop in-house manufacturing capabilities that can be switched to different production runs without too much difficulty, so that a component shortage from a supplier triggers a move to a different product that does not require the impacted component. However, this is only a short-run solution, since the company will eventually run out of the product that it can no longer manufacture.
- *Hedge prices.* A business may find that its financial results are worse than expected due to a run-up in the prices of its raw materials. The problem can be combatted with hedging arrangements that commit the entity to long-term purchases at the current prices, thereby eliminating the prospect of future price increases. The problem is when the current prices are at historic highs, so the company is committing to keep buying at prices that may subsequently drop. Yes, the hedging will keep the company from paying even higher prices, but the likelihood of a continuing price spiral is probably remote, so the hedging will likely cost the company even more money. Thus, hedging is only profitable in certain circumstances.
- *Redesign products.* A longer-term solution is to redesign products so that the use of certain components is minimized or eliminated. However, it may take an entire product cycle to carry through with this solution.
- *Offer free risk analyses.* A company could offer to send its engineers or an outside consulting group to its suppliers for free, with the intent of identifying risk issues for the suppliers and assisting with their risk mitigation efforts. Doing so eventually results in a more robust supply chain that is less likely to fail.

## Project Completion Risk

An organization may be concerned that a supplier cannot complete a major project on time. For example, a company is planning to depart its current premises on June 1, and so needs to have its new corporate headquarters completed by the same date. To mitigate the risk that the new facility will *not* be ready, the company can require the building contractor to post a *surety bond.* This is a contract guaranteeing that a legal agreement will be completed. It is commonly used to ensure that construction performance is completed. A bond agreement involves the participation of the following three entities:

- *The principal.* This is the party that is supposed to perform in accordance with the requirements of a contract.
- *The obligee.* This is the party receiving the obligation; typically, it is the counterparty to the contract with the principal.
- *The surety.* This is a third party that does not directly perform the requirements of the contract, but rather who guarantees the performance of the principal under the contract.

Thus, a surety bond is a promise to pay the obligee if the principal does not perform under the contract. The surety makes the payment to the obligee. In exchange for this service, the principal pays a fee to the surety for as long as the surety bond is outstanding. In cases where the financial resources of the principal are in doubt, the fee will be quite high, or the surety will insist that all or most of the bond be kept in escrow during the term of the bond.

If there is a claim by the obligee for reimbursement under the surety bond, the surety will investigate the claim, pay it if the claim is valid, and then turn to the principal for reimbursement.

There are several types of surety bonds, including the following:

- *Bid bond.* The principal guarantees that it will enter into an agreement with the obligee if awarded a contract.
- *Performance bond.* The principal guarantees that it will perform the services specified in a contract.

While a surety bond does show that a business has a certain amount of capital, it also acts to block smaller competitors unable to obtain a surety bond from bidding against them. Thus, a surety bond tends to reduce competition.

## Shifting Risk into the Supply Chain

When a company elects to build products or supply services, it is taking on the risk of changes in the prices of the associated materials or labor. To mitigate this risk, it may be possible to shift work to contractors or subcontractors who are then paid on a fixed-price basis. The result is that the company knows it will incur a fixed amount, with no price variation. This eliminates the risk of a price increase, but also eliminates the potential benefit to be gained from a decline in prices.

The shifting of risk into the supply chain is not free. When faced with a proposal to supply goods or services under a fixed-price arrangement, an experienced contractor or subcontractor will build into the bid price an extra margin that compensates it for the risk of increasing prices.

A company could elect to keep work in-house during periods of falling commodity prices, so that it benefits from the reduced prices, and then outsources during periods of increasing commodity prices, so that this risk is borne by contractors.

## Summary

The main concept to take away from this chapter is that the level of information sharing that an effective supply chain engages in should be extremely high. Only by constant discussions of current and prospective ordering needs can a group of suppliers be converted into an effective tool that provides a business with a strong competitive advantage. In addition, a company should engage in a detailed evaluation of its suppliers, to see if there are weaknesses in the supply chain that can be mitigated or eliminated. Finally, it is helpful to periodically examine potential events that could disrupt the supply chain, and to take mitigation steps in advance to reduce their effects. By addressing all of these areas, a company can nurture a robust supply chain that provides it with just enough of the highest-quality inventory to meet the needs of its customers.

# Chapter 14
# Inventory Management

## Introduction

The operations manager will usually have to deal with some amount of inventory. This can be a concern, because inventory requires a significant investment in working capital, presents the risk of inventory obsolescence, and also takes up valuable storage space. However, it also provides a convenient buffer to cover for hiccups in the production process, as well as for unexpected spikes in customer demand. Consequently, the operations manager is always striving to balance the inventory investment against the associated costs and risks. In this chapter, we cover the nature of and need for inventory, its cost, and how to keep inventory investments at a reasonable level.

## The Nature of and Need for Inventory

At the most general level, inventory can be defined as those assets that a business has or will have available for sale. Inventory is usually classified in more detail as raw materials, work-in-process, or finished goods, to reflect its state of completion. This classification is commonly used in the accounting records, and so has become the standard form of identification. However, these terms do not reveal the functional reasons *why* inventory is being held. The following classifications do a better job of revealing why an organization needs inventory:

- *Batch replenishment inventory*. Some inventory is created simply because the production system is designed to create inventory in batches, rather than one at a time. For example, if the setup interval for a machine is quite lengthy, the production manager may elect to process 1,000 units of inventory through it in order to justify the long setup, rather than the 100 units that are actually needed at the moment. The remaining 900 units are batch replenishment inventory, and will sit in the warehouse until needed at some later date. The same logic applies to volume discounts that can be obtained from a supplier. The purchasing manager buys 500 units at a discounted price, instead of the 50 units that are actually needed. The 450 unused units are all batch replenishment inventory.
- *Safety stock*. Some inventory is kept on hand as a buffer to guard against shortages. For example, the high variability of customer demand dictates that 80 units of a green widget be maintained to avoid imposing backorders on customers. Similarly, if there is a risk of having a shortfall of raw materials before a supplier can replenish them, a certain amount of safety stock is maintained. Safety stock is also useful to guard against production failures, such as broken equipment or staff shortages. The need for safety stock is eliminated

if a company has perfect information about future customer orders, knows exactly how long it will take for a supplier to fulfill an order, and has excess production capacity to guard against equipment failures. Since the reduction of lead times reduces forecasting uncertainty, such a reduction also reduces the need for safety stock.

- *Seasonal inventory.* When sales are seasonal, production continues through low-sale months, so that inventory levels will be high enough to sustain customer orders during high-demand months. A company may elect to avoid some of this inventory by instead incurring overtime costs to produce for longer periods of time during high-demand months.
- *Work-in-process inventory.* This is the only case where the accounting designation for inventory matches its actual function. This inventory type refers to the inventory passing through the production system. Large amounts of work-in-process inventory tend to build up between work stations in a production process. This buildup can be caused by the distance between work stations, and can be mitigated by compressing the distance.
- *Investment inventory.* Some types of inventory can increase in value over time, such as wines, precious metals, and precious stones. Oil and gas and other commodities may also be held over the short term in order to take advantage of spikes in spot rates. If management wants to engage in this type of speculation, it may hold substantial amounts of inventory for prolonged periods.

In addition to these operational issues, a business may incorporate a certain need for inventory (or exclusion of inventory) into its strategy, as described in the following sub-sections.

## Replenishment Strategy

A company can pursue a strategy of replenishing its inventory at a rate much faster than its competitors. This means that the total stock of inventory is being replaced by new inventory during a period when competitors are still offering older goods for sale. By doing so, a business can achieve the following advantages:

- *Investable cash.* The company can maintain the same order fulfillment rate as competitors, while investing far less money in inventory. The difference can be used elsewhere to gain a competitive advantage, such as by increasing spending on new product development, loosening credit to expand sales, or by investing in more efficient production equipment.
- *Broader product line.* The company can choose to match the total inventory investment of competitors, but because it is replenishing inventory much more quickly, the result is a broader product line from which customers can choose.
- *Faster product replacement.* Since inventory is being flushed out of the company much faster than for competitors, the company can choose to replace its

product line at more frequent intervals. This is a particular advantage in fashion or trend-oriented businesses, where sales can spike and suddenly decline within very short periods of time. A fashion business can use fast replenishment to test designs without having to build up unwanted stock that it might otherwise need to sell off at a steep discount. Also, faster product replacement allows the seller to lock up the best distributors, since distributors want to differentiate themselves by offering the latest product innovations.

---

**EXAMPLE**

Quest Adventure Gear has achieved an inventory turnover rate that is double the rate attained by its competitors. By doing so, Quest has reduced its investment in inventory by $5,000,000. The management team decides to use this advantage by creating a new product line, which will require $2,000,000 of development costs to create and $3,000,000 of an investment in inventory to support. Competitors cannot match this action, unless they raise $5,000,000 through an equity offering or obtain $5,000,000 of debt (for which interest payments must be made).

---

In addition to the advantages already noted, it is possible that the following ancillary benefits may also be gained from a fast replenishment strategy:

- *Reduced obsolescence cost.* If inventory is being flushed out of a company at an accelerated rate, it is possible that there will be a reduced amount of loss from product obsolescence. However, obsolescence can still occur, since a few products may only sell poorly, irrespective of the overall inventory turnover rate. Also, some raw materials may still become obsolete if they are not used up prior to the official termination of a product.
- *Increased prices.* If a company markets its accelerated replenishment strategy properly, customers will come to appreciate their ability to buy the freshest product concepts from the company. This can be a powerful branding tool that may allow the company to charge higher prices than competitors.
- *Reduced forecasting uncertainty.* If inventory is being replaced with great rapidity, this means that product demand only needs to be forecasted for a relatively short period of time. Since forecasting tends to be more accurate over the short-term, this means that a company is at much less risk of adopting a production schedule that mandates the manufacture of goods that will not be sold.
- *Better reseller penetration.* When the supplier can replenish the stocks of a retailer or distributor within a few days, this means that the retailer or distributor can keep less inventory on hand to guard against stockout conditions. The retailer or distributor therefore invests less cash in inventory, and so will be more likely to buy goods from the fast-replenishment supplier. Further, retailers and distributors can use the savings from reduced funding to grant

easier credit to *their* customers, which in turn increases the orders they place with the supplier.

---

**EXAMPLE**

Quest Clothiers produces clothes designed for the adventure market, specifically focusing on women's products. Changes in this market are more rapid than for men's adventure clothes, with styling changes occurring in as little as three months. Quest has concentrated on increasing the replenishment speed of its inventory by forcing a key supplier to locate a facility a short distance away from Quest's headquarters. The result is an ability to issue new fashions in just six weeks, which is twice the speed of every other competitor. This triggers an immediate increase in market share, as competitors struggle to keep up with Quest's continuing product line changes.

---

**Tip:** Reduced forecasting uncertainty is particularly important when a company forecasts demand too low, since this equates to lost sales. Consequently, in industries where forecasted demand is especially prone to error, it can be especially important to pursue a rapid replenishment strategy with the specific target of shortening the forecasting period.

## Fulfillment Strategy

A company may elect to be a full-service provider of goods to its customers. This means being the monolithic supplier of as many goods as possible. This approach can be comprehensive, such as being the sole supplier of maintenance, repair and operations (MRO) supplies. Alternatively, it can mean being the sole supplier of a particular category of goods, such as the supplier of all air filters to large industrial suppliers, no matter what type of filter is required.

The fulfillment strategy may call for a large investment in inventory, in order to ship most customer order line items on the same day of receipt. Alternatively, it may mean that the seller can improve upon the promised ship dates of its competitors, as may be the case when products are configured for a specific customer. This strategy also involves building relations with a financially sound and reliable group of suppliers, so that they can forward materials and goods to the company in an extremely reliable manner. The outcome of these actions is to present to customers a business that can comprehensively meet their needs on the shortest possible delivery terms, as reliably as possible. In exchange for pursuing this strategy, a company can expect the following outcomes:

- *Increased market share.* As customers realize the reliability of the company, they will allocate a greater percentage of their spend to the company, resulting in an ongoing increase in market share.

- *Reduced unit costs.* As market share expands, the company can increase its production volumes, which means that fixed costs are spread over more units, resulting in a decline in average costs and therefore increased profits.

However, this strategy is not without its risks. The company must carefully monitor its inventory levels, since it may be committing to maintain much larger stocks of inventory than might normally have been the case. Also, customers may ask the company to act as primary supplier for a whole range of products, which means that the company must have the managerial skill to coordinate the actions of a number of secondary suppliers.

**Tip:** To reduce the risk of obsolete inventory, a company following the fulfillment strategy should request access to the purchasing plans of its key customers, thereby reducing the uncertainty of its own production and procurement forecasts.

## Customization Strategy

Some customers want products that vary somewhat from the standard offerings that a seller provides. These customers may be more than willing to pay a premium for their non-standard demands, and will be especially willing to do so if the seller can provide customized goods within a short period of time. If a company can refine its order-handling and production systems to provide somewhat customized goods within a compressed time frame, this can be an excellent strategy. In addition to the pricing advantage, here are several other benefits of the inventory customization strategy:

- *Loyalty.* Few companies are willing to provide customized goods within a short time frame. Those that can do so garner high levels of customer loyalty, which translates into repeat business. Further, these customers may be so impressed with a company's service that they go out of their way to refer other potential customers – which reduces new customer acquisition costs for the organization.
- *Broader purchases.* A customer that has had a good experience with a customized product purchase is more likely to buy other, more standardized goods from the same seller. Thus, the use of customization can be used as a wedge to obtain all types of additional sales.

Further, customization does not have to be considered a niche strategy that only applies to small segments of a market. If a company can redefine its systems to handle modest amounts of customization for many orders, it can become the dominant player in an industry.

This strategy only applies to markets where customers value differentiated products. For example, a company could successfully pursue the customization of electric guitars or skis, but would be less successful in customizing cleaning products.

## Showrooming Strategy

A business may choose to operate showrooms in which customers can view, touch, and try on its products, after which they are directed to a website to make actual purchases (possibly from a kiosk within the showroom). This approach has three advantages. First, the company can concentrate its inventory in a small number of warehouses, from which all sales are shipped. This is especially important when the customer base is spread across a large area, since stocking local stores to service them would otherwise require a massive inventory investment. Second, customers have a chance to examine the goods before placing on-line orders, which makes it more likely that they will select the right product options on the first order, requiring fewer product returns. And third, showrooms can be smaller than regular retail outlets and require fewer staff. Given their lower cost structures, it is possible to set up a large number of showrooms, possibly in lower-population areas that would not support a retail store.

The main downside of the showrooming strategy is that the purchasing process now has two steps – viewing the product and then placing an order, possibly at a later date. This more extended purchasing process could mean that fewer sales are realized. Another potential problem is that some customers may not be comfortable shopping online; a smaller number of more traditional retail outlets may be needed to service these customers.

## Startup Outsourcing Strategy

The founders of a company may choose to invest their limited funds in only a small number of key areas, such as product design and marketing, and outsource all other activities. Since the production and warehousing of goods can require a large amount of funding, these activities are more likely to be outsourced. If so, the startup company trades off a higher per-unit cost to a third-party contract manufacturer in exchange for reduced funding requirements. There is also a risk that the manufacturer will learn so much about the company's products that it can eventually become a direct competitor. However, if the company does an adequate job of branding its products, this can be a lesser concern.

The startup outsourcing strategy does not always work for the entire life cycle of a company. As the business grows, management may realize that a large part of the company's profits are being handed to suppliers. Also, customer concerns over the quality of goods and/or the speed of product delivery may lead the company to take over control of its production and warehousing. Nonetheless, avoiding all contact with inventory can be a smart strategy for a small startup operation.

## The Cost of Inventory

Much of the management effort associated with reducing inventory is based on its cost, which can be substantial. Inventory cost includes the costs to order and hold inventory, as well as to administer the related paperwork. Inventory costs can be classified as follows:

- *Ordering costs*. These costs include the wages of the procurement department and related payroll taxes and benefits, and possibly similar labor costs by the industrial engineering staff, in case they must pre-qualify new suppliers to deliver parts to the company. These costs are typically included in an overhead cost pool and allocated to the number of units produced in each period.
- *Holding costs*. These costs are related to the space required to hold inventory, the cost of the money needed to acquire inventory, and the risk of loss through inventory obsolescence. Most of these costs are also included in an overhead cost pool and allocated to the number of units produced in each period. More specifically, holding costs include:
- *Cost of space*. Perhaps the largest inventory cost is related to the facility within which it is housed, which includes warehouse depreciation, insurance, utilities, maintenance, warehouse staff, storage racks, and materials handling equipment. There may also be fire suppression systems and burglar alarms, as well as their servicing costs.
- *Cost of money*. There is always an interest cost associated with the funds used to pay for inventory. If a company has no debt, this cost represents the foregone interest income associated with the allocated funds.
- *Cost of obsolescence*. Some inventory items may never be used or will be damaged while in storage, and so must be disposed of at a reduced price, or at no price at all. Depending on how perishable the inventory is, or the speed with which technology changes impact inventory values, this can be a substantial cost.
- *Administrative costs*. The accounting department pays the wages of a cost accounting staff, which is responsible for compiling the costs of inventory and the cost of goods sold, responding to other inventory analysis requests, and defending their results to the company's internal and external auditors. The cost of cost accounting personnel is charged to expense as incurred.

As the preceding list reveals, the cost of inventory is substantial. If not properly monitored and adjusted, inventory costs can eat into profits and cash reserves. Given these concerns, it should be no surprise that several tools have been developed to assist managers with a number of inventory decisions, such as when to order additional raw materials and components, and how many units to buy when orders are placed. These tools are discussed in the following sections.

## The Reorder Point

A reorder point is the inventory unit quantity on hand that triggers the purchase of a predetermined amount of replenishment inventory. If the purchasing process and supplier fulfillment work as planned, the reorder point should result in the replenishment inventory arriving just as the last of the on-hand inventory is used up. The reorder point is designed for goods that experience independent demand.

The reorder point can be different for every item of inventory, since every item may have a different usage rate, and require differing amounts of time to receive a replenishment delivery from a supplier. For example, a company can elect to buy the same part from two different suppliers; if one supplier requires one day to deliver an order and the other supplier requires three days, the company's reorder point for the first supplier would be when there is one day's supply left on hand, or three days' supply for the second supplier.

The basic formula for the reorder point is to multiply the average daily usage rate for an inventory item by the lead time in days to replenish it.

---

**EXAMPLE**

ABC International uses an average of 25 units of its green widget every day, and the number of days it takes for the supplier to replenish inventory is four days. Therefore, ABC should set the reorder point for the green widget at 100 units. When the inventory balance declines to 100 units, ABC places an order, and the new units should arrive four days later, just as the last of the on-hand widgets are being used up.

---

However, this formula for the reorder point is only based on *average* usage; in reality, demand may spike above or decline below the average level, so there may still be some inventory on hand when the replenishment order arrives, or there may have been a stockout condition for several days.

To guard against the latter situation, a company may alter the reorder formula to add a safety stock (see the next section), so that the formula becomes:

(Average daily usage rate × Lead time) + Safety stock = Reorder quantity

This formula alteration means that replenishment stock will be ordered sooner, which greatly reduces the risk that there will be a stockout condition. However, it also means that a company will have a larger investment in its on-hand inventory, so there is a trade-off between always having available inventory and funding a larger inventory asset.

## Safety Stock

Some inventory is kept on hand as a buffer to guard against shortages, which is known as safety stock. For example, a company may usually receive an average order total of 100 units of a widget per week. However, actual customer demand can vary around this 100-unit level by as much as 25 units. Thus, orders may be received for 75 units in one week and for 125 in the next week. To guard against a stockout condition, a company could incorporate into its required on-hand balance an additional 25 widgets, so that the company will be able to meet the maximum possible level of customer demand.

The amount of safety stock to be maintained is usually loaded into a company's materials planning system, after which this information is promptly forgotten – unless there is still a stockout, despite the amount of safety stock listed in the system. Safety stock is a laudable idea, since it ensures a higher level of customer service. However, it comes at the cost of an increased investment in working capital. To mitigate this cost, it can be worthwhile to examine demand levels for each product over a full year, to see if the variability of demand changes over time. It is quite possible that there are demand spikes only during limited time periods, with much reducing ordering variability in other periods. If this is the case, consider altering the safety stock level to coincide with expected changes in demand variability.

If the materials planning system does not automate an ongoing reset of safety stock levels, it will be necessary to do so manually. If so, conduct the safety stock investigation and reset only those inventory items for which the company has a significant investment. It is not worthwhile to periodically reset safety stock levels for low-investment goods, since the impact on working capital will be immaterial.

Another way to deal with safety stock is to segment the reasons for its use among different customers. It is possible that the ordering histories of only a small number of customers are highly variable. If so, the company is essentially maintaining extra safety stock just for these customers. In this case, there are several possible courses of action:

- Calculate the cost of holding the extra safety stock for these customers, and include the cost in an analysis of customer profitability. If the extra cost makes a customer unprofitable, drop the customer.
- Approach the customer about paying the company a fee in exchange for maintaining a reserve of inventory for their specific use.
- If the company earns a large profit percentage on the sale of a product, it makes more sense to maintain a large safety stock than if the profit is inconsequential.
- There may be a contractual obligation to provide a certain speed of fulfillment to a customer. If the company cannot deliver goods on a timely basis, it may be under default, and is contractually penalized. If so, there is no way to avoid retaining a large amount of safety stock.
- If there is strong competition for a customer, the company may be forced to maintain a large safety stock for that customer; otherwise, someone else with a better fulfillment speed may obtain the business.

**Tip:** If management wants to maintain a certain average fulfillment rate, it can address the issue in aggregate, by always maintaining sufficient safety stocks for high-volume items, and never maintaining stock for a certain proportion of low-volume items. The result is that some items will always be backordered, while the overall fulfillment rate remains high.

## Safety Time

Safety time is a variation on safety stock. Rather than focusing on a certain amount of buffer stock, we focus on having a buffer for a certain period of time. Safety time is an important concept when demand varies by a significant amount over time. For example, a company sets a safety stock level of 500 units, based on variability of approximately 500 units around an average monthly order volume by customers of 2,000 units. However, this safety stock level was originally calculated during the summer months, when the average monthly demand was peaking. During those months, a 500-unit safety stock equaled one quarter of a month of total demand. In the winter, average monthly demand plummets to 600 units. If the company continues to maintain the fixed safety stock level of 500 units, the amount now equates to 5/6ths of a month. If the company were to instead focus on having safety stock of one-quarter of a month throughout the year, this means the amount of safety stock kept on hand during the winter months would be only one-quarter of 600 units, or 150 units.

## Economic Order Quantity

The economic order quantity is a formula used to derive that number of units of inventory to order that represents the lowest possible total cost to the buyer. It essentially creates a least-cost balance between the cost of ordering inventory and the cost of holding inventory. The formula is designed for situations in which there is a recurring and consistent rate of demand for goods, and the lead time is known. The economic order quantity is derived from the following formula:

$$\text{EOQ} = \sqrt{\frac{2(\text{Annual usage in units})(\text{Order cost})}{(\text{Annual carrying cost per unit})}}$$

The inputs to the model are noted within the formula.

---

**EXAMPLE**

Smithy Smelter uses 100,000 pounds of aluminum ingots per year, and the cost to place each order is $15. The carrying cost for one pound of aluminum ingots is $5 per year. The economic order quantity, based on this information, is the square root of:

(2 × 100,000 Pounds of ingots × $15 Order cost) ÷ $5 Carrying cost

= 775 Units economic order quantity

---

It is useful to test variations on the ordering cost and annual carrying cost to see how they impact the economic order quantity. It is possible that driving down the annual carrying cost of inventory can significantly alter the economic order quantity. A key factor in this analysis is determining which carrying costs actually vary with inventory volumes, and which are unrelated fixed costs. If they are unrelated, do not include them in the denominator of the calculation.

The EOQ model is subject to alteration in certain circumstances. Any of the following situations may limit its applicability:

- *Long-term supply.* A large recommended purchase volume may not be practicable if doing so results in such a long-term supply that there is a risk of obsolescence, or there is a risk that demand levels will become more uncertain. In this case, a smaller purchasing quantity is indicated.
- *Shelf life.* There may be a short shelf life on goods that constrain the maximum amount of units that can be ordered. In this case, the actual amount ordered may be much less than the optimum amount indicated by the model.
- *Storage constraints.* There may be an upper limit on the amount of storage space available for a particular item. This situation most commonly arises for a rarely-used item for which the warehouse manager does not want to reserve extra space. If so, a smaller purchase quantity is needed.

The economic order quantity is not used in a "pull" manufacturing system, where components are ordered from suppliers only as needed and in the quantities needed; thus, a pull system tends to order fewer components than would be indicated by the economic order quantity formula.

## Dependent Demand Reordering Systems

When goods have dependent demand, the need for them is dependent on the stock levels of a different, related inventory item. Thus, if a company sells a widget to a customer, all of the components used to manufacture that widget have dependent demand that is based on the sales of the widget. The demand for these items can be planned with great precision through a computer system called *material requirements planning* (MRP).

The goal of an MRP system is to always have sufficient components on hand to support the requirements of a company's production schedule. To do so, an MRP system follows these steps:

1. Create a production schedule that states the quantities of goods to be produced, and the dates on which production is scheduled.
2. Using a *bill of materials* (i.e., a list of the parts used to manufacture a product), break down the scheduled goods into their component parts, which creates a listing of all the parts needed to support the production schedule.
3. Compare this list of required parts to the on-hand inventory of parts that are not already allocated for other needs.
4. If there are any shortages that must be filled by suppliers, calculate the amount of lead time required to obtain the goods and place orders with the relevant suppliers.

The MRP system is extremely computer-intensive, which means that the information used to construct orders to be placed with suppliers must be accurate. For the system to operate properly, the production department must commit to produce exactly in accordance with the production schedule, while both the bill of material and inventory records must have extraordinarily high accuracy levels. Otherwise, the system will generate nonsensical orders to suppliers (or no orders at all), possibly resulting in the inability to produce goods and/or excessive raw material inventory quantities.

Conversely, if the information used as input to an MRP system is accurate, the result can be quite low raw material inventory balances on hand, since only enough is kept on-site to deal with planned production. Also, the ability of a business to manufacture on a timely basis is heightened, since all component parts are available on time.

A different type of dependent demand reordering system is provided by a just-in-time (JIT) system. A JIT system is designed around the concept of only producing goods if there is a customer order. If there is no order, there is no production. This is a general target that is not always achieved; in reality, estimates of expected customer orders may also be used.

A JIT system uses very short production runs. Since the goal is to immediately produce to the requirements of a single order, it may be necessary to manufacture just a single product in a production run. From an inventory perspective, this means that a small amount of component parts may be needed at any time for immediate production purposes. Accordingly, a notification is sent to suppliers whenever a product is to be manufactured, which calls for an immediate delivery from a supplier, preferably straight to the production area, and only for the amount immediately needed. The notification sent to a supplier is usually an electronic one, to eliminate transit times.

## Visual Reordering Systems

The reorder point described in an earlier section is designed for goods having independent demand, and for which quantities are tracked in real time through a computer system. If there is no up-to-date tracking system in place, a visual reordering system should be installed instead. There are two variations on the same concept that work well:

- *Two bin system.* Goods are stored in two bins, one of which contains working stock and the other containing reserve stock. The amount of inventory kept in the reserve stock bin equals the amount the company expects to use during the ordering lead time associated with that item. To use this system, reorder goods as soon as the working stock bin is empty, and replacement parts should arrive before the reserve stock bin is empty. It is possible to fine-tune the inventory investment by altering the amount of goods kept in the reserve stock bin. The calculation for the amount of inventory to keep in the reserve stock bin is:

  (Daily usage rate × Lead time) + Safety stock = Reserve bin quantity

- *Order line system.* This is the same as the two bin system, except that only a single bin is used. A line is drawn across the back of the bin. When the stock level in the bin declines to the point where the line is visible, additional inventory is ordered.

Which of these two versions is selected may depend upon the storage configuration; if there is not enough room for a two bin system, the single bin version is used. However, the single bin version requires larger bins, so the space savings is not that large.

---

**EXAMPLE**

Entwhistle Electric experiences weekly usage of 500 units of a purple cell battery, so the daily usage rate is 100 units. The lead time for the battery is three days. The reserve storage bin should contain at least 300 batteries, to cover expected usage during the three-day lead time.

In addition, the company assumes that usage levels can vary by as much as 25% from the average usage rate. Consequently, 75 additional batteries are kept in the reserve storage bin. This is calculated as 300 reserve units × 25% safety stock allowance. Thus, the total reserve stock is 375 units.

---

**Tip:** A visual re-ordering system may also be used for dependent demand items whose on-hand balances are not tracked through the inventory computer system. This approach is commonly used for incidental items, such as fittings and fasteners.

A visual reordering system suffers from a major flaw, which is the assumption that someone will periodically conduct a visual review of on-hand balances. If this does not happen, or there is confusion about who is responsible for re-ordering, there can be an unanticipated stockout condition. This issue can be addressed in two ways:

- *Responsibility.* Assign reordering responsibility for every bin using a visual reordering system. With just one person responsible, there can be no confusion about who places replenishment orders.
- *Card trigger.* Include a reorder notification card in the reserve stock bin. The card is removed when an order is placed, and is returned when the bin is refilled. Therefore, if there is no card in the bin, an order has been placed.

## Summary

There are a number of valid needs for inventory within a business, ranging from the use of volume purchasing discounts to ensuring that bottleneck operations continue to function at all times. In addition, inventory may be used as a competitive weapon. These needs may justify a hefty investment in inventory, as well as comprehensive systems for ensuring that more inventory is acquired at regular intervals. The trick to monitoring this investment is to ensure that management understands the specific reasons for maintaining inventory, and that there are adequate policies and procedures in place to ensure that the inventory investment is a prudent one.

# Chapter 15
# Operations Improvement

## Introduction

The operations area is always in need of improvement. No matter how refined a business may already be, its circumstances are continually changing, which calls for corresponding adjustments to its operations. Indeed, operations improvement is typically built into the budget, where there is an expectation every year that costs will be reduced in some way by a few percent; given the size of the operations budget, this typically constitutes a significant proportion of the total budgeted profit figure for the year. In this chapter, we explore how operations improvements can be found and implemented.

## The Need for Operations Improvement

Every activity within the operations area may seem to operate smoothly already, so why should management try to rip things up to enhance the system even further? After all, there is always a risk that an "improvement" does the reverse and actually hinders operations. There are multiple reasons for engaging in improvements. Consider the following:

- *Competitiveness*. Everyone else in the industry is trying to enhance their operations in order to be more competitive. On an annual basis, the changes they make may improve operations only by small amounts – perhaps a percent or two. However, these improvements pile up over time, so that within a few years, a company that has not achieved any improvements will find itself in a significantly uncompetitive position, and may be forced out of business. In addition, new competitors may enter the market who have found different ways to compete, and so can undercut the established businesses. The firm needs to improve itself to guard against these new interlopers. Thus, operations improvement becomes a survival issue.
- *Technology enhancements*. There are always new technologies being created, some of which could have a profound impact if they can be properly integrated into operations. For example, the advent of 3-D printing technology has resulted in the wholesale replacement of existing production equipment in some industries, allowing those firms installing it to offer a greater variety of products in any batch size.

When there are many best practices available and they are well understood by competitors, a company is forced to implement them just to stay in the same competitive position in relation to the others. In order to gain a longer-term competitive advantage, a firm must focus on internal research and development activities to create breakthrough changes that no one else has even considered. These changes may call for the use of innovative technologies that are so bleeding-edge that there is a significant risk of failure if they are not implemented properly, but which push the company so far forward in terms of its performance objectives (quality, speed, performance, dependability, flexibility, and cost) that it is worth the risk.

The much more common approach to operations improvement is to make many small, incremental improvements that cumulatively result in significant gains over an extended period of time. For example, a product design can be altered to share more parts with other company products, thereby reducing the number of parts kept in stock; this reduces the inventory investment by a small amount, and also reduces the risk of parts obsolescence if the product is discontinued at a later date. Similarly, the standardized response scripts used by an inbound call center can be refined to exclude a word or two, thereby saving a few seconds on each call. These gains are incrementally tiny, but they add up when a large number of them are made throughout the operations area. There are likely to be thousands of these small improvement possibilities scattered throughout an organization, and which can be implemented relatively painlessly on an ongoing basis. For continuous improvement to be successful, management needs to push it as an ongoing initiative that never stops, so that there is organizational momentum behind it.

This continuous improvement process is known as *kaizen*. There are two variations on the basic concept, which are:

- *Kaizen blitz*. This is a tight focus of kaizen activities on a particular process, with the intent of implementing a large number of small changes within a short period of time.
- *Kaizen burst*. This is the application of a specific kaizen technique on a process.

The basic process flow for enacting kaizen is to first assess an existing system, then plan the changes to be made, then enact the changes, and finally evaluate the results of the change. Kaizen facilitators receive training and certification before they are allowed to engage in kaizen activities.

## The General Approaches to Operations Improvement

There are a number of general approaches to operations improvement, each of which has its proponents and detractors. In this section, we provide an overview of three of the more popular improvement approaches, which are improvement cycles, business process reengineering, and Six Sigma.

## Improvement Cycles

The basic flow for operations improvement is to question how each aspect of a process works, locate and install improvements, and then do it again – over and over. This is known as the plan-do-check-act cycle, which describes the process of continuous improvement needed to enact change. It is particularly useful when applied to high-volume processes, since even small changes to these processes can translate into substantial gains for an organization. The cycle involves a series of steps, which are followed iteratively to ensure that change is reinforced over time. The steps are as follows:

1. *Plan*. Study the current process to determine where it is failing and how it can be improved.
2. *Do*. Enact change, preferably on a small scale.
3. *Check*. Measure the outcome of the implemented change.
4. *Act*. If the measured result represents an improvement, go ahead and implement the change across the organization. If the check stage results in failure, then go back and try a different improvement plan.

The lessons learned from each iteration of the cycle are incorporated into the next iteration, so that the process improves over time.

The plan-do-check-act cycle was developed by William Edwards Deming in the 1950s.

## Business Process Reengineering

Business process reengineering (BPR) revises workflows to optimize processes and eliminate non-value-added activities. A comprehensive re-engineering project could result in the complete replacement of an existing process. It is common for such a project to fully integrate the use of the latest information technology, so that automation can take the place of manual labor.

A key underlying concept of business process reengineering is that an existing process may have to be completely torn out and replaced. By doing so, an organization can dispense with antiquated notions of how transactions should be dealt with that have more of a basis in tradition than the realities of how a business should compete.

The main problem with BPR is that the type of radical change that is a normal outcome of the process is difficult to impose on an organization. The issue is particularly difficult when a series of BPR changes are required, since they can result in significant downsizing that leads to an employee revolt. A typical outcome is an initial group of BPR changes, after which the effort bogs down and is eventually abandoned. Due to the radical nature of BPR, it works best in an environment where employees understand that a company faces bankruptcy if it cannot overhaul its systems to meet or exceed the performance of competitors.

### Six Sigma

The Six Sigma concept is a set of management techniques that are intended to improve processes by greatly reducing the probability that an error or defect will occur. A Six Sigma process is one in which 99.99966% of all opportunities to produce some feature of a part are statistically expected to be free of defects; this is a defect level of less than 3.4 defects per million opportunities. In essence, Six Sigma is designed to deliver virtually zero-defect objectives.

Six Sigma strategies are intended to improve the quality of the output of a process by identifying and removing the causes of defects and minimizing variability in manufacturing and business processes. Each Six Sigma project carried out within an organization follows a defined sequence of steps and has specific value targets, such as reducing process cycle time, minimizing pollution, reducing costs, increasing customer satisfaction and enhancing profits. The Six Sigma doctrine asserts the following:

- Continuous efforts are needed to achieve stable and predictable process results.
- Manufacturing and business processes have characteristics that can be defined, measured, and improved.
- Achieving a sustained level of quality improvement requires a commitment from the entire organization.

One of the key innovations of the Six Sigma concept is its professionalization of quality management by setting up specific roles within a business to engage in Six Sigma projects. Master black belts act as in-house Six Sigma coaches. They assist lower-level personnel in Six Sigma tasks. Black belts operate under master black belts to apply Six Sigma methodology to specific projects, with an emphasis on project execution. Green belts work on Six Sigma project implementations along with their other job responsibilities, under the guidance of black belts.

A key problem with Six Sigma is its expense. The substantial amount of training required in a range of techniques can be too expensive for smaller firms, especially given the number of people who need to be classified as black belts (about one person per 100 employees is considered optimal). Another concern is that the level of perfection required under Six Sigma calls for a level of perfection that may be too difficult for some companies to attain. In reality, a lower level of perfection will still result in substantial benefits for a business.

## Improvement Techniques

Thus far, we have covered the general approaches to operations improvement, without addressing the tools that are available for identifying specific problem areas. A representative sampling of these tools appears in the following sub-sections.

## Business Process Diagrams

A business process diagram (BPD) graphically depicts the flow of business processes. The intent is to generate a simplified, easy-to-understand overview of a process, which can then be used to identify problem areas. A minimal number of symbols are used in a BPD, usually just a rectangle to describe activities and arrows to indicate the flow of activities. A sample BPD for the purchase of goods appears in the following example.

When preparing a BPD, consider using the following best practices to generate higher-quality diagrams:

- *Standardize the flow.* The information in a BPD should begin at the top or in the top left corner and proceed to the bottom or bottom right corner, thereby establishing a standard flow.
- *Minimize information.* Ideally, a BPD should contain much less information than a narrative description of a system, so that only the highlights of the basic process steps are revealed.
- *Eliminate insignificant items.* Strip out minor steps that are rarely used. It makes more sense to focus on those aspects of the system that are used on a repetitive basis.
- *Terminate the BPD.* If any activities or documents continue off the bottom of the BPD, identify the name of the chart in which the description continues. Otherwise, the reader does not gain a complete understanding of the underlying process.
- *Conduct a walkthrough.* Conduct a joint walkthrough of the BPD with someone else who is knowledgeable in the targeted system, to see if there are any errors or omissions that need to be corrected.
- *Simplify the format.* Since this is a high-level diagram, simplify it as much as possible by only using two columns. The first column states who is engaged in an activity, while the second column describes their activities.
- *Stay high level.* A BPD is constructed at such a high level that there is no need to delve into the details of exactly which documents are used, or which software is employed to process data. This means that a BPD is much less likely to require revision as certain aspects of a system are altered over time.

## Purchasing Business Process Diagram

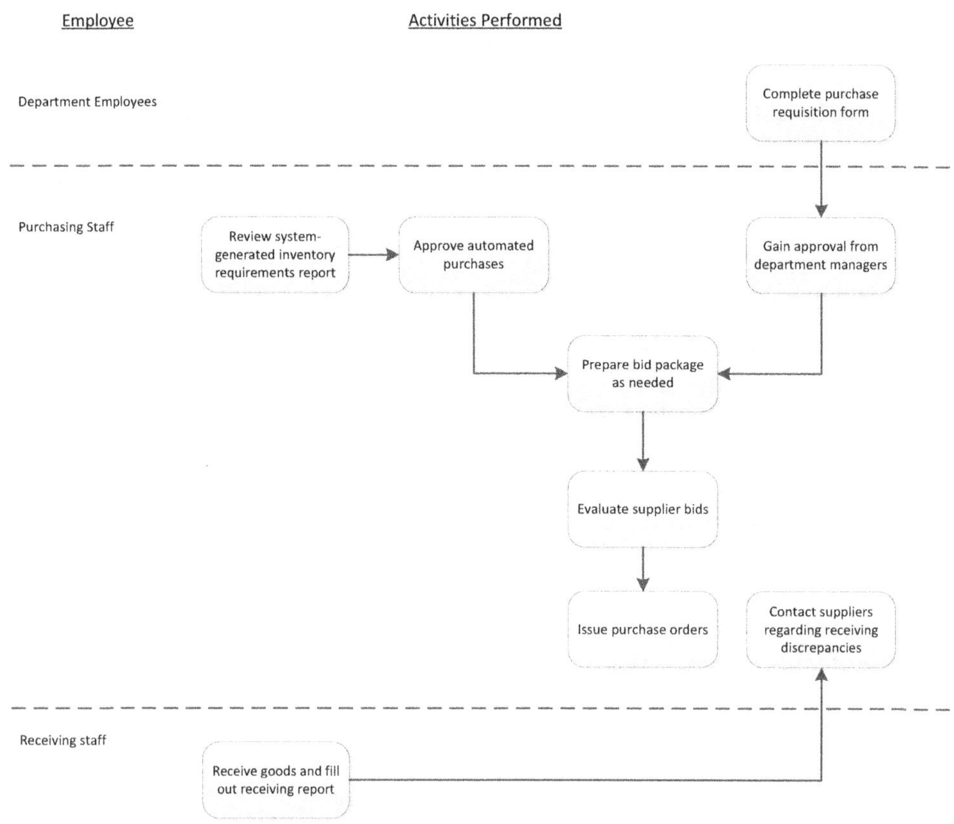


## Cause-and-Effect Diagrams

A cause-and-effect diagram is a visual layout of the possible causes of a problem. It is structured to show a number of branches, and so looks somewhat like a fish skeleton (hence its alternate name of *fishbone diagram*). A cause-and-effect diagram begins with a single line, at the end of which is stated the problem to be solved. Then a number of branches are added that denote the general areas in which the causes of problems may be found. The generic headings most commonly used for these problem areas are:

- Methods (procedures)
- Machines (equipment)
- People
- Materials
- Measurement
- Environment

With this basic structure in place, a facilitator then collects possible causes from the team assigned to the problem, and writes them into the diagram. The outcome is a diagram similar to the following sample. This approach does a good job of organizing information about the causes of a problem.

**Sample Cause-and-Effect Diagram**

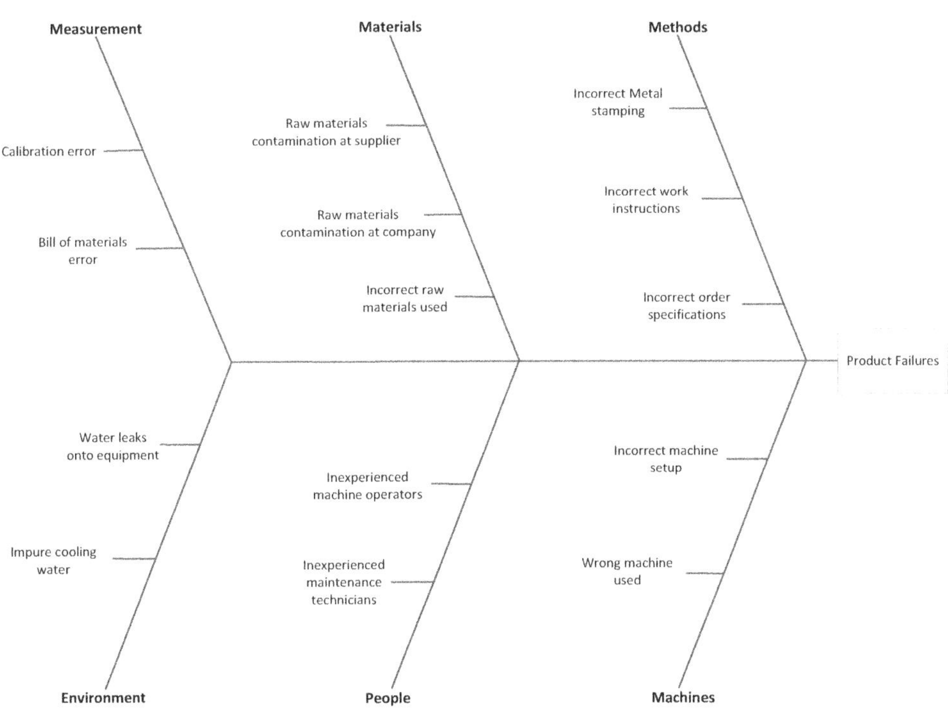


## Control Charts

A control chart is a statistical control used to analyze process variables and monitor their effects on performance. A control chart states upper and lower control limits, which are used to detect a trend of plotted values. If the plotted data points are all within the control limits, then a process is considered to be in control. If some data points fall outside of the control limits, then the process is considered to be out of control. The upper and lower control limits are set at the highest and lowest (respectively) values that would be impacted by common causes of variation. A visual examination of a control chart reveals whether defects are occurring randomly or systematically; in the latter case, corrective action is required.

**EXAMPLE**

The Christmas Candy Cane Factory manufactures candy canes. A problem has been detected in the production line, for which a project team is created to find a solution. The team finds that the normal processing time to combine white and red batches of candy, twist and stretch the batch, clip off individual candy canes and bend them into an arc is 10 minutes. There are modest variations in this time period that are caused by operator expertise. A sample control chart for the process follows.

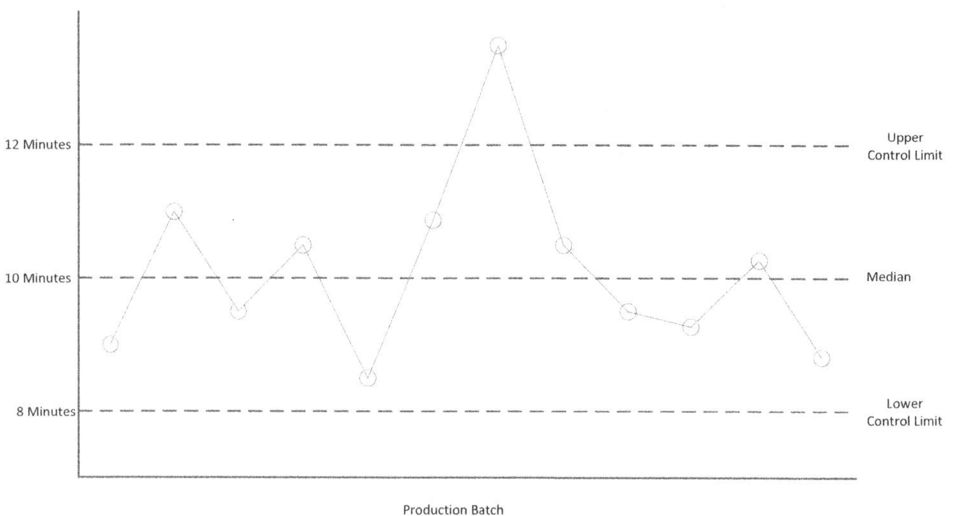


In the chart, there is one massive spike in the data. This was caused by an incorrect batch formulation that softened the candy cane batch, requiring extra processing time to let the batch cure. If management wants to act on this variation, it can set up a procedure in the batch formulation process to ensure that the correct ingredients are used.

---

A common finding when control charts are used is trend patterns, where one can see that a series of measurements are pointing toward an out-of-condition event. These trends point toward looming mechanical problems, such as a machine beginning to wear out or which is in need of adjustment. The following control chart shows such a trend, where the pattern is clearly visible well before a measurement actually breaches the upper control limit.

## Sample Control Chart with Trending Data

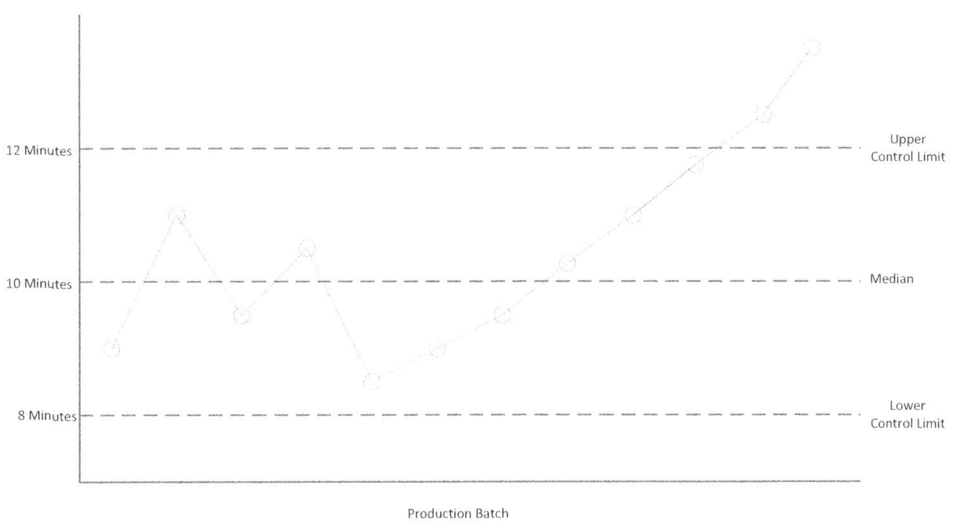


## Pareto Analysis

Pareto analysis is a method of analysis based on the concept that 20% of the variables included in an analysis are responsible for 80% of the results. For example, 20% of all customers are responsible for 80% of all customer service activity, or 20% of all inventory items comprise 80% of the inventory value. Pareto analysis is used to concentrate management attention on those issues having the greatest impact on an organization. It is also called the 80/20 rule.

Pareto charts are bar graphs in which the longest bars are positioned on the left and the shortest to the right. This arrangement tells the viewer which situations depicted by the bars are the most significant. The chart may also contain a cumulative total, which appears as an ascending line across the top of the chart. The vertical axis represents the frequency of occurrence, while the horizontal axis identifies the different types of events being tracked by the bars.

A Pareto chart is used when examining the frequency of problems. It is especially useful when there are many problems to sort through, since it draws attention to the most frequently-occurring issues. For the same reason, it is an excellent mode of communication.

In the following sample Pareto chart, a company is trying to determine the frequency of different types of customer complaints, using as a database the customer complaints received in the past month. The chart begins with the most common issue (broken packaging), and then proceeds through a series of additional complaints that are of declining importance to customers. If a project team wanted to eliminate those issues causing nearly all customer complaints, it should focus its attention on just the first two items (broken packaging and incorrect order fulfillment), since the remaining problems represent a minimal proportion of the total number of customer concerns.

**Sample Pareto Chart**

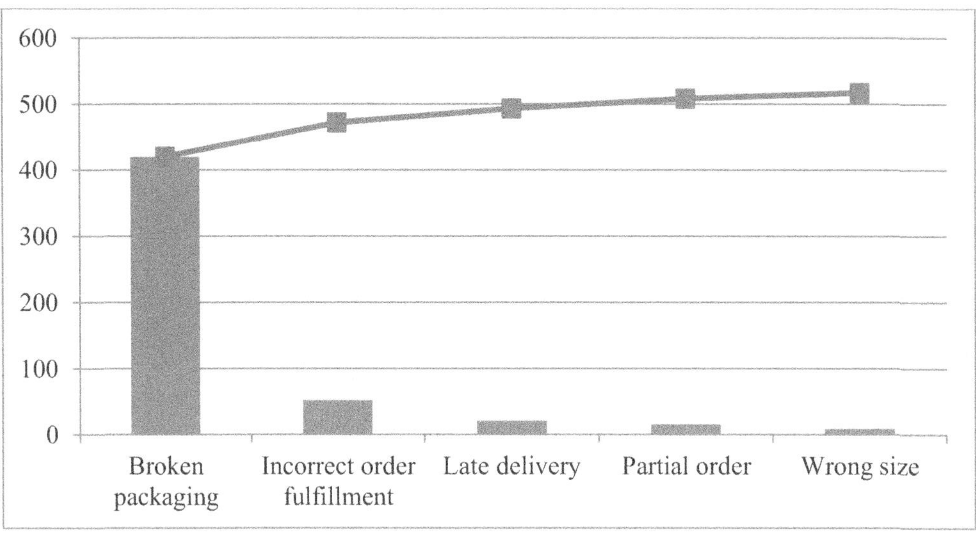


## Root Cause Analysis

Root cause analysis is used to identify the root cause of a problem by asking the question "why" multiple times. This approach is useful for peeling away the layers of symptoms to arrive at the root cause of a problem. By correcting the underlying root causes of problems, the incidence of the problems can be greatly reduced or eliminated. This approach can be used to uncover issues related to the failure of a system, an error by a person, or an organizational issue (such as an incorrect work instruction). The basic process steps to follow in a root cause analysis are as follows:

1. *Define the problem.* State the issue that requires correction, including a specification of the nature, magnitude, timing, and location of events. A high degree of specificity makes it easier to find a root cause.
2. *Obtain evidence.* Collect data pertaining to the problem. The information obtained should relate to every behavior, condition, action, or inaction relating to the problem.
3. *Ask why.* In going through the collected data, inquire into the factors that directly resulted in an effect. This may involve drilling down through a series of "why" questions.
4. *Eliminate causal factors.* A causal factor is an action or inaction that caused an incident or exacerbated an incident. These are simply triggering events and not root causes, and so no action is taken. For example, an employee turns on a laptop computer, which then explodes. Turning on the laptop was not the root cause, but rather something within the device. In short, we must sort

through the data and eliminate causal factors, which leave root causes in the data.

5. *Identify corrective actions.* Note those actions that will likely prevent a recurrence of the defined problem.
6. *Identify usable actions.* From the initial set of corrective actions, identify those that are within the control of the business, are cost-effective, and will probably not introduce a new set of problems. When there are several possible actions that meet these criteria, pick the simplest one, since it is easier to implement and maintain.
7. *Implement usable actions.* Obtain the required resources and implement those actions considered usable.
8. *Examine outcome.* Review the process to see if the changes are having a positive impact on the identified problem.
9. *Repeat.* If the problem has not been entirely corrected or at least reduced below a threshold level, repeat the process to identify and implement other usable actions.

It is quite possible that finding and correcting a single root cause will not completely eliminate a particular problem. If so, root cause analysis can be conducted on a recurring basis, to gradually locate and eliminate a series of issues. Eventually, the number of times the triggering problem arises may decline to the point where additional effort is considered unnecessary, though there may be additional root causes still causing problems; the remaining issues are simply considered too immaterial to pursue, or their correction is not cost-effective.

Root cause analysis may require a considerable amount of detailed investigation, not only to find a root cause, but also to generate several possible solutions that will correct the root cause. The solution selected will usually be the simplest or least expensive alternative available, and one that does not trigger a new root cause that leads to a new problem or reinforces an old problem.

Root cause analysis suffers from several problems. A key concern is that project teams tend to find problems that they already suspect. Thus, they tend to select and interpret data that supports their existing opinions, which means that new and unique root causes may not be found. Also, this type of analysis does not identify the severity of a root cause, only the existence of the root cause. When there are several possible root causes, this means that management may choose to spend time and resources eliminating an issue that may prove to have a relatively minor impact on a problem. Finally, root cause analysis can be quite time-consuming, since it may involve a large amount of data gathering and investigatory work.

## XY Charts

The XY chart, which is also known as a scatter graph, is a graph of plotted points that can be used to show the relationship between two sets of data. This can be a useful tool for conducting a visual search for causation. For example, the number of calls made to customers by the collection staff can be plotted against the amount of overdue receivable collections to see if these two data sets are positively correlated. An example appears in the following exhibit, showing a very high degree of correlation between the number of collection calls made and the number of payments received from customers.

**XY Chart**

## Operations Improvement Considerations

When using any operations improvement tool, one should consider in advance their impact on various issues, to see if it makes sense to employ them. In the following bullet points, we note several relevant issues:

- *Impact on customers*. An improvement should either be invisible to customers or improve how the company deals with them. When an improvement is going to harm any one of the company's performance objectives relating to customers, then it should not be installed. For example, if a prospective change will increase the amount of time required to deliver goods to customers, it should not be installed. However, this rule comes with a caveat, which is that the current performance levels with customers may be so expensive that the company must cut back in order to avoid losses. For example, a business may have built up inordinately large reserves of finished goods inventory in order to fulfill all customer orders within one day of order receipt. When it becomes apparent that the associated working capital investment is killing the company's finances, then it makes sense to draw down the inventory and accept a longer customer order fulfillment period.

- *Process simplification.* Whenever possible, it is better to use operations improvements to simplify a process, rather than making it more complex. Doing so reduces the amount of employee training time and also reduces the variability of the outcomes generated by the process.
- *Process variability.* The errors generated by a process can require a significant amount of time to correct, and also can damage relations with customers (if the processes are customer-facing). Therefore, any operations improvement targeted at reducing process variability can be considered a useful improvement.
- *Inventory reduction.* It is generally better to reduce inventory levels within a business. Inventory tends to act as a buffer to smooth over process irregularities, so by reducing inventory levels, these irregularities can be exposed and corrected. The main exception to inventory reduction is the inventory buffer positioned in front of the bottleneck operation, to ensure that it is operating at all times.

## Management of the Operations Improvement Process

An effective improvement process requires a well-defined and clearly articulated vision of what the company wants to achieve, which is well-organized and thoroughly implemented. To arrive at this high level of managerial competence, a business needs to attend to the following issues:

- *Gain senior management support.* Operations improvement always starts with the senior management team. They must have a firm understanding of how it relates to the overall corporate strategy, communicate the need for it to the entire organization, and actively participate in the improvement process. It is especially important to tie improvement projects back to the corporate strategy, so that resources are being applied in areas that will advance the interests of the company as a whole.
- *Integrate into the culture.* The process of continually improving operations has to be deliberately built into the culture of a business. When every employee understands that ongoing improvement is simply part of the way in which the company does business, they will be more likely to initiate and support change initiatives.
- *Avoid consulting hype.* Consulting firms like to develop their own systems for operations improvement and then peddle them (for high prices) to anyone willing to listen. It is critical to sort through these possibilities to determine which ones make sense for the company, and ignore everything else. Otherwise, the company will be in danger of continually hopping around among the latest improvement trends, without committing to anything over the long term. Also, jumping among fads tends to sour employees on the whole concept of operations improvement, since they are continually being pulled in different directions.

- *Copy others*. Many of the best ideas for operations improvement come from other businesses, both within and outside of the industry. The greatest positive impact from copying others is when an idea is being introduced into the industry for the first time, since the early implementors gain an immediate advantage over the competition. A later implementation has a reduced advantage, since it merely brings the company up to the level of other competitors who have already installed a best practice. One of the most common ways to copy the ideas of others is through *benchmarking*, which involves comparing the policies, procedures, products and processes of a business to those of other firms.

## Summary

Generally, the ongoing implementation of incremental improvements is easier on a company than the more radical overhaul advocated under the concepts of business process improvement, which means that improvement cycles and Six Sigma are more viable long-term approaches to operations improvement. Process reengineering is more likely to be used when a company is in dire straits, either because its competitive position is failing or because its financial results are in a state of rapid decline; in this case, reengineering might be the only way to keep the business afloat.

# Chapter 16
# Quality Management

## Introduction

A key sales advantage for any company is to provide products to their customers with a noticeably higher level of quality than those offered by competitors, especially if this difference can yield a higher price. In addition, by installing the systems needed to assure higher quality, a company will find that it is actually *less* expensive to do business, since a number of administrative, warranty, and rework costs are reduced. This chapter explores the types of quality, the costs of quality, quality reporting, and how to improve quality.

## Types of Quality

What is product quality? A customer perceives a product as having a high level of quality if it conforms to his or her expectations. Thus, high quality is really just making sure that a product does what a customer expects it to do.

---

**EXAMPLE**

Rapunzel Hair Products has designed a comb made of titanium, and markets it as a light weight product for the frequent traveler. Not only is the comb made of titanium, but it is also stamped with the world-famous RHR logo, and has a special low-friction coating that keeps hair tangles from being trapped in the comb. It sells for $20, and costs $16 to manufacture. The margin is unacceptably low, so the product manager is searching for ways to reduce the cost.

He surveys comb owners, and finds that their perception of quality is not that the comb is made of titanium, but simply that it is light weight. After some research, the product manager finds that titanium is twice as strong as aluminum, but is 60% heavier than that metal. Product testing reveals that aluminum is sufficiently strong to prevent bending. Aluminum is also ten times less expensive than titanium.

Consequently, Rapunzel changes the composition of the comb to an all-aluminum version that it can produce (with some extra heat tempering steps) for just $4. Since the weight of the product has declined, customers perceive the comb to have a higher quality level than the titanium version.

---

Based on this definition, quality is *not* having the highest possible standards for creating the ultimate product. Thus, if management insists on creating a mahogany interior for a car's glove box when the customer only wants it to be big enough to store documents, then it has just gone to considerable expense to create something that a customer does not define as being of high quality. Conversely, if the customer expects a car's steering wheel to be heated and it is not, then there is an adverse gap between customer expectations and what is being provided – which is an opportunity for improvement.

This view of quality means that a company can eliminate any costs that customers have no quality perceptions about. The cost reduction can impact a great many areas. For example, it may be perfectly acceptable to use lower-quality or thinner materials, or to allow blemishes in areas where customers cannot see them, or to allow production at a lower tolerance level than is currently the case (which eliminates some rework costs).

There are two types of quality that a company should be concerned about, one of which originates in the engineering department, while the other is the responsibility of the entire organization. They are:

- *Quality of design.* This is the ability of a company to design a product that conforms to the quality expectations of a customer. In other words, the quality that customers expect is designed into the product. This type of quality requires a considerable amount of interpretation of what engineers think customers want, and how these wishes are integrated into the final product design. If quality is not designed into the basic structure of a product, there is no way to improve the quality situation later, short of replacing the product with a new version.
- *Quality of conformance.* This is the ability of a company to produce a product that conforms to the original product design. This type of quality is not just the responsibility of the production department; the procurement staff has to acquire the correct materials, the shipping department must deliver it without damage, and the marketing department must communicate the attributes of the product that matter most to customers.

---

**EXAMPLE**

Rapunzel Hair Products wants to create a hair straightener for women who travel frequently. A survey of such travelers reveals that their views of quality for such a product encompass light weight, the ability to operate at different voltages, a variable temperature setting, and a power cord that will not break or pull away from the unit.

Of these four quality issues, three are entirely design issues – the engineering staff must design for low weight, a variable voltage capability, and a variable temperature setting. Only one of the quality issues is entirely a quality of conformance issue, which is the power cord. The purchasing department must obtain a sufficiently robust power cord to ensure that it will not break.

The quality of conformance does have a secondary role in ensuring the quality of this product, however. The procurement staff must be sure to acquire power transformers and temperature rheostats that will continue to work properly for a long period of rough handling.

---

## Costs Impacted by Quality

There are several types of costs that are impacted by the quality of a product. They are:

- *Prevention costs*. These are costs incurred to avoid product failures. These costs include production procedure development, staff training, product testing, preventive maintenance on the machinery used to create products, and supplier qualification assessments.
- *Appraisal costs*. These are the costs of inspection needed to reduce the risk of sending defective products to customers. These costs include supplier component testing, quality control product testing, process analysis, and the cost of any testing equipment.
- *Internal failure costs*. These are the costs associated with defective products that are uncovered prior to delivery to customers. These costs include rework of the defective products, additional testing of the reworked products, scrap, purchasing replacement parts, and the lost profit on products that must be sold as seconds.
- *External failure costs*. These are the costs associated with defective products that are uncovered subsequent to delivery to customers. These costs include lost revenue from customers who will not buy from the company again, the processing of returned goods, administering warranty claims, field service costs, liability lawsuits, and possibly even a comprehensive product recall.

It is more cost-effective to pay for cost improvements in-house, rather than waiting for customers to discover defects. The primary reason is that customers are much less likely to buy from the company again if they discover defects, which can make external failure costs more expensive than all of the other costs combined.

Modern accounting systems are not designed to compile information about the cost of quality, and so managers have no idea how serious the problem can be. Studies of the cost of quality have generated wildly varying amounts, ranging from five percent of sales all the way up to 30 percent of sales. No matter where the actual amount may lie within this range, the potential cost savings are enormous – among the highest that can be achieved from any management initiative.

## Quality Management Techniques

A business can employ a number of techniques to manage the quality levels being experienced by its customers in a cost-effective manner. Consider the following options:

Customer-focused Changes

- *Alter advertising.* Customers may be expecting a certain level of quality because that is what the company is communicating in its advertising. If the advertising does not reflect the reality of the product or service being provided, then tone down the advertising. Doing so reduces customer expectations to what they will really experience.
- *Provide a service guarantee.* Offer to pay customers for substandard service. Doing so is useful for overcoming any customer doubts about the company, which is especially important when dealing with new customers. It is also a useful way to gain insights into service problems, since the company is essentially paying its customers to report them.

Cost-focused Changes

- *Inspect before the bottleneck.* The bottleneck production operation controls the amount of profit that a business can generate, so it makes sense to weed out any inferior products before they enter it. By doing so, no bottleneck time is wasted on products that will not be sellable.
- *Inspect before high-cost processing.* A good cost-reduction measure is to inspect work-in-process before it enters a processing step that has a high added cost component. By doing so, inferior products are removed from processing before the company invests even more money in them.
- *Inspect on a sample basis.* Inspecting goods on a sample basis is usually a sufficient indicator of product quality, as long as the number of units sampled is statistically significant. The company is using sampling to decide whether a process is operating as it should be; if the measured output is too variable, then the underlying process needs to be examined in more detail.

## Reporting on the Cost of Quality

It is cost-prohibitive to create a cost of quality tracking system that is absolutely comprehensive. Such a system would require a massive amount of data collection, and may very well offset any benefits to be gained from the system. Instead, eliminate any costs that are inordinately difficult to measure, assess what the resources are for measuring the remaining costs, and finally discuss with management which specific types of quality-related costs they wish to monitor. The result will likely be a cost collection system that varies over time, redirecting its focus to different costs as management gradually tackles and improves upon each one.

One way to aggregate cost of quality information is to create new accounts for them in the chart of accounts. However, it may be difficult for the accounting staff to discern which costs to assign to these accounts, so in many cases it may make more sense to track the costs on a project basis only; by doing so, one can undertake a small collection effort and store the information in an electronic spreadsheet. Afterwards, if the results of the project indicate that there can be long-term cost reductions to be gained from continual cost collection efforts, it may be worth investigating the use of general ledger accounts in which to store this information.

Once the cost of quality information has been collected, format it into a report structure that presents the maximum amount of actionable information to management. The following example uses a format that aggregates costs into the four types of quality costs already described – prevention, appraisal, internal failure, and external failure. This format not only shows management where most of its quality costs lie (clearly in the external failure cost area), but also the sub-categories of expenses from which these costs are originating. This report format tells management roughly where to look if it wants to reduce its cost of quality.

---

**EXAMPLE**

The president of Rapunzel Hair Products commissions a cost of quality analysis to determine where the company incurred the bulk of its quality-related costs over the past three-month period. Her intent is to use the results of this study to focus more closely on reducing costs in the areas where most costs are incurred. The results are noted in the following table.

| Cost Type / Cost Line Item | Cost Line Item Results | Summary Totals |
|---|---|---|
| **Prevention Cost Category** | | |
| Production procedure development | $6,500 | |
| Staff training | 5,000 | |
| Product testing | 2,000 | |
| Preventive maintenance | 12,000 | |
| Supplier qualification assessments | 19,000 | |
| | | $44,500 |
| | | |
| **Appraisal Cost Category** | | |
| Supplier component testing | $4,200 | |
| Quality control product testing | 5,000 | |
| Process analysis | 7,100 | |
| Testing equipment | 3,000 | |
| | | $19,300 |
| | | |
| **Internal Failure Cost Category** | | |
| Rework of defective products | $23,000 | |
| Testing of reworked products | 3,800 | |
| Purchasing replacement parts | 1,900 | |
| Lost profit on products sold as seconds | 25,000 | |
| | | $53,700 |
| | | |
| **External Failure Cost Category** | | |
| Processing of returned goods | $61,000 | |
| Administering warranty claims | 23,000 | |
| Field service costs | 5,900 | |
| | | $89,900 |
| Total | | $207,400 |

The report reveals that internal and external failure costs comprise 69% of the company's $207,400 total cost of quality, with the processing of returned goods being by far the largest cost incurred.

---

This report can also be converted into a percentage of sales format, which is useful if sales are varying a great deal over the reporting timeline. The cost of quality varies with sales volume, so if sales are fluctuating, only a percentage of sales format will show if a cost of quality reduction campaign is really working.

The preceding cost of quality report tells management what types of general quality costs a company is incurring, but it does nothing to inform them about where specific quality problems are arising. Locating such information requires detailed investigative work. It may be necessary to conduct a separate root cause analysis for each problem encountered, such as the one in the following example. This report tells management what is causing a quality cost and the proportion of total incidents. They use this report to take immediate action steps. Thus, the report in the preceding example is needed to give them a general view of where quality costs occur, and the root cause analysis to create a cost reduction action.

---

**EXAMPLE**

The president of Rapunzel Hair Products reviews the cost of quality report and decides that the rework of defective products (which costs $23,000) is the most troubling. She asks an operations analyst to delve further into this specific area, and create a root cause analysis report.

He investigates the situation, targeting the reasons why products become defective. He finds that there is roughly a 50/50 split between problems arising from purchased goods and from goods manufactured in Rapunzel's own facilities. From this analysis, he investigates further and then generates the following report:

| Proportion of Incidents | Root Cause | Recommendation |
|---|---|---|
| **Purchased Goods Issues** | | |
| 39% | Performance specifications were incorrect | Tighten the tolerances on purchased product specifications (may result in cost increase) |
| 32% | Damaged in Rapunzel warehouse | Change putaway and picking procedures. Also require suppliers to ship in more robust packaging |
| 18% | Supplier quality too low | Institute supplier certification system and prepare to change suppliers |
| 11% | Other issues not investigated | |
| 100% | | |
| **Manufactured Goods Issues** | | |
| 41% | Inferior quality raw materials | Purchase higher grade resin (may result in cost increase) |
| 29% | Scratches incurred during internal moves | Replace move containers with padded versions |
| 13% | Machine tolerances incorrect | Revise machine setup procedures |
| 17% | Other issues not investigated | |
| 100% | | |

The report indicates that there will be a cost associated with several of the proposed fixes, which will require a management decision. Another major cause of problems is the packaging and handling of products, which will likely require further analysis to determine precise causes.

---

The preceding report gives management detailed information that it can act on, or which at least takes it well down the path of finding the root cause of a quality problem.

## Summary

The cost of quality is spread throughout a company – there are related costs everywhere, including administration, engineering, production, and customer service. Since the cost of quality is so pervasive, it is clearly an excellent source of potential profits. If management can improve product and service quality, then related costs decline throughout the organization.

Given the massive potential impact on profits, one should be well aware of the types of quality-related costs, make an attempt at constructing at least a rudimentary cost of quality data collection and reporting system, and make periodic efforts to educate management about how quality impacts profits. If management takes action, an organization could experience a significant profit boost.

# Chapter 17
# Risk Management

## Introduction

Risk equates to uncertainty regarding a future outcome. The operations area of a business is filled with uncertainty, for there are few situations in which the outcome can be predicted with complete reliability. For example, a business requires a key commodity as a raw material in the construction of a product – can it predict exactly what the price of this commodity will be in one year? Or, it will cost $250 million to develop a new drug and have it approved – but how certain is the approval? In these cases, it is impossible to predict the exact outcome.

Uncertainty is pervasive, and yet managers routinely ignore the concept of variable outcomes. Instead, they use budgets to derive a single view of the future, and are then perturbed when they cannot force their organizations to deliver results that precisely match the outcome predicted in the budget. This is because there may be thousands of uncertain events that all impact the financial results of a business. Despite management's best efforts, it is nearly impossible to deliver actual results that match the original budgeted prediction.

A better way to see the impact of risk is to view an organization as a portfolio of risks, each of which is derived from any number of management decisions made in the past. Some decisions, such as expanding an existing product line, are more likely to result in modest profits or losses. Other decisions, such as the funding of a portable fusion reactor product, could be spectacularly successful or drive a firm into bankruptcy. Some may produce offsetting gains and losses, resulting in modest net changes. One should be cognizant of the more crucial of these risks, sometimes to take advantage of them and at other times to reduce them.

In this chapter, we describe the concept of risk management, the risk management process, and contingency planning.

## Benefits of Risk Management

There are a number of reasons why an organization should manage its risks. The central issues are the ability to smooth out earnings or to enhance earnings.

Risk management can be used to mitigate the occurrence of unusual expenses, so that the actual expenses incurred are much closer to budgeted expectations. A benefit of this is that reliable earnings attract lenders, so that a business is more likely to be offered reasonable interest rates and longer-term lending arrangements. Lower interest rates reduce the cost of a firm's capital, so that it can invest in more projects that have lower projected returns. Having longer-term debt arrangements means that it can more easily weather market crises, since it does not have to constantly roll over its debt into new loans.

One can enhance earnings by actively identifying opportunities that are risky, but which also generate high returns. For example, an organization might choose to start doing business in a country where profits could be substantial, but where there is also a risk of a currency devaluation. Taking this approach can result in higher profits, but those profits are also likely to be more variable – very high in some periods, but with notable losses in others. This use of risk management works well when the management team is willing to aggressively pursue profits.

The most likely scenario in a well-managed business is that management takes advantage of both types of risk management. They are well aware of the risks to which the business is subjected, and take steps to mitigate risks in certain areas while accepting the risk associated with selected business opportunities.

The amount of risk taken on by a business depends on the comfort level of the management team. Some may prefer a highly stable environment from which the probability of risk has largely been reduced, while others are more comfortable taking large chances throughout the organization in order to pursue the possibility of maximizing profits.

## The Interrelationship between Risk and Strategy

The two preceding benefits of risk management can be incorporated into an entity's strategic planning. When the management team considers the strategic direction of a business, a major part of the analysis should center on the risks that are linked to each possible strategic alternative, and how to handle those risks. Since there may be a number of strategic alternatives with many risks attached to each one, the planners will need to focus on just the most critical risks associated with each strategy, and develop the following information:

- The likelihood of occurrence
- The cost per occurrence
- Mitigation alternatives

Ideally, each proposed strategy should outline key risks, how risks are to be mitigated or off-loaded, *or* the cost of retaining the risks. The senior management team can then review this risk summary as part of its analysis of strategic alternatives.

**Tip:** When evaluating the risks associated with strategic alternatives, consider any circumstances that could amplify the likelihood or cost of risks. If the amplified risk turns out to have a massive loss potential, this could influence the decision to avoid a strategic direction.

## Risk Retention Strategy

Not all risks can be successfully mitigated. Some types of risk can be expensive to guard against, perhaps with relatively expensive hedging contracts. Consequently, there should be some level of risk that it is more economical over the long-term for a business to retain.

The amount of risk that a business is willing to retain is strongly influenced by its financial position. For example, a company with significant market share, profitability, and cash reserves can easily withstand the financial losses associated with risk. Conversely, a company that is highly leveraged and which uses much of its cash to pay off loan principal can afford to retain very little risk.

This ability to retain risk can have a profound impact on the overall strategy of a business. In essence, a financially stable entity is in a much better position to dabble in new lines of business that offer major upside potential, but which also run the risk of significant losses.

---

**EXAMPLE**

The management team of the thermometer manufacturer Kelvin Corporation has just completed a leveraged buyout of the founder, which involves taking on $10 million of high-cost debt that must be paid off within the next five years. For this period, the sole focus of the management team is on paying off the debt. The company cannot afford to risk any funds on new product development.

At the same time, Celsius Corporation has just raised money through a major new stock offering, and is risking $5 million on the development of a new lineup of remote temperature sensors that use the theory of quantum entanglement to track temperature readings from thousands of miles away. There is a significant risk that the development project will fail, but the upside potential is complete patent protection in a large new market.

Given the financial circumstances of the two companies, Kelvin cannot afford to take on any risk, while the management of Celsius has so much money that it can take on highly risky projects.

---

## Risk Analysis as an Opportunity

The analysis of potential risk to which a business is subjected should not be a casual affair, but rather a studied one. This means keeping a running list of problems that other companies have encountered within the industry and in adjacent industries, and reviewing the list at regular intervals to see if events have made any risks more or less likely.

The identification of risks may present opportunities; a company could launch initiatives in new areas that competitors might consider excessively risky. This is particularly likely when a higher level of risk is accompanied by a greater chance of reward.

---

**EXAMPLE**

There is a general dearth of storefronts near a certain section of coastline, since it has been hit by three hurricanes in the past ten years. A real estate company is fully aware of the hurricane risk, and develops a new building design that mitigates the risk of storm damage by elevating the first floor of the building, leaving room for storm waters to flow under the building. The company successfully builds and operates these structures, which survive several additional hurricanes with minimal damage. In this case, the company is fully aware of the risks, and chooses to proceed in a manner that mitigates them.

**EXAMPLE**

A CPA firm has just been devastated by a major tornado that wiped out a large part of the city in which it is located. It could take the prudent path of following the other CPA firms out of town, to relocate to a safer city. Instead, the partners decide to construct a robust safe room for the employees that will also contain client files, and markets this upgrade as a document storage facility for clients. The result is a major boost in business, especially since most of the other CPA firms have fled the city.

---

A reverse way of looking at risk-related opportunities is to evaluate when to exit an excessively staid business. A low-risk environment tends to also generate low returns, so it can make sense to see if any product lines or customers that have a combination of low risk and low reward should be eliminated.

---

**EXAMPLE**

Gulf Coast Insurance is evaluating its hurricane insurance to see if there are any opportunities to improve its overall rate of return. An examination by geographic region discovers that the Tallahassee area has not borne the brunt of a hurricane for some time, which has resulted in a gradual decline in the insurance rates that can be competitively set in this area. Management concludes that the margins are too low in this region, so it elects not to renew policies in this area, and instead focuses its sales force on other areas where the claim risk is higher, but where prices are also higher.

---

## Types of Risk

Any company is subject to a large number of risks. To better understand them, it is useful to classify them into different categories. By doing so, one can adopt category-specific tactics to mitigate or transfer risk. Common risk categories are:

*Business risk* – The organization does not generate sufficient financial results to satisfy its owners. For example:

- A business reports unusually low earnings per share, resulting in the sale of its shares by many investors, which lowers the share price substantially.
- A retailer reports a decline in same-store sales, after which investors vote for a change in the board of directors, which in turn fires the entire management team.

*Compliance risk* – The organization violates the law, and incurs penalties as a result. For example:

- An airline suffers from several plane crashes. A government probe finds that the airline was skimping on its maintenance procedures, and forcibly shuts down the business.
- An oil drilling company suffers a major underwater drilling failure, resulting in a million-barrel oil spill into the ocean. The affected government immediately sues the company for several billion dollars.

*Credit risk* – The organization's customers, suppliers, or counterparties to other transactions do not meet their obligations to the business. For example:

- A major customer goes bankrupt, leaving the seller with a massive bad debt that likely cannot be recovered.
- A supplier takes a large advance payment for a custom order and then goes bankrupt, leaving the buyer with little prospect for a recovery.
- A supplier is only able to ship part of an order to the buyer, because it does not have sufficient cash to buy the raw materials needed to complete the order, resulting in disruptions in the buyer's operations.

*Liquidity risk* – The organization does not have sufficient cash to meet its obligations. For example:

- A company grows so fast that its working capital requirements soak up all available cash. As a result, the business cannot pay its employees, so a competitor scoops up the firm during bankruptcy proceedings.
- The credit market unexpectedly tightens, so that a company cannot renew its line of credit or find an alternative lender.
- A company's credit rating is unexpectedly downgraded, making it much more difficult to sell bonds to investors.

*Market risk* – The market prices of goods and services, loans and investments, and other financial instruments that an organization depends on move in an unfavorable direction. For example:

- A company takes on a large amount of short-term debt in order to fund a production line expansion. Interest rates then increase, and the company finds that its new venture does not return enough cash to pay the higher interest rate.
- A company buys expensive equipment from a foreign supplier. By the time the invoice is due for payment, the relevant foreign exchange rate has moved sharply in an unfavorable direction, resulting in a much larger amount for the company to pay.
- A business buys petroleum products in bulk and converts them into plastic goods. Its input prices can vary substantially, while it is constrained from passing price increases through to its customers.

*Operating risk* – The organization suffers losses from failures by its employees, processes, or systems. Acts of nature fall into this category. For example:

- A treasury employee manages to transfer several million dollars of company money to his private account in Grand Cayman.
- Flooding in Thailand destroys a factory that a business was depending on for the electronic components used in its products.
- A bank's computer system crashes, wiping out the records of its depositors and borrowers.

The most dangerous type of risk is *strategic risk*, which interferes with a company's business model. A strategic risk undermines the value proposition which attracts customers and generates profits. For example, if a company's business model is to be the low-cost provider of a product and a competitor from a low-wage country suddenly enters the market, the company will find that its value proposition has been destroyed. Examples of strategic risk scenarios are:

- A new product fails catastrophically
- A major acquisition fails
- A customer gains massive market share and then has an inordinate ability to set prices
- A supplier gains monopoly control over supplies and raises raw material prices
- A key product goes off patent
- There is a sudden shift in technology that makes the company's products obsolete
- The contamination of company products with a hazardous substance leads to brand erosion

- The government changes its tax policy, which eliminates a key pricing advantage built into a firm's business model
- A trade agreement reduces barriers to entry, resulting in a flood of new competitors into the market
- Company assets are nationalized
- Terrorist attacks reduce sales or destroy property

The types of risks to which a business is subjected will vary considerably by company, since risk is based on such factors as geography, industry, product type, and employee relations. Thus, the risk mix is unique to every business. For example, a mining company is subject to the risk of a local shutdown by people who object to local pollution issues, while a business in the apparel industry may face a customer revolt over the working conditions of employees at its foreign clothing factories.

Now that we have a general knowledge of the types of risks to which a business is subjected, we will review the process needed to manage those risks.

## The Risk Management Process Flow

There should be a consistent process for identifying, quantifying, and dealing with risk. A more scattershot approach is likely to result in significant risks never being addressed. The general flow to follow is:

1. *Identify risks*. This can involve employee surveys or questionnaires, and/or the use of consultants who have a deep knowledge of the industry. If the management team has many years of experience in the industry, it might limit itself to using internal meetings to derive risks, without polling employees outside of this group. It is useful to view an organization from many perspectives to extract all possible risks. For example:

    - *Internal capacity*. Are the various functional areas of the company able to handle increased sales or other types of transactions? For example, what would happen to the accounting department's ability to operate if management were to engage in a minimum of three acquisitions per year?
    - *Inherent internal risks*. Are there risks that "come with the territory" in certain departments; these risks cannot be sidestepped or mitigated. For example, there is a high risk of losing IT personnel, due to shortages in the market for their skills.
    - *Impact of supply chain*. What would be the impact on the business if a major supplier or the supplier of a strategic part were unable to make deliveries? For example, a supplier might be purchased by a competitor, which intends to reserve all of the supplier's output for itself.
    - *Impact of customers*. Is the business able to support additional customers? For example, how would the organization deal with the demands of a large retail chain? There may not be sufficient customer

service personnel, and returns may increase by several orders of magnitude.

- *Future trends.* Are there discernible trends that can alter risks? For example, will the increased amount of social media usage increase the number of poor on-line reviews for a business?
- *Historical risks.* Comb through the industry records to see if certain risks have appeared, even if only a few times or just once. The circumstances may change enough for these issues to appear again, though perhaps in a modified form.
- *Competitor risks.* Are competitors noting any unusual risks in their financial reports or investor communications? If so, these risks may soon trouble a company's own operations.

These risks can be summarized into a risk profile, which is described later in the Risk Profile sub-section.

2. *Rank risks.* There may be hundreds of possible risks that could impact an organization, so they must be prioritized to focus attention on the key items. This is typically based on their frequency and severity, which can be plotted on a grid that uses frequency and severity as the axes. Severity can be measured by conducting a what-if analysis that reveals the full impact of a risk event on a business. The outcome should show the extent of losses and any reduction of cash reserves.
3. *Mitigate risks.* There are a variety of internal actions that can be taken to mitigate risk, such as moving a factory away from a flood plain or selling off a subsidiary that might otherwise be nationalized. Or, if there is a risk of product failure in the marketplace, consider developing two products at the same time. As another example, the risk of expropriation can be dealt with by halting the investment in the at-risk country or even selling off facilities in that country.
4. *Accept risks.* The likely payout from a risk may be so small that the company can easily bear the risk of loss. Alternatively, the offsetting amount of profit may be so high that the company is willing to accept a substantial amount of risk. For example, there could be a potential for massive profits from a new technology, though the development process could fail.
5. *Transfer risk.* If management cannot mitigate a risk and is unwilling to accept it, the remaining option is to transfer it to another party, usually an insurer.
6. *Report on the status of risks.* The management team must know if risks are changing, especially in a more frequent or more severe direction. Accordingly, there should be a reporting system in place that focuses attention on key risk "movers," without bogging down the reporting with other risks whose status is unchanged.
7. *Repeat.* Repeat the process at regular intervals and especially when there are major changes in a business that might strip away existing risks or introduce new ones, such as entry into a new market or the launch of a new product line. The iterative nature of the risk management process flow cannot be

overemphasized, since an organization can learn from its actions in previous iterations to arrive at better risk management solutions in the future.

**Risk Rankings**

The ranking of risks can be difficult, for they cannot always be quantified. For example, the risk of a product recall can probably be quantified in terms of a range of product repair costs, but cannot be quantified in terms of the damage to the brand. The first figure could be reliably stated as falling somewhere between $800,000 and $1,000,000, but the cost of brand damage could extend for years and involve many lost customers who will no longer automatically turn to the company for replacement products. Consequently, an analysis of the frequency and severity of risks will require a significant amount of judgment, rather than hard numerical analysis. This hardly means that a ranking system should be ignored – judgment can be based on many years of experience, and may result in risk rankings that prove to be fairly accurate.

Given the difficulty of quantification, it can be difficult to assemble an exact ranking of which specific risks are more critical than others. Instead, it can make more sense to use a simple scale to measure a risk's frequency and severity, and concentrate attention on the cluster of risks that score the highest. We illustrate this concept in the following chart, which uses a zero-to-five scale to rate each risk.

Note in the sample table that there is a clear differentiation between three key risks (supplier damage, delivery disruptions, and bottleneck issues) and the remaining risk topics, which would certainly direct management's attention toward these items. At a lesser degree of risk, the chart shows a high frequency for commodity price swings, as well as high severity levels for hurricanes at one location and the risk of a pollution-related shutdown. The remaining risks are a combination of low severity and low frequency, and so would likely receive less management attention.

**Sample Risk Rankings Chart**

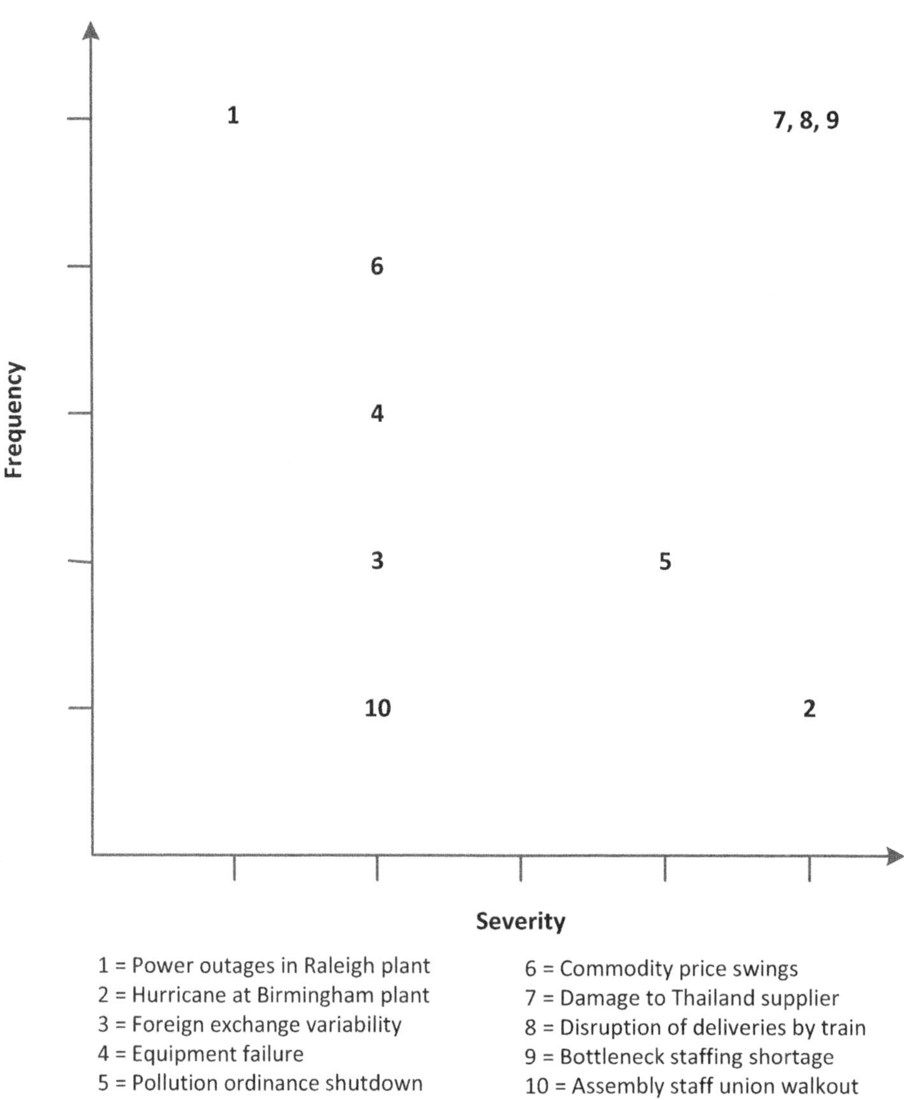


1 = Power outages in Raleigh plant
2 = Hurricane at Birmingham plant
3 = Foreign exchange variability
4 = Equipment failure
5 = Pollution ordinance shutdown
6 = Commodity price swings
7 = Damage to Thailand supplier
8 = Disruption of deliveries by train
9 = Bottleneck staffing shortage
10 = Assembly staff union walkout

The zero-to-five scale used in the sample chart can be clarified in greater detail, so that those people deriving scores for risks can set scores with a fair degree of reliability. For example, the following frequency scoring system sets ranges for each of the scores from zero to five.

### Frequency Scoring Guidelines

| Score | Description | Time Guideline |
|---|---|---|
| 5 | Frequent activity | Weekly |
| 4 | High activity | Quarterly |
| 3 | Normal activity | Annually |
| 2 | Modest activity | Every 2-3 years |
| 1 | Low activity | Every 5+ years |
| 0 | No activity | No historical activity whatsoever |

The same approach can be applied to the severity of a risk, as described in the following severity scoring system. In the sample scoring guidelines, the table notes multiple ways in which to set a zero-to-five score, since it is not always possible to define a risk based on a single set of criteria.

### Severity Scoring Guidelines

| Score | Description | Sales Reduction | Expense Increase | Order Fulfillment Rate in 24 Hours |
|---|---|---|---|---|
| 5 | Potentially business threatening | Sales terminated | 50% increase | 0% |
| 4 | Major disruption | 50% decline | 25% increase | 50% |
| 3 | Concerning to stakeholders | 20% decline | 10% increase | 75% |
| 2 | Material impact | 10% decline | 5% increase | 80% |
| 1 | Minor impact | 5% decline | 2% increase | 90% |
| 0 | No impact | < 1% decline | < 0.5% increase | 98% |

Note that in the preceding severity scoring guidelines table, the percentages listed for a sales reduction are higher than the percentages used for an expense increase. The reason for the difference is that the effects of a sales reduction are reduced by the cost of goods sold, which will not occur if there is no sale. This means that the severity scoring will vary, depending on the gross margin that a company earns. For example, a potential sales reduction of 10% may be considered to have a material impact if the contribution margin is high, since most of the sale passes through to profits. Conversely, a potential sales reduction of 10% might be considered to have a minor impact if the contribution margin is relatively low, since only a small part of each sale appears in profits.

## Risk Quantification Issues

Some risks initially appear so vague that it may not seem possible to assign any value to them at all. For example, what is the cost of the loss of a company's reputation? While certainly difficult, it may be possible to estimate these costs by examining what happened to other companies that experienced the same or similar problems in the past. Examples of risks that certainly pose quantification difficulties are:

- Losses from a customer boycott
- Reduced sales from a decline in the perception of a brand
- Difficulty in hiring high-grade employees because of a reputational issue

Other risks are considerably easier to quantify, since a specific action should result in a tightly-defined cost. For example, if a factory is located in a flood plain, flooding damage will be limited to the complete replacement of the factory, along with lost profits from sales that could not be fulfilled from that factory. Similarly, asset expropriation can be tightly defined; the assets located in the at-risk country will be taken.

The cost of some risks will fall midway between the two extremes just noted, and may encompass expenditures that a business has not been accustomed to dealing with in the past. For example, a company dealing with a loss in reputation may need to factor in the cost of a lobbyist, extra security personnel to protect company property, a community relations manager, payments to the local populace, an advertising campaign, a public relations advisor, incentive packages to retain or hire employees, and so forth.

Once risks have been quantified, there may be a temptation to multiply the expected cost range by the probability of occurrence, which results in an expected value. For example, if the probability of an event is 10% and the cost of an unfavorable outcome is $1 million, we multiply the cost by the probability to arrive at an expected value of $100,000. The trouble with the expected value concept is that it tends to hide the sheer size of some risks. For example, a risk may have a cost of $100 million but a probability of only ¼%, so anyone examining the expected value report would reasonably conclude that the risk is worth only $250,000. In reality, management should be made aware of the total projected cost of a risk, even if the risk is small, to see which risks are hefty enough to bring down a business. This means that both the probability and cost information for each risk should be disseminated.

## The Risk Profile

A risk profile is a categorization of the main risks that can impact an organization. A risk profile document is useful for focusing the attention of management on those risks that can cause significant turmoil for the entity, either in terms of financial losses or operational difficulties. The types of categories used can vary by organization. Here are a number of risk categories that might be used:

- *Brand.* Includes issues that can cause the perception of a company's brand to decline, such as a product recall, a marketing flop, bad publicity, negative product reviews, and public squabbles with business partners.
- *Catastrophic.* Primarily includes natural disasters, such as hurricanes, earthquakes, tornadoes, and floods.

- *Environmental*. Includes fines and remediation costs related to pollution, as well as damage to the environment.
- *Financial*. Includes the risks of customer nonpayment, foreign exchange rate variability, capital availability concerns, and employee fraud.
- *Human resources*. Includes the loss of key employees and the lack of properly directive leadership.
- *Industry risk*. Includes factors that can alter the competitive profile of the industry, such as changes in the entire size of the market that the industry serves, the rate at which the industry is consolidating, and the ability of new competitors to enter the market.
- *Information technology*. Includes factors that do not allow an organization to have responsive IT systems, such as being tied to legacy software and having a significant amount of systems downtime. Can also include system breaches that result in the loss of key data.
- *International*. Includes factors caused by doing business in other countries, such as employee kidnappings, terrorist attacks, asset expropriation, political unrest, and sanctions.
- *Legal and regulatory*. Includes new laws or regulatory requirements, such as changes in available tax credits and increased filing requirements for publicly held companies. Can also include internal legal issues, such as being unable to lock down trade secrets.
- *Operational*. Includes factors that impact the ability to produce a sufficient number of quality goods and services, such as inadequate peak capacity, low fulfillment rates, high scrap rates, and processes not being followed.
- *Strategic*. Includes risks arising from the decisions that management makes to follow certain strategic directions. Examples of these risks are bringing new products too late to market, being unable to secure key distribution channels, and selling a product mix that does not attract a sufficient number of customers.

The risk profile document can be combined with the preceding risk rankings chart to yield a good overview of the risks to which a business is subjected. This report can be used as the basis for risk management planning, budgeting, and presentations to the board of directors and the investment community.

## Risk Management Themes

There are several general themes that well-managed businesses usually follow, and which keep them from adopting risky behavior patterns. If the management team adheres to the following concepts, it is much less likely to experience major losses or participate in highly risky, high-return enterprises. These themes are:

- *Deep knowledge of the business*. Risky behavior is much less likely to arise when every employee of a business has a deep knowledge of his or her own responsibilities, and also how the organization as a whole operates. When there is a well-trained work force, many more people can spot anomalies that may lead to losses, and will also recognize the associated risks that accompany new business proposals. This level of detailed knowledge should cover absolutely everyone – from the board of directors down to production-line employees. This level of knowledge can only be obtained through the long-term training of all employees on all aspects of the business. It also requires basic business policies to promote employee retention, such as excellent benefits, a commitment to retain staff during business downturns, and promoting from within.

---

**EXAMPLE**

Creekside Industrial hires a hot new prospect into the purchasing department who comes from a leading university, and who wants to experiment with many new ways to save money for the company. One of her proposals is to use hedging strategies to mitigate swings in the costs of several metals that Creekside uses in its production processes. The idea is interesting, but no one else in the business has any experience with the hedging concept. What steps should Mr. Haley, the purchasing manager, take?

Creekside has had a long-term commitment to ensuring that there is a thorough understanding of every aspect of its business. Since hedging is entirely new, Mr. Haley takes the following steps to reduce the associated risk of hedging:

1. Discusses the matter with the risk management committee and gains their preliminary approval of the concept.
2. Hires a consulting firm to make presentations to the board of directors, risk management committee, and purchasing department regarding the mechanics of the hedging process and the risks that can arise.
3. Retains the consulting firm to engage in a small number of hedging transactions on a pilot basis, instructing the purchasing staff about the process. This includes creating policies and procedures.
4. The consulting firm then switches roles and oversees several purchasing employees as they engage in more hedging transactions and provides corrective advice as needed.
5. The internal audit department is brought in and examines the proposed process flow. The internal audit manager devises several audit procedures that will be conducted periodically to ensure that the hedging process is operating as planned. The external auditors are notified of the hedging initiative and examine the initial process flow, as well as the internal audit team's proposed examination plans. The external auditors provide advice regarding any issues found.
6. The risk management committee and then the board of directors give their formal approval of the hedging activity, and both request an initial quarterly milestone review meeting to discuss the outcome of initial hedging activities.
7. Hedging activities begin.

Mr. Haley has acted correctly in bringing numerous parties into the discussion of a hedging initiative, while also obtaining expert advice from a third party. He then ensures that the hedging activities are properly described and monitored, and that many people both inside and outside of the purchasing department are made aware of this activity.

The worst action that Mr. Haley could have taken would be to allow the new hire to solely pursue the hedging concept, which would have the dual negative effects of concentrating knowledge of the process with one person, and of creating the risk of an incorrect hedge that might be mistakenly entered into because the individual has no direct experience in hedging transactions.

---

- *Infrastructure commitment.* A proper level of risk management requires deep controls in selected parts of an organization – even if those controls are expensive and/or interfere with the efficient processing of transactions. In a business that focuses excessively on streamlining operations and cutting out costs, it is likely that key controls will be removed, thereby making it more likely that high-loss incidents will occur. This issue is less likely when responsibility over processes and controls is kept away from profit center managers, so there is no temptation to reduce controls in order to increase profits. A strong commitment to infrastructure is especially important when there is a drive to re-engineer processes, since the newly reformulated systems are likely to contain fewer controls than the predecessor systems.
- *Activity boundaries.* Many business transactions can be taken to excess, so it is necessary to set boundaries to limit them. For example, it may be acceptable to write 1,000 insurance policies for flood damage in Louisiana, but writing 100,000 of them will expose an insurer to a potentially massive loss if the Mississippi River overflows its banks. Similarly, it may be unwise to double the amount of credit available to a customer, if the amount of this increase would expose the seller to a large enough bad debt to destroy the business.

---

**EXAMPLE**

The president of Henderson Industrial has retired, so the board of directors conducts a search and hires an outsider, Mr. Blinker. The new president negotiates for an expanded range of authority, which gives him a high level of overriding control over the entire business, with few checks and balances.

After a few months, the chief risk officer notes a number of circumstances in which controls have been overridden by Mr. Blinker, which were specifically allowed when his three-year contract was negotiated. Specifically, he has mandated increased production levels and then offered promotions to distributors to buy goods now. He has also offered much longer payment terms to key customers, and is planning an expansion into a country that all of Henderson's competitors have abandoned due to the level of unrest in that region. Mr. Blinker's reasoning in taking these steps is to boost sales. However, the added sales come at the risk of higher returns from distributors, more bad debts from customers, and outright business failure in the new sales region. In short, the president is accepting much more risk in exchange for increased sales. The risk levels taken on all of these activities exceed the boundaries set by his predecessor, who advocated no channel stuffing, reasonable payment terms, and no foreign sales activity.

The chief risk officer takes his concerns to the audit committee, which brings the matter to the attention of the board of directors. Shortly thereafter, the company issues a press release that Mr. Blinker is leaving the company to pursue other interests.

---

- *Performance targets.* The management team should set reasonable performance targets for a business. By doing so, employees can set a reasonable and sustainable annual pace at which to grow sales. If targets are set too high, and especially if compensation systems match the high targets, then expect employees to engage in increasingly risky behavior, if not outright fraud, in order to meet the imposed targets. The performance targets to be set depend on the stage in the life of a product or business. Early sales may increase at a prodigious growth rate until the market reaches maturity, at which point vastly lower performance targets should be set. This is also a function of the gross sales level of a business – that is, an organization with $1 million in sales may reasonably expect to double its sales in one year, but a $10 billion business is extremely unlikely to duplicate this feat.

---

**EXAMPLE**

Medusa Medical sells a special blend of rapeseed oil through retail stores that specialize in home health care products. Since its founding four years before, the company has experienced 50% average annual sales growth. A venture capital fund has invested several million dollars in the company, in the belief that the business can grow at an even faster rate.

To meet the inflated sales figures that the founder used to attract the venture capitalists, the sales target for the next year is set at a level 80% higher than the year before. To achieve this goal, the company hires an appropriate number of sales representatives, but does not plan on an adequate ramp up period in which to train the new hires. Also, there is an incorrect assumption that additional sales can be squeezed from the existing sales regions, which proves not to be the case. As a result, all of the new hires find that they are falling far behind their sales quotas, and so resort to making sales pitches to financially questionable retailers. The resulting orders trigger a much higher level of bad debt losses than the company had experienced in the past. At year-end, sales do not reach the anticipated levels, while profits actually decline due to the extra costs of the new hires and bad debts.

**EXAMPLE**

In the past year, the price of oil increased to an all-time high, so the senior management team of Franklin Drilling decided to implement a new bonus plan that compensates the entire management team based on the number of new wells drilled from which there is a minimum threshold amount of oil flow per day. The intent is to greatly increase the volume of oil that Franklin can sell in the next year, presumably reaping massive profits. The company plans to invest an average of $2.5 million in each hole drilled.

Seeing massive bonuses in their future, the management group enthusiastically leases land in prime drilling areas and invests in the drilling of dozens of wells. In the meantime, the price of oil plummets. However, the management team continues to drill, since their incentive plan does not account for changes in the price of oil – they are only interested in producing more oil. By the end of the year, the company has invested over $100 million in new wells and $5 million in bonus payouts, but is forced to cap many of the wells, because the market price of oil now makes it unprofitable to extract the oil.

A better approach would have been to tie overall performance to profitability, since doing so would have accounted for variations in the market price of oil.

---

## Contingency Planning

Contingency planning is a set of activities taken to contain damage and minimize injuries to employees. In the following sub-sections, we note many steps that can be taken to improve the ability of an organization to survive a major physical event. We begin with employee-related issues and then move to event detection and damage mitigation topics.

### Disaster Communications

A standard approach to informing employees about disruptions to the business is the phone tree, which involves having employees call other employees to inform them of a situation. The callers may be department managers, or simply someone who is assigned the task. Consider giving employees a complete directory of all employee phone numbers, so that anyone can be involved in a phone tree.

A key concern with the use of phone trees is that many people only use cell phones, so the loss of cell towers in the area where employees are located will disrupt the phone tree system. In this case, several alternatives are:

- *Internal postings.* Post on the company's internal website the status of the business, as well as the contact information for those who can supply more detailed responses. This information should be kept on an internal website, so that the general public cannot gain access to critical operating information.

- *Texting.* The lowest-bandwidth form of communication over the phone system is to send text messages. These messages can sometimes get through when voice calls are rejected or dropped.
- *Bulletin board.* If the company's internet servers are not operational, consider shifting to messages on an electronic bulletin board that is hosted by a third party.
- *Rerouting.* Contact the phone company and have phone calls to the organization re-routed to an alternate location.

### Disaster Drills

If there is a history of specific types of problems within the area, such as flooding or wildfires, then create a disaster drill that is tailored to the most likely event. The drill should be practiced at reasonable intervals (such as testing a flood evacuation plan at the start of the rainy season). These drills are not only useful so that employees know what to do and where to go, but also so that any flaws in the plans can be spotted and corrected.

### Safety Procedures Training

Designate those individuals responsible for employee evacuations, as well as those maintenance and engineering personnel tasked with shutting down systems. Then conduct periodic training classes with them to ensure that they thoroughly understand evacuation and shutdown procedures. This training must be revised whenever building configurations are changed or employees move into new facilities.

### Emergency Response Team

Designate a group of qualified employees to be the emergency response team, with responsibility to contain problems during their early stages before outside assistance arrives. This group should be well-trained in remediation techniques, and also thoroughly supplied with all necessary equipment, such as water vacuums, portable generators, and sand bags. They should also have access to a complete medical kit and be properly trained in its use.

### Worker Flexibility

In the wake of a major disaster, employees may be able to return to the office physically, but they may be quite distracted by the effort required to reassemble their personal lives. If the entire area has been affected by a disaster, assume that a good portion of employee time will be spent contacting family members, arranging with contractors to make repairs, and dealing with insurance claims. Management should tone down its expectations for employee performance during this period, and also provide assistance by allowing for extra time off during the recovery period. It may even be more efficient to allow for *extra* time off, since this allows employees to settle their affairs more quickly and return to work.

### Automatic Detection Systems

Fire and water detection systems are a normal part of the local building code, and also make sense from a contingency planning perspective. Even when it is not necessary to install detection equipment in order to comply with the building code, consider adding detectors wherever they can give early warning of a potential problem. In addition, conduct a periodic inspection of all detectors to verify that they are all functioning properly.

### Preventive Maintenance

The use of preventive maintenance has been touted as a key tool for increasing the productive capacity of a business, but it also has a major side benefit – fewer dangerous equipment failures. When equipment is periodically inspected as part of an ongoing program of preventive maintenance, potentially dangerous incipient failures can be detected and corrected.

### Boiler-Related Activities

Boiler failures tend to be catastrophic, so a number of preventive measures are needed. For example, verify that automatic shutoff valves are installed on all incoming lines, so that an explosion will not be rendered worse by additional water or fuel. These valves should be tested regularly. Also, develop a list of local boiler repair and welding firms, along with their contact information, so that they can be brought in to effect repairs. Finally – and most importantly – conduct regular inspections of the boiler, using the most conservative intervals recommended by the manufacturer.

### Hazardous Materials

When a business uses hazardous materials as part of its ongoing operations, there should be an examination of how they are stored, to see if these items can be properly secured in the event of an emergency. For example:

- *Covers*. Ensure that all containers for hazardous materials are properly covered, so that a sudden imbalance (such as would be caused by an earthquake) would not cause a spill.
- *Dikes*. Build dikes around hazardous materials storage locations, so that spills can still be contained.
- *Containment supplies*. Maintain containment supplies near hazardous materials storage areas, such as absorbent materials, gloves, and empty containers.

### Mechanical Drawings

In the event of a major emergency, it may be necessary to shut off water lines, gas lines, feed lines from hazardous materials tanks, and so forth. If so, prepare mechanical drawings of these systems and store them in several readily-accessible locations. Ideally, note the system shutoff points on these drawings, and how to reach them.

### Equipment Positioning

In a flood-prone environment, position vulnerable equipment and inventory off the floor. In an earthquake-prone environment, position towers, utility poles, and signs away from buildings so that they cannot collapse onto these structures. Also, anchor or brace equipment so that it will not fall over or collapse.

### Safe Room

A well-designed safe room can provide a significant improvement in safety to employees. A safe room should have dense walls, sufficient water, food, and first aid supplies for a short stay, enough space to accommodate all employees, and also enough ancillary space in which to retain the most crucial records.

### Flood Mitigation Activities

In flood-prone areas, install water pumps in all basement areas. Also, consider building floodwalls around key buildings. Where possible, shift the most vulnerable equipment and inventory onto the higher floors of buildings. Further, adopt a procedure for regularly cleaning gutters and drains, so that rainwater is properly routed away from the building.

### Hurricane Mitigation Activities

In addition to the flood mitigation activities just noted, create covers to place over all windows. This prevents window breakage, as well as the entry of rain into the facility.

### Replacement Facilities

It may be necessary to open a replacement facility if an existing company location is destroyed. At a minimum, consider having an off-site location to which the company's information technology department can switch on short notice. If the information systems continue to be available, then employees may be able to work from home. This approach works best in a knowledge industry such as consulting or auditing services.

## Core Reports

No matter what type of operations a business may conduct, the management team should always be provided with a periodic losses report and incidents report. The losses report notes the amount of money lost in the period from different causes, while the incidents report summarizes the incidents that occurred in the period, irrespective of the amount of money lost (if any). In addition, the insurance claims report summarizes the types of claims made and the related settlement amounts.

### Losses Report

All types of losses can be reported to management. These losses should be a central focus of the management team, since they should either be recognized as the offshoot of a high-risk strategy or as losses for which mitigation tactics might be employed. However, reporting losses does not mean that the report recipients should be buried with detail. Instead, pare away all minor losses that do not meet a certain threshold. Also, consider aggregating losses into different categories for easier perusal, such as losses linked to customer credit, commodity prices, and exchange rates. Additional useful information could be to track losses against expectations, both for the reporting period and on a cumulative basis. These extra refinements are useful for highlighting unusual losses that require further investigation.

### Incidents Report

The problem with the preceding losses report is that it only focuses attention on activities that actually lose a notable amount of money. Other events may not immediately lose money, but could do so in the future, and so should also be presented to management. Incidents that might appear in such a report are the theft of inventory or petty cash, the filing of a lawsuit against the company, a network failure during non-working hours, an equipment fire that was immediately extinguished, and an employee injury that was covered by workers' compensation insurance. These incidents could be indicative of larger problems, so it can be useful to attach an analysis that points out trends or perhaps correlations between different incidents.

### Insurance Claims Report

Some risk will be offloaded to insurers, so it makes sense to summarize in a claims report the types of claims made and the settlement amounts. By doing so, one can see the size and frequency of insured losses. It can be useful to issue this report as a summary page, with details on attached pages regarding the nature of the various claims. Management can then spot an item on the cover page and drill down through the attachments to locate additional information. A sample insurance claims report summary page follows.

**Sample Insurance Claims Report**

| Claim Date | Claim Description | Event Location | Claim Amount |
|---|---|---|---|
| 1/05/XX | Boiler claim \| Steam valve broke and flooded area | Thornton facility | $48,000 |
| 1/28/XX | Auto claim \| Rolled over in high winds | On Interstate 25 | 42,000 |
| 2/09/XX | Directors liability claim \| Shareholder awarded damages | Headquarters | 100,000 |
| 2/10/XX | Property claim \| Hail damage to warehouse roof | Little Rock facility | 63,000 |
| 2/17/XX | Property claim \| Fire damage to office furniture | Miami office | 15,000 |
| 3/07/XX | Inland marine claim \| Sales exhibition destroyed in transit | In transit to Dallas | 30,000 |
| 3/15/XX | Business interruption \| River flooding shut down subsidiary | Omaha retail store | 120,000 |

If there are many claims, it can make sense to not include in the report any claims below a threshold level. Doing so keeps the reader focused on the largest loss events.

An option to consider for this report is to also include the deductible loss that the company absorbed, as well as any additional losses for which no insurance claim could be made. If these amounts are minor, it may not be worth the administrative effort to accumulate the additional information.

## Summary

Management needs to have a clear idea of the risks to which the business is subjected, as well as which risks it is deliberately undertaking in order to gain a strategic advantage. This information comes from an ongoing examination of the business and its environment, with a particular focus on any changes that may alter the risk profile of the entity. Further, the risk management mindset should be driven deep into the fundamentals of the business, so that it is routinely considered as part of many operations decisions.

A risk management mindset is not intended to destroy the entrepreneurial spirit of a company. There must always be a willingness to take risks in the pursuit of a new market or the release of a new product. However, operations employees must be made aware of the risk implications of their actions, so that they can make properly balanced judgments about what to do.

A business should have an action plan for how to survive a major emergency, including such topics as employee evacuations, saving key equipment, and keeping inventory safe. Even when such a plan has been developed, be sure to evaluate it at regular intervals, since the circumstances may mandate an alteration to the plan. For example, a recent buildout of a production facility may call for a different fire drill evacuation route, or the installation of new production equipment may have introduced additional gas lines into the facility, for which the shutoff valves should be noted in the plan. Whenever changes are made to the plan, use a drill to test whether the revisions are adequate.

# Chapter 18
# Project Management

## Introduction

A *project* is a series of tasks that must be completed within a fixed time frame in order to achieve certain objectives. Projects are essential, being the primary tool for change. For example, when there is a need to increase the sales of a business, the management team will likely initiate a series of projects – to add a distribution channel, add a sales region, build a new production facility, or design a new product. Projects are also needed to react to change. For example, if a competitor disrupts the industry with a low-cost product, a company may have to follow by designing and rolling out a similar product, and as soon as possible. Thus, if an organization wants to prosper, it must have a project management capability. In this chapter, we discuss the activities associated with project management, including project phases, planning, and control.

## Project Phases

A properly organized project goes through a series of phases, from its inception to eventual completion. A *phase* is a cluster of related activities that result in a deliverable. Phases are needed to ensure that a project is properly organized. There is usually a set of unique tasks associated with each phase, over which the project manager exercises control. Once the activities within a phase result in a deliverable, it is handed off to the tasks comprising the next phase. The end of each phase is a good place to conduct a review, to see how well the project is progressing and to alter the remaining work, if necessary.

The number and nature of each phase can vary by company; some organizations have found that they achieve better results by making modifications at certain spots, usually based on prior experience. These adjustments are intended to improve upon the results of each successive process.

In this section, we cover the characteristics of each project phase.

### Phase 1 – Project Concept

The initial project phase is to develop a concept of what the project is supposed to do. The concept is comprised of a project objective, general constraints that could impact the project, and a very rough estimate of a budget. This is a high-level statement that is used as the basis for further documentation of the project. For example:

> The company wants to develop an electric car that can travel 500 miles on a single charge, with the first cars being sold in 20X3. A key constraint is the level of knowledge regarding batteries within the company. The intent is to develop all prototypes and the final production-ready model for no more than $250 million.

This concept statement is then examined to see if it is feasible. If not, the concept may be tweaked to bring it into alignment with the realities of the situation. For example, the preceding sample statement could be revised to reduce the number of miles driven on a single charge, delay the sale date, or increase the budget. Once there is general agreement that the concept can be achieved, the project moves to the next phase.

### Phase 2 – Project Definition

The project definition phase requires the development of more detail regarding the project. The documentation should include the following topics:

- Personnel requirements
- Asset requirements
- Space requirements
- Expected timing
- Projected budget, with a relatively high degree of accuracy

The intent behind this phase is to delve into a sufficient level of detail to be reasonably sure that there are no issues with resource requirements. If no issues are uncovered, the project moves to the next phase.

### Phase 3 – Project Planning

The project planning phase requires a high degree of specificity. The plan is quite detailed, noting exactly which tasks must be completed, who will complete them, and when each task must be begun and completed. The roles and responsibilities of each person are stated. Funding sources are clearly identified, as well as the amounts that will be needed. Further, the plan states the organizational structure to be used to manage the project, and identifies the people who will occupy the management slots. A deep level of detail is needed, since adequate planning in this phase correlates to a higher level of project success.

**Phase 4 – Preliminary Studies**

At this point, there is still a risk that the project could fail due to a faulty assumption that is incorporated into the project plan. The preliminary studies phase is used to unearth these assumptions. These studies could encompass a number of activities, depending on the nature of the project. For example:

- Interview an expert in the field to obtain advice regarding the achievability of the project.
- Collect information, both internally and from outside sources, regarding issues that others have encountered in the general area.
- Consult with others in the company who have engaged in related projects to learn about the types of issues that arose in the past.

If these studies indicate the presence of certain risks or potential problems, then the project plan can be revisited and adjusted to incorporate their effects.

**Phase 5 – Project Performance**

As the name indicates, the next phase is to actually conduct the work. The project manager activates the plan, calling in all necessary resources, and monitors the progress of the project. The manager routinely adjusts resources or the plan to keep the project moving forward.

Project performance typically absorbs 90 percent of the resources of a project, and yet it is only the fifth of six project phases. The reason we incorporate so many steps in front of the project performance phase is to minimize the risk of having a failed project. All of the preceding steps are designed to identify any issue that could have a negative impact on the project. If any of the preceding steps were to be shortened or skipped, a possible outcome is that a large amount of resources could be wasted in the project performance phase, working on the wrong tasks or working in a less efficient manner. The following exhibit shows how the uncertainty level is highest at the beginning of a project, while the cost of changes is lowest at that point. As the project progresses, the situation reverses. That is, the residual level of uncertainty declines, but the cost to make changes increases dramatically. Thus, one must spend time upfront, exploring risks and identifying alternative ways to complete a project.

**Levels of Project Uncertainty and Risk over Time**

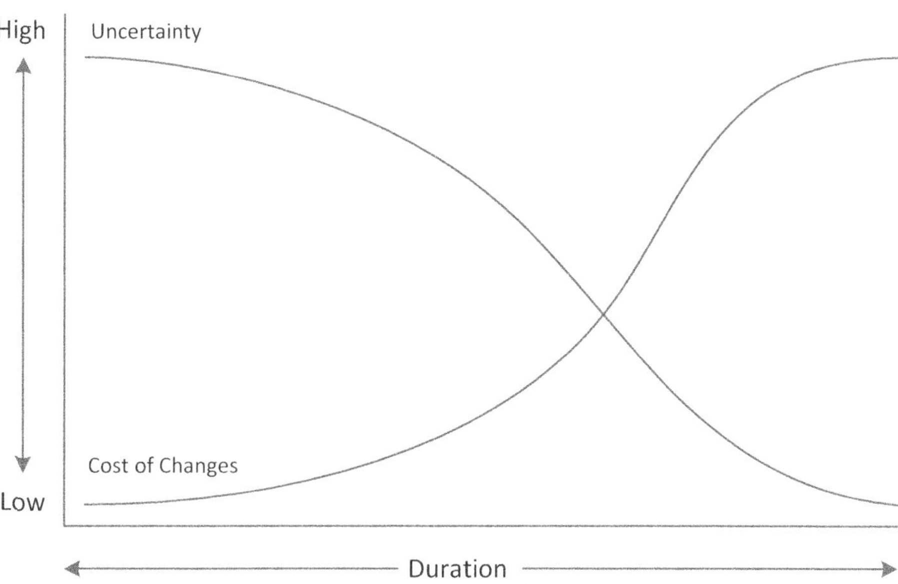


### Phase 6 – Project Post-Completion

Once a project has supposedly been completed, there are still several activities to complete as part of the post-completion phase. The first is to ensure that the project has met its original goals. This requires a comparison of the measured outcome to the expected outcome. If there is a difference, it should be investigated. The result may be a continuation of the project until the original goals have been achieved.

There should also be a post-implementation review to determine whether there were any problems or achievements that should be shared more broadly with the organization. By spreading the news of these issues, the organization can learn from each successive project, building upon its successes and learning from its failures.

Another part of the post-completion phase is to reassign employees to other work within the business. This activity does not just occur at the end of a project. It is quite possible that specialists may be employed for only a short period of time, and then shift away to other non-project work. Thus, there may be work reassignments at any time over the course of a project.

Finally, all documentation relating to the project is completed and properly stored. This can include a summary report by the project manager, reviews of those employees who worked on the project, and an analysis of monetary and time variances.

## The Project Planning and Control System

A project planning and control system translates a project objective into a work breakdown structure, which is then analyzed using such network scheduling tools as Gantt charts, the critical path method (CPM), and the program evaluation and review technique (PERT). The outcome of this process is a detailed work schedule and project budget. Once a project begins, hours worked and costs incurred are tracked against the work schedule and project budget. This tracking results in reports that are sent back to the project manager and project stakeholders. Based on this information, the project objective may be adjusted. Thus, the process is a continual loop. It appears in the following exhibit.

**Project Planning and Control System**

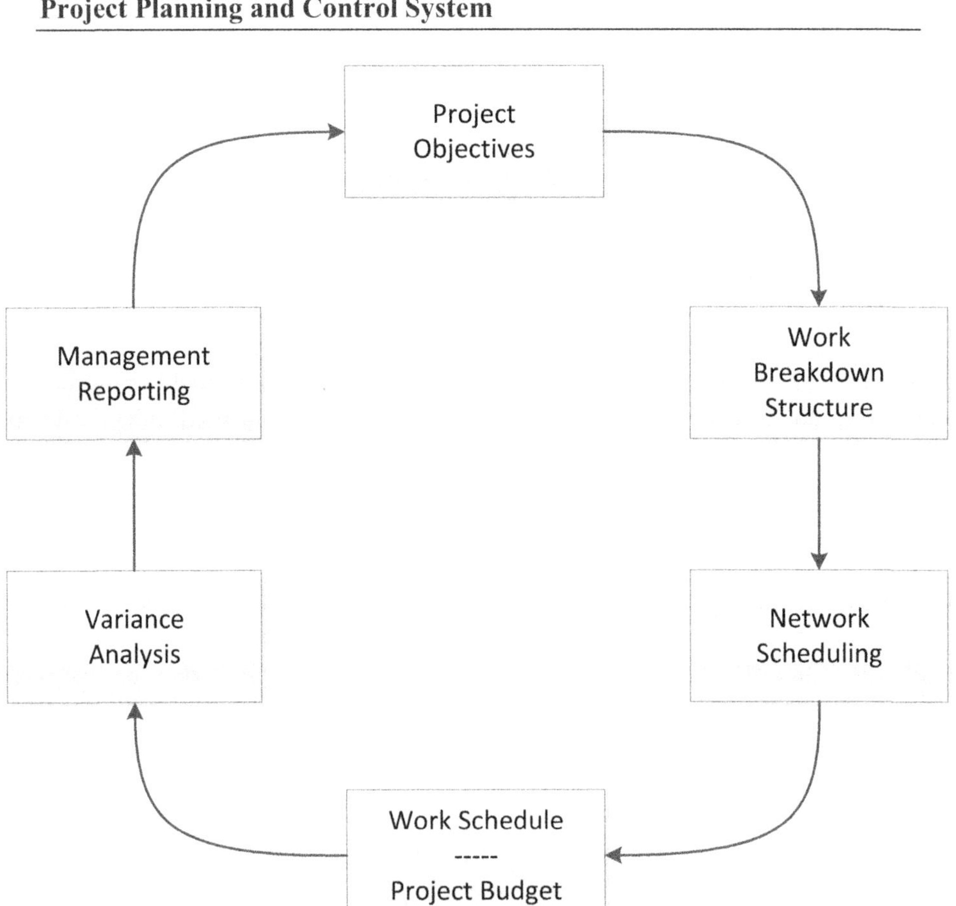


In the following sections, we focus on the work breakdown structure and network scheduling segments of the planning and control system.

## The Work Breakdown Structure

Some projects are inordinately large, making them quite difficult to manage. This issue can be addressed by employing the work breakdown structure, which identifies every task in a project. This process of identification breaks down a project into a cluster of bite-sized pieces that are easier to manage. Each task is listed in an outline format, so that a great many tasks can be clearly stated within a relatively small document. With this information in hand, a project manager can more easily do the following:

- Clearly state all aspects of a project's scope
- Monitor the completion stage of each identified task
- Compile the cost of each task
- Develop work assignments for each task

The work breakdown structure of a project divides activities into *summary tasks* and *work packages*. A summary task describes a set of activities (work packages). A work package is a group of activities for which work is estimated, scheduled, monitored, and controlled. A work package defines work at the lowest level for which cost and duration can be estimated and managed. For example:

- Constructing a shed is a summary task, while laying the foundation, constructing a frame, and building a roof are all work packages within the summary task.
- Installing a purchasing software module is a summary task, while loading the software, porting over existing purchasing data, and testing the new software are all work packages within the summary task.
- Training employees in a new safety program is a summary task, while writing the training materials, training the trainers, and conducting training classes are all work packages within the summary task.

In each of the preceding examples, when all of the work packages are complete, the summary task is also accomplished. A sample work breakdown structure for the construction of an office building appears in the following exhibit.

**Sample Work Breakdown Structure for an Office Building Construction Project**

---

**1.0 Design building structure**

**2.0 Lay foundation**

2.1 Dig hole
2.2 Build concrete forms
2.3 Pour concrete

**3.0 Construct home**

3.1 Construct frame
3.2 Add exterior walls
3.3 Add plumbing
3.4 Add wiring
3.5 Add interior walls
3.6 Add roof
3.7 Add carpeting and hardwood floors
3.8 Add windows

**4.0 Install lawn**

4.1 Dig trenches
 4.1.1 Have the local utility mark all gas lines
 4.1.2. Identify trench lines
 4.1.3 Rent trench digging equipment
 4.1.4 Dig trenches
4.2 Install sprinkler pipes
4.3 Cover sprinkler system
4.4 Plant lawn seed
4.5 Plant shrubs

---

In the preceding exhibit, the top-level activities (noted in bold) are the summary tasks. These are known as *level one* items. All of the indented activities are the work packages. The indented activities can be indented further to denote additional levels of detail, as we noted for the "dig trenches" work package. In that work package, "Dig trenches" was a *level two* item, while "Have the local utility mark all gas lines" was a *level three* item. These extra levels of detail are useful for providing a high level of refinement to a project.

The easiest way to construct a work breakdown structure is to start with the highest-level tasks that are listed on a project's statement of work, and list them as top-tier items (summary tasks) in the work breakdown structure. Then list all tasks required to complete each summary task. It is easiest to state each task beginning with a verb, which denotes that an action is required.

The project manager may find that he or she does not have a sufficiently detailed knowledge of the task steps to develop a complete listing of work packages. If so, consult with other members of the project team who have the requisite skills. In some cases, it may be necessary to consult with outside experts who can fill in any gaps in the plan. When a project is quite large, the project manager may only be able to complete the first level or two of the structure, and must then hand it off to specialists to complete the lower levels.

The work breakdown structure should be fully fleshed-out before a project is allowed to proceed. The reason is that working through the levels of detail required to fully understand a project may uncover areas in which there is uncertainty about what to do. By addressing these areas in advance, the project manager may be able to avoid tasks that might otherwise have caused problems for the project.

When creating a work breakdown structure, follow these best practices to improve the odds that the outcome properly reflects the actual project:

- Does the summary task matter? The costs of the work packages underneath a summary task are aggregated at the summary task level. Will anyone review this summary-level information or be responsible for it? If not, try reconfiguring to arrive at a more meaningful summary task.
- Should a work package be linked to a certain summary task? Verify that all work packages are actually associated with the summary task under which they are listed. If not, move the work packages under a more applicable summary task.
- Does a work package result in a product? There should be a specific outcome associated with each work package. Thus, "evaluate bidders" is not a work package, since there may be no end to this activity. Instead, use "select a bidder," which implies that there is a solid outcome to the activity.
- Is a work package too large? When a task is estimated to require a massive number of hours, the daily monitoring of the work does not tell the project manager if there is any real progress. Instead, many hours may pass before anyone realizes that there is a problem. To correct this problem, break the work package down into smaller segments that can be more easily tracked on a daily basis. As a general rule, try to restrict all work packages to no more than two weeks.
- Has the work breakdown structure been stated at too fine a level of detail? When there are too many work packages for a large project, this may result in thousands of charge codes, which take time to set up and monitor.
- Is it too difficult to estimate the duration of a work package? If so, chop the package into smaller segments and try again. Smaller work packages are easier to estimate.

A reasonable minimum duration for a work package is eight hours. This keeps a project manager from delving too deeply into the realm of micromanagement, while still staying close to some of the more critical tasks. However, there are instances in which much smaller time intervals should be scheduled, usually when the work involves a bottleneck activity that has a broad impact on the general operations of the business, or when there are many small steps involved.

---

**EXAMPLE**

The Twister Vacuum Company has a bottleneck in its production operation, where a plastic extrusion machine is not quite able to keep up with the flow of production. An hour of production lost at this machine costs the company $10,000 of profits.

A project manager has been assigned the task of installing a process monitoring system on this machine, which will require that the machine be shut down for at least 20 hours. Given the significant cost to the company of this shutdown, the manager decides to create a work breakdown structure that states work packages in increments of as little as 15 minutes. Doing so allows her to precisely monitor the status of the project.

---

## Task Relationship Identification

Once a work breakdown structure has been devised for a project, one must then determine how the various work packages within it relate to each other. Certain tasks must be completed before others can begin. For example, pouring a foundation must be completed before constructing the framing for a building, while the framing must be completed before the roof can be added. There are several types of these relationships. One is the *finish-to-start* relationship, where a preceding task must be completed before the next task can begin. For example, a piece of furniture must be stained before varnish can be applied to it. The finish-to-start relationship is the most common relationship. Another relationship is the *start-to-start* relationship, where both the preceding and successor tasks can start when the preceding task begins. For example, in a physical inventory count, received inventory count tags can be verified and tabulated at the same time. These relationships are useful when tasks can be overlapped to compress the duration of a project. Another relationship is the *finish-to-finish* relationship, where the successor task can only be finished when the preceding task ends. For example, a project to prepare a large, multi-course meal requires that the various components of the meal be ready for consumption at the same time – at the end. Thus, one could turn on the oven and begin baking potatoes (the preceding task), and then add a pie to the oven a short time later (the successor task).

When a task is not dependent upon the completion of a prior task, it has no *sequence constraint* – that is, the task can start at any time. Also, it may be possible for several tasks to be addressed at the same time. If so, these are *concurrent tasks*. An example appears in the next exhibit, where the tasks and sequence constraints are described for a project that involves the installation of production equipment.

**Sample Sequence Constraint Table**

| Task Number | Task Description | Predecessor |
|---|---|---|
| 1 | Pour concrete pad | None |
| 2 | Position equipment | 1 |
| 3 | Install electrical | 1 |
| 4 | Conduct a test run | 2, 3 |
| 5 | Write an operations manual | None |
| 6 | Conduct employee training | 4, 5 |

In the table, note how tasks 2 and 3 can both proceed at the same time, though only after task 1 has been completed. Tasks 2 and 3 have a sequence constraint in relation to task 1, but can be considered concurrent tasks in relation to each other. The full set of relationships is noted in the following network diagram. In the diagram, writing an operations manual is not considered to have a sequence constraint, so it can begin as soon as the project starts. Finally, employee training has multiple sequence constraints, since the trainer needs both an operational machine and an operations manual in order to conduct the training.

**Sample Network Diagram**

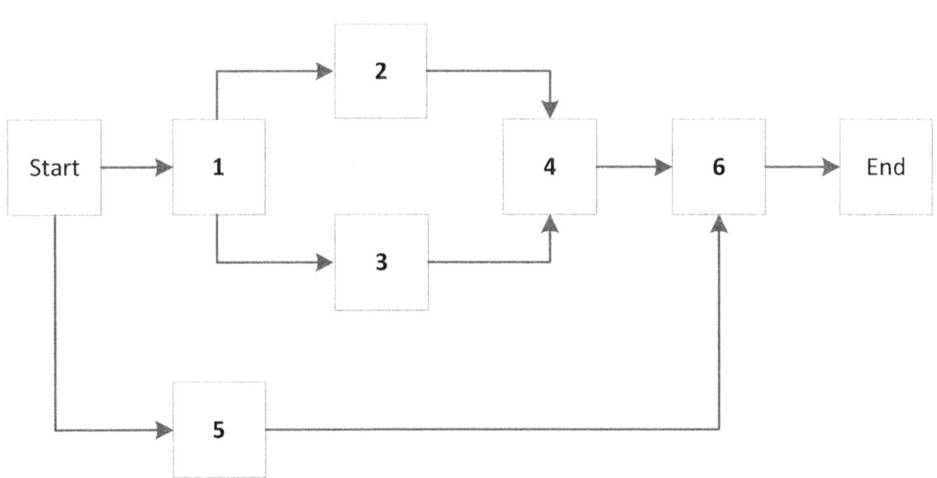


Another possibility to factor into a task relationship analysis is the existence of an *external dependency*. This is an input from an external source that is required before a task can proceed. This dependency frequently takes the form of an approval. For example:

- A government agency must issue an operating license to a power plant before the facility can be turned on. The license is an external dependency.
- A customer must review the progress of a project and give his approval before he will release funds to pay for the next summary task. The approval is an external dependency.
- A building inspector must issue a permit before the wiring for a building will be approved. The permit is an external dependency.

The main concern of the project manager is the existence of sequence constraints, where one task must be completed before another task can begin. If a single predecessor task cannot be completed, it may prevent an entire project from advancing. External dependencies can be particularly difficult to manage, since they typically involve a decision by an entity that is outside of the control of the project manager.

## Bottom-Up Estimating

Once a work breakdown structure has been built and task interrelationships identified, one can construct estimates of costs and time requirements for each work package. This work is conducted for each individual work package and then rolled up into a grand total for the project. Because the estimating work begins at the lowest level of detail, it is referred to as *bottom-up estimating*. If these numbers had instead been imposed from above by company management, stakeholders, or the project manager, they would be referred to as *top-down estimating*. Top-down estimating is not recommended, since it is not based on the underlying detail of a project, and so may be wildly incorrect.

The cost estimates for a project must include cost information from all possible sources, including all factors that could ratchet up these costs. For example:

- *Labor cost*. Calculate the labor cost based on the number of hours that will be needed, factoring in the different labor rates for people with higher or lower skill sets. On more critical projects, there is a tendency to use higher-grade people in order to ensure that tasks are completed on time; if so, estimate a higher hourly rate. If additional hours will be needed and people are paid on an hourly basis, estimate a reasonable amount of overtime pay.
- *Contractor bids*. When contractors will be working on a project, include the amount of their fixed-price bids as a separate cost. If they are working on an hourly basis, include their cost in the preceding labor cost category.
- *Materials cost*. A construction project is likely to require a massive amount of materials, while other services-related projects may not require any materials. This cost is derived from the project specifications, not from the work breakdown structure.

- *Equipment cost.* It may be necessary to rent or purchase tools and equipment for a project. If there is an expectation that these may need to be acquired on a rush basis, include rush fees in the acquisition cost. Also include the operating costs required to run the equipment, such as gasoline for powered equipment. Further, include the costs of any tools that will be consumed during the project. If equipment is being purchased for use on several projects, prorate its cost over the projects.

---

**EXAMPLE**

Monique Ponto designs and builds high-end watches for women. A project manager working on a new design project wants to buy an advanced graphics workstation for $100,000 to assist in the design work. However, the cost of the workstation is too large. Instead, he learns that six other projects could all use the workstation and negotiates a deal with them to apportion the cost among the seven projects, based on hours of actual usage.

---

Both time and cost estimates must be compiled for a project with the greatest care. The reason is that cost and time frame are major constraints that directly impact the eventual outcome of a project. If the cost turns out to be higher than expectations, or if the duration is longer than expected, it is possible that the project scope will be reduced. By doing so, the project cost and/or time frame can be reduced back to a level that meets the expectations of stakeholders.

Estimates should be very specific, so that one can evaluate costs and durations at a fine level of detail. In the following exhibit, we note the cost calculation for the personnel needed to complete a few of the tasks noted earlier in the work breakdown structure for a home construction project.

**Sample Cost Calculation**

| Task | Unit | Headcount | Days | Hours | Cost/Hour | Extension |
|---|---|---|---|---|---|---|
| **2.0 Lay foundation** | | | | | | |
| 2.1 Dig hole | Staff hour | 3 | 6 | 144 | $40 | $5,760 |
| 2.2 Build concrete forms | Staff hour | 3 | 4 | 96 | 48 | 4,608 |
| 2.3 Pour concrete | Staff hour | 2 | 2 | 32 | 60 | 1,920 |
| | | | 12 | 272 | | $12,288 |

The time requirements developed through bottom-up estimating are worth a careful review, especially when there is a need to complete a task within a short period of time. In a case where there is little time available, the project manager can budget for extra staff or longer working hours to ensure that tasks are still completed on time.

---

**EXAMPLE**

Cantilever Construction replaces bridges. One of its assigned tasks is to remove an aging bridge as part of a project to build a new bridge. The local government, which is funding the project, has stipulated that the state road over which the bridge passes cannot be closed for more than ten hours during the demolition work. For every additional hour of road closure over the ten-hour threshold, the government will fine Cantilever $10,000.

Given the large penalty, the project manager has a substantial incentive to minimize the road closure. The first pass at an estimate for the bridge demolition is that the road will be closed for 14 hours. To complete the work four hours faster and eliminate the penalty, the project manager must add six more people to the project for the preceding two days, which will cost an additional $2,500. The extra cost is well worth the amount of the saved penalty.

---

A useful outcome of this analysis is the occasional discovery that adding more staff to a task will not necessarily shorten its duration. For example, when a task requires highly skilled labor for a short period of time, the only way to complete the task may be with those already assigned to it. Adding more staff merely takes time away from the existing staff to train the new arrivals, and so may even extend the task duration. Consequently, this analysis will likely uncover several instances in which there is an absolutely minimum amount of time required that cannot be compressed further.

There may be other instances in which a large number of people can be added to a task, with a reasonable expectation that the outcome will be a significant reduction in the duration of the task. This typically occurs when the required skill level is low, so that the training period is insignificant and a person is fully functional almost at once. For example, in a project to cut back foliage in a fire zone, many people could be added at once with great effect, since the skill level is so low.

Yet another variation on personnel planning is to recognize cases in which a person is being pulled in multiple directions by the demands of several jobs. This is quite common when a person is working on a project while also working on his normal day job at the same time. When a person is multi-tasking in this manner, his efficiency level tends to decline. In this situation, having the person assigned full-time, with no other responsibilities, may be the best way to shorten the duration of a task.

Once estimates of time and cost have been developed, the work breakdown structure and task relationships can be translated into a project schedule. This schedule is commonly presented using a Gantt chart, the critical path method, or the program evaluation and review technique, which are described in the following sections.

## Gantt Charts

A Gantt chart is a visual portrayal of the task assignments and task durations within a project. This information is displayed in the form of a horizontal bar chart. The chart can be enhanced with shading to show the level of completion of each task, or a vertical line through the chart that shows today's date. The chart can also show dependencies between the different activities, where one task must be completed before the next task can begin; this means it is relatively easy to identify critical tasks or bottlenecks that might prevent a project from being completed by its planned due date. A simplified Gantt chart that outlines the tasks associated with setting up a production work center appears in the following exhibit.

**Sample Gantt Chart**

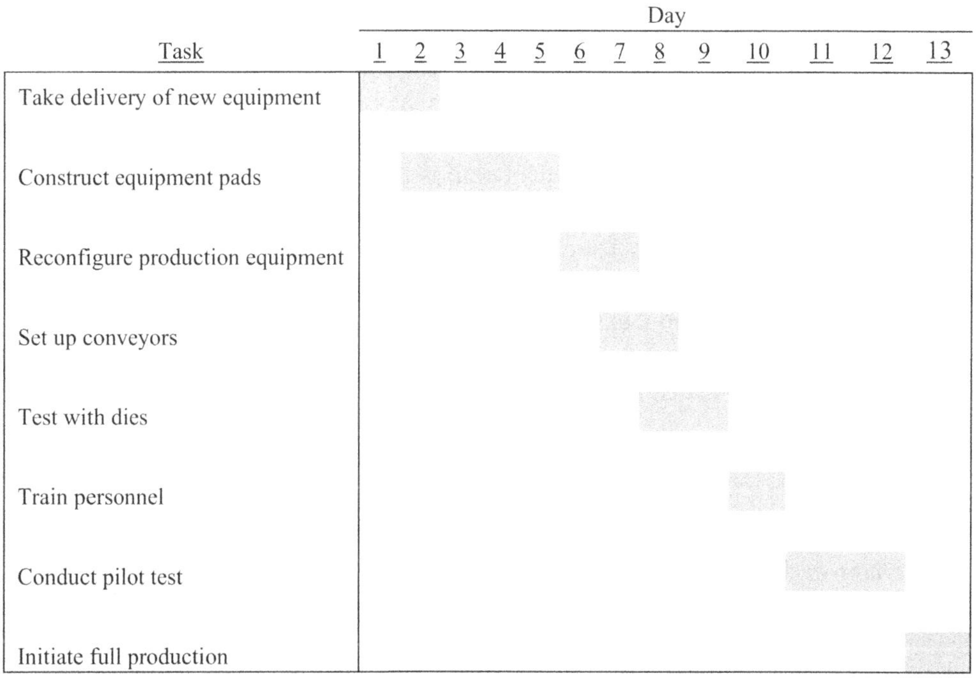

| | Day | | | | | | | | | | | | |
|---|---|---|---|---|---|---|---|---|---|---|---|---|---|
| Task | 1 | 2 | 3 | 4 | 5 | 6 | 7 | 8 | 9 | 10 | 11 | 12 | 13 |
| Take delivery of new equipment | | | | | | | | | | | | | |
| Construct equipment pads | | | | | | | | | | | | | |
| Reconfigure production equipment | | | | | | | | | | | | | |
| Set up conveyors | | | | | | | | | | | | | |
| Test with dies | | | | | | | | | | | | | |
| Train personnel | | | | | | | | | | | | | |
| Conduct pilot test | | | | | | | | | | | | | |
| Initiate full production | | | | | | | | | | | | | |

In the sample chart, note that certain tasks are dependent upon the completion of prior tasks. For example, the reconfiguration of production equipment cannot begin until the equipment pads have been completed. Similarly, employees cannot be trained until the product dies have been tested. These dependencies are critical to project completion, since a delay earlier in the process has a ripple effect that pushes dependent tasks further out into the future. However, other tasks can be worked on concurrently, since there is no dependency between them. There is more likely to be an overlap in the timelines for these tasks. For example, work can progress on setting up conveyors even before the production equipment with which it will be associated has been re-configured.

The Gantt chart is one of the simplest project management tools, and yet can be quite effective, especially when dealing with a relatively uncomplicated project. Conversely, the complexity of a larger project might instead call for the CPM or PERT techniques, which are described later in this chapter.

## Critical Path Method (CPM)

When a project contains many tasks that must be closely coordinated, a better planning technique than a Gantt chart is the critical path method. Under CPM, each task is arranged in sequential order, along with a time estimate for how long it will take to complete the task. An *event* occurs when a task either begins or is completed. This information is then displayed on a CPM chart. This chart is useful for determining how delays will influence the completion of a project, where there is slack in a project, and which tasks are crucial for meeting the project due date.

*Slack time* occurs when there are activities that can be completed before the time when they are actually needed. The difference between the scheduled completion date and the required date to meet the critical path is the amount of slack time available. The project manager should always be aware of where slack time exists in a project, since this time can be used to reshuffle the schedule to support the critical path. For example, if there is slack time in a task not located on the critical path, resources can be shifted from that task to tasks located on the critical path, thereby bolstering the most crucial tasks. One can also keep track of the trend in available slack time for each task. If the trend is declining, it can indicate that work is taking longer than expected.

---

**EXAMPLE**

It takes three weeks to complete a task. The task must be completed in five weeks, which is when it will be needed to support the critical path of a project. The two week differential is the slack time for this task. The project manager has several options for how to deal with this slack time, including the following:

- Delay the start of the task for two weeks
- Proceed as normal, which leaves the two week buffer at the end of the task in case something goes wrong
- Reduce the resources assigned to the task so that it now takes the full five weeks to complete

---

A CPM chart is also useful for "what if" analysis, to see where delays are more likely to crop up in a project, and the impact of those delays.

A CPM chart is organized in a specific way, which calls for the use of rules to display information on the chart. Those rules are:

- Each task is represented by an arrow, and each circle represents an event. For example:

- A linked series of arrows and circles means that the subsequent tasks cannot be completed until the earlier tasks have been completed. In the following example, this means that testing the machine cannot be initiated until the machine has been built.

- The general direction of progress is from left to right.
- When several tasks end at one event, the next event cannot be initiated until all of the preceding tasks have been completed. In the following example, obtaining a construction permit and building an equipment pad are both precursors to testing the equipment.

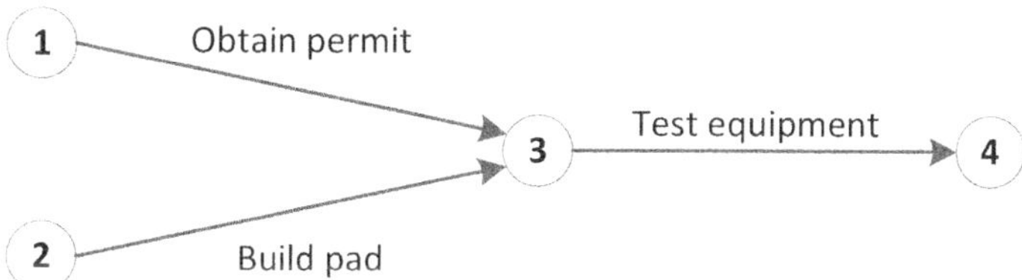


Of particular interest in the chart is that those tasks that could hold up the project are identified as critical. By arranging the chart to focus attention on the critical tasks, one can forecast the time required to complete the entire project. A simplified CPM appears in the following example, to illustrate the concept.

**EXAMPLE**

The engineering manager of Mule Corporation is planning a design change to the muffler used on the company's iconic "Bad Ass" motorcycle, requiring a reconfiguration of a key work cell. This will call for completion of the following steps:

| Step | Task | Duration |
|---|---|---|
| A | Design muffler mold | 2 weeks |
| B | Reconfigure muffler work cell to receive mold | 4 weeks |
| C | Acquire tooling and parts for the work cell | 3 weeks |
| D | Install production equipment | 1 week |
| E | Test new equipment with new muffler mold | 1 week |

The engineering manager shifts this information into a CPM chart, which appears next. In the chart, the bold line indicates the minimum amount of time needed to reconfigure the work cell, which involves steps A, C, D, and E. This is the project's critical path. If the manager wants to shorten the amount of time required to complete the project, he will need to focus his attention on reducing the duration of one or more of these four steps. Step B, reconfiguring the work cell, is not on the critical path, since it requires only four weeks to complete and there are five weeks available. This means step B has one week of slack time associated with it. Conversely, if step A, C, D, or E is delayed, this will increase the duration of the entire project.

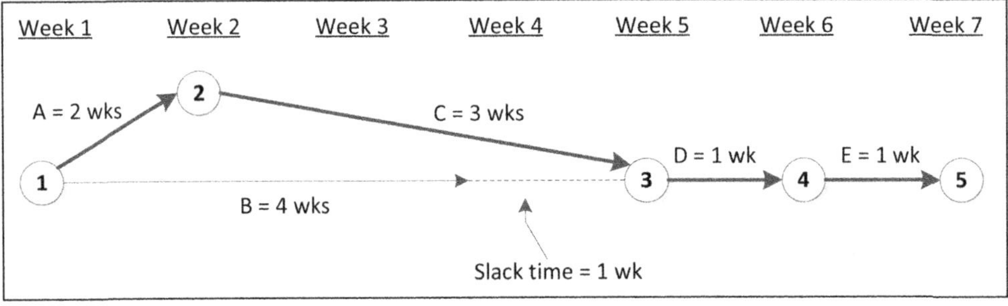


The example presented the concept of the *critical path*. The critical path is the longest path through a network. There is no slack in any task on the critical path, so if there is a delay in any of these tasks, the completion of the entire project will be delayed. Consequently, a project manager's attention is heavily focused on ensuring that each task along the critical path begins and ends on time.

It is possible that there are several near-critical paths associated with a project. If the tasks within these paths become prolonged and their float is consumed, it is entirely possible that one of these paths will become the new critical path, supplanting the original critical path. If this happens, the attention of the project manager is then focused on the new critical path. When there is a near-critical path, it behooves the project manager to watch it closely over time and evaluate the risk that it may become the new critical path.

When a complete work breakdown structure and a CPM analysis have been completed, it is entirely likely that a negative float will be revealed. A *negative float* occurs when the critical path will result in project completion after the mandated completion date. If a negative float is indicated, it should be brought up with the project sponsors at once, which should trigger a negotiation over what should be changed: the completion date, the project cost, or the project scope. Continuing a project with negative float makes no sense, since it is guaranteed to fail (where failure is defined as not meeting the completion date).

The sample CPM chart was based on the conditions present at the start of the project. The durations and types of tasks will change over the course of the project, as well as the relationships between the tasks, so the chart must be continually updated over the course of the project, possibly on a daily basis. By doing so, the project manager has the best idea of where to allocate resources and reschedule tasks.

There is project software available that allows a manager to enter a massive number of project tasks and provide a complete CPM evaluation as output. This software requires a significant amount of time to maintain, so larger projects may have a CPM software person whose full-time job is to maintain the CPM model.

The CPM method works best when a project is well-defined and there are relatively few uncertainties. These conditions make CPM an ideal tool for construction projects. When there is more uncertainty, PERT may be a better tool. It is described in the next section.

## Program Evaluation and Review Technique (PERT)

The program evaluation and review technique is a more complicated version of CPM. PERT allows for the inclusion of variable amounts of time for each task. Thus, each task has a most likely, pessimistic, and optimistic duration attached to it. The optimistic and pessimistic durations should have a probability in the 10-20% range. These three estimates are then combined to arrive at a single estimated duration for each task. The calculation of this expected task time is:

$$\frac{(\text{Optimistic estimate} + (4 \times \text{Most likely estimate}) + \text{Pessimistic estimate})}{6}$$

In effect, the calculation gives a heavy weighting to the most likely estimate, but does incorporate the high and low time estimates. A potential problem with this approach is that there may be little historical information on which to base optimistic, most likely, and pessimistic estimates. Conversely, if the project repeats activities that have been completed in the past, then this information may be available.

The outcome of a PERT analysis is placing a focus on where the greatest effort should be made to keep a project on schedule.

---

**EXAMPLE**

A project manager at Milford Sound is conducting the preliminary planning for the construction of a new sound stage. One of the tasks is to assemble the scaffolding for the stage. The manager assigns an optimistic estimate of 12 days to this task, 16 days to the most likely estimate, and 32 days to the pessimistic estimate. Using the formula just noted for the estimated task duration, the manager calculates the following expected task time:

$$\frac{(12 \text{ Days optimistic} + (4 \times 16 \text{ Days most likely}) + 32 \text{ days pessimistic})}{6}$$

$$= 18 \text{ Days estimated task duration}$$

---

The estimated task duration is stated underneath each task description in the PERT chart. For example:

1 → Build machine / 5 days → 2

In addition, the early start (ES), late start (LS), early finish (EF) and late finish (LF) times are added to each task. For example:

2 → ES = 2.0 / LS = 2.9 — Build machine / 5 days — EF = 6.5 / LF = 9.7 → 3

In the preceding example, the assumption is that building the machine is the second task in a series of tasks; this allows for the addition of early and late start information for the task. The project manager knows that the machine building task could begin as early as two days into the project, or as late as 2.9 days. She also knows that the build task should take five days. However, if the early start is achieved, then the best possible early finish will be after 6.5 days. Similarly, if the late start occurs, then the latest possible finish for this task will be in 9.7 days. The concept is extended in the following exhibit, where we follow the early and late finishes for each task through several consecutive tasks:

2 → ES = 2.0 / LS = 2.9 — Build machine / 5 days — EF = 6.5 / LF = 9.7 → 3 → ES = 6.5 / LS = 9.7 — Test machine / 3 days — EF = 8.8 / LF = 13.5 → 4

In the preceding example, note how the early finish estimate of 6.5 days for the machine building task becomes the early start estimate for the next task, which is testing the machine. Similarly, the estimated 9.7 day late finish for the machine building task becomes the late start estimate for the next task. In this manner, the project manager can work through the various sequential tasks and estimate high-low values for project completion dates. As the earlier tasks are completed, their actual finish dates are plugged into this model, which results in a different set of estimated early and late finish dates.

When there is a difference between the early start and late start amounts for a task, this means there is slack in the system. In the preceding example for the machine testing task, there is a 3.2 day difference between the 6.5 day early start and the 9.7 day late start. This is the maximum amount of leeway in a task that will not delay the completion of the entire project.

When there is slack in the projections, this means the task is not on the critical path. Critical path tasks have no slack at all, so the early start and late start figures will be the same. Similarly, the early finish and late finish figures will be the same for a critical path task.

The length of a path in a PERT chart is the sum of the expected task times on that path. There may be several paths within a chart, each comprised of a different set of interrelated tasks that must be completed. Whichever path has the longest duration is the critical path, since shrinking this path will compress the duration of the entire project.

The main problem with PERT is the large amount of data that must be incorporated into the planning process. This makes it expensive to maintain, which usually limits its usefulness to larger and more complex projects.

## Differences between CPM and PERT

There are several key differences between the CPM and PERT methods. First, the CPM method employs just one time estimate, which represents the normal amount of time in which tasks are expected to be completed. The PERT method uses three time estimates to derive an expected time, which are the optimistic, most likely, and pessimistic durations. Second, the PERT method employs probability in deriving estimates, since three time estimates are used to derive durations. Third, the PERT method is used on projects in which it is difficult to determine the completion percentage, except when completion milestones are reached. The CPM method is more likely to be used on projects where the percentage of completion can be derived with some degree of accuracy. Thus, the essential difference between the two methods is the ability to incorporate a primitive probability distribution into a PERT analysis, thereby making it the more useful method when there is a higher level of uncertainty.

## Resource Leveling

Many of the preceding planning techniques can assist in completing a project on time. However, they may not optimize the use of people and equipment while doing so. Instead, there may be tasks that require an inordinate amount of effort to complete within a short period of time, which can result in overtime charges and burned-out people who will then work at suboptimal levels or require time off. Or, a mass of temporary workers are brought in to work intensively on a few tasks for a short period of time, after which they are dismissed from the project. These people must be trained, and the value of that training is lost as soon as they leave the project.

A better approach is to maintain a high level of efficiency by keeping the same people working on a project for as long as possible, avoiding the use of overtime and excess staff. By doing so, the project gains from having a smaller number of well-trained and experienced personnel who work on it from start to finish.

An additional consideration is that certain types of equipment may only be available for use within narrowly defined time periods. For example, construction equipment may only be available to be leased for a few months, after which someone else has reserved the equipment. If so, the schedule needs to accommodate these restrictions.

Another possibility is that personnel or equipment may be underutilized on a project. When this happens, there is a risk that an individual or key equipment will be shifted off to another project. Or, an employee might be laid off from the company. When this happens, it may be difficult to get these resources back at a later date, which could interfere with the timely completion of the project. By being cognizant of these issues, the project manager may be able to compress work for valuable resources, so that they are fully employed for a reduced period of time, after which their work is done and they can leave for other projects.

To engage in resource leveling, identify the peaks in resource usage that are clearly excessive. Then follow these three steps:

1. *Delay tasks*. During the period in which there is excessive resource usage, delay noncritical tasks. The amount of this delay cannot exceed the float for those tasks – otherwise there is a risk of extending the duration of the entire project. This delay shifts work out of high-usage periods. The adjacent periods to which the work is being shifted may also have a fairly high amount of scheduled resource usage, which may in turn call for shifts further along the timeline – thus, resource leveling can have the effect of ripples spreading out through a schedule.
2. *Adjust resources*. The preceding step may still leave a number of resource peaks that are clearly excessive, or declines in resource usage that might normally call for the elimination of resources. When there is a resource usage spike, add resources to the plan (such as more employees). When there is a decline in resource usage, schedule fewer resources. For example, if two people have been scheduled for a month and there is not enough work for them,

would it instead be possible to schedule just one person for a longer period of time?

3. *Extend completion date.* If the preceding steps do not result in an adequate amount of resource leveling, the remaining option is to extend the completion date. Doing so allows for more time in which to complete tasks, thereby spreading the resource load over a longer time period.

These steps will likely require multiple iterations before a reasonable amount of resource leveling can be achieved. It is possible that the outcome will involve having several tasks that have considerably reduced floats. This can be a dangerous situation, since there is now less buffer built into the schedule that is available for absorbing unforeseen problems. When the amount of residual float is small, it may make more sense from a risk management perspective to retain the float and add more resources, even though this entails some additional cost.

---

**EXAMPLE**

A project manager at Norrona Software is planning an upcoming project for the development of a warehouse management system. She notes that a volume testing task is currently scheduled to require 80 hours of staff time in one week, with one person assigned to the task. This task is not on the critical path, and so has a float of an additional two days. The project manager could expand the task by two days, thereby greatly reducing the employee's hours of work per day. However, an analysis of project risks indicates that there is a 30% chance that the software will fail the volume test and so will require additional testing. Given this risk, the manager wants to retain the float. Instead, she chooses to assign an additional person to the task. Doing so eliminates the resource spike and preserves the float, though at the cost of the additional person.

---

Resource leveling is especially useful when there is no particular rush to complete a project, since tasks can be readily stretched to accommodate overloaded resources. Leveling is also a useful option when there is pressure to keep the project cost low, since overloaded resources tend to increase costs.

## Optimizing the Schedule

Once a project schedule has been completed, go back and examine it for the following issues, with the intent of correcting errors and optimizing the schedule:

- *Verify time estimates.* Look for time estimates that are not sufficiently realistic, and correct them as necessary. Pay particular attention to the time estimates on the critical path, since they will have the largest impact on the ability to complete the project on time.

- *Verify relationships.* When a task does not appear to be dependent upon the completion of a prior task, verify that this is really the case. In many instances, there is at least some peripheral relationship.
- *Spot missing tasks.* Have some tasks been missed? The absence of a task can be quite difficult to spot. A task may be missing because there is an assumption that work has already been completed. For example, the installation of a new software package may include an assumption that the software developer has already constructed a procedures manual to go along with the software – which may not be the case.
- *Spot bottlenecks.* Every project contains a bottleneck. Locate it and ensure that the bottleneck is being properly managed to reduce its impact on the outcome of the project.
- *Spot overcommitted resources.* A key resource (usually a person) may be spread too thin across multiple tasks. There may be undue reliance on overtime, or a lack of consideration for holidays and personal time off. This can be a major problem if the person is working on a bottleneck task.
- *Match against budget.* If the amount of funds allocated to a project is limited by period, it may be necessary to prolong certain activities in order to delay certain expenditures. By doing so, they can be matched against the funding that will be available in later periods.
- *Match against company activities.* See if there are other company activities (such as the year-end crunch) that will impact staffing levels on the project, and schedule around them.
- *Match against holiday and vacation schedule.* Compare the company's holiday schedule and the schedule of planned employee vacations to the project schedule. It may be necessary to alter the project schedule to accommodate these other uses of employee time.

The schedule will need to be optimized on a regular basis, as any number of changes force the schedule to be altered. These alterations will require the team to reconsider its estimates of required durations and the resources that will be needed, and whether the changes now cause conflicts with other company activities. The result will be continual fine-tuning of the schedule, right through its completion date.

One can also calculate variations on the schedule that are designed to optimize different things. For example, if management wants to keep the total amount of costs incurred to a minimum, a schedule could be run that focuses on least cost. This schedule will likely have a longer duration, to take advantage of longer supplier lead times and to avoid rush fees. Or, a schedule could be run that focuses on the shortest possible duration. This schedule will likely have the highest cost, since it will allow the incurrence of rush fees and overtime in order to accelerate the schedule.

## Project Constraints

It can be exceedingly difficult to bring a project to fruition, because the project manager is being asked to deal with three constraints that may be mutually incompatible. They are:

- *Time frame*. This is the project duration within which the scope is expected to be accomplished.
- *Cost*. This is the total budgeted cost assigned to the project.
- *Resources*. This is the availability of people, equipment, or materials for a project.

These three items can be impacted by problems at any time over the course of a project. If so, the project manager will need to balance the relationship between these constraints, which may result in a reduction of the project scope. For example, the scope must be reduced in order to bring the project in on time and within budget. Or, the time frame must be extended in order to give the project team enough time in which to complete all deliverables; and when the time budget expands, it is likely that the cost will increase, too. These can be uncomfortable choices, and are usually driven by management's needs and the amount of available resources, as noted in the following examples.

---

**EXAMPLE**

Micron Metallic has just experienced a catastrophic failure of one of its stamping machines. It cannot be repaired. Since much of the company's revenue is derived from this machine, a project is initiated to replace the machine as soon as possible. In this case, the scope and time frame variables must be met, so the company is willing to spend more (the cost variable) in order to ensure that the project is completed.

**EXAMPLE**

Luminescence Corporation is working on a project to bring it into compliance with a new safety standard that will become law in three years. The project is initially forecast to take one year to complete. There have been no safety incidents related to the new standard, so management is in no rush to complete the project. In this case, the scope must be completed eventually and preferably within the original cost budget, so management is willing to let the time frame variable slip quite a bit in order to meet the cost objective.

**EXAMPLE**

Henderson Industrial is engaged in an industry roll up, where it is acquiring a number of competing firms. The acquisition integration team only has three months at each acquiree to integrate operations as much as it can. In addition, Henderson does not have much excess cash, so the budgeted funds for each integration effort cannot be expanded. This means that the variable management is most willing to move is the scope of each integration project. Accordingly, the team is instructed to integrate as much as it can in three months, and then move on to the next acquiree.

---

These variables are noted in more detail in the following sub-sections, along with discussions of project scope and the amount of pressure placed on employees and contractors.

### Time Frame

The time frame of a project can be critical if the output from the project must be available as of a certain date. For example, a Mars satellite must be ready by the time the launch window arrives, or the payload delivery may be delayed by many months. Or, a stage must be set up in time for a concert, or else the scheduled performance cannot proceed. Or, a deliverable is supposed to be sent to a customer by a certain date, or the company will incur a penalty. When the completion date is critical, costs tend to escalate, since it may be necessary to incur rush fees and overtime to ensure that the delivery date is met.

The time frame is still an issue even when the delivery date is not critical. The reason is that scope changes will require the retention of people on a project for longer than had been anticipated. When these people have scheduling conflicts, they may need to work on both commitments at the same time, which delays completion of the project task. Or, they must be replaced, which may require a training period for their replacements that adds to the time frame of the project. Also, when materials must be procured as part of a scope change, there may be a lead time requirement before the materials can be delivered, which extends the duration of the project.

### Cost

The cost of a project can vary, based on several factors. First, if a project is being completed in rush mode, suppliers may demand rush fees to deliver materials by the dates required by the accelerated project schedule. Conversely, when the project schedule is relaxed, one can schedule around supplier lead times to minimize the costs of materials. The same concept applies to staffing, where an immediate need for contractors may result in only being able to hire excessively qualified people whose billing rates are higher, rather than waiting for less-expensive people to become available.

### Resources

Resources are the people who work on a project, the equipment that may be needed to create deliverables, and the materials needed to construct physical goods. Obtaining personnel for the scheduled duration of a project can be quite difficult, especially when employees have significant duties elsewhere, such as working on other projects at the same time. This is a particular concern when people can only work within specific date ranges, in which case some aspects of a project may need to be scheduled around them.

Equipment can occasionally be considered a resource constraint. This is most common in the construction industry and especially in an overheated market, where there is not enough construction equipment available for all of the projects in the area. In this situation, entire projects or just certain tasks may be delayed until the equipment is available for use.

Materials are not usually a resource constraint, since they are assumed to be a commodity. However, there are cases in which a supplier is in a monopoly position, and so has little incentive to increase its capacity to meet sudden surges in demand. In this case, a business may find that materials are simply not available, or only at a very high price.

## Summary

The planning process is essential for even the smallest project, since it provides a baseline for evaluating progress and is an excellent tool for scheduling resources. At a minimum, a work breakdown structure must be created, along with the identification of task relationships and the use of bottom-up estimating. This information is needed to gain a clear grasp of the flow of activities for smaller projects. When there are many tasks to be completed and the level of project uncertainty is low, the critical path method can be used to clarify where the project manager should be focusing the bulk of his or her attention to ensure that the project is completed on time. In a very complex and uncertain environment, the program evaluation and review technique can be employed.

A project manager will almost certainly have to deal with the trade-offs associated with changes in a project. There will be issues related to every possible constraint, which may eventually result in a scope change. When dealing with these issues, always keep the project sponsor and stakeholders fully informed of the situation. None of these parties wants to be blindsided by an unexpected cost increase, delayed completion date, or reduction in scope. As long as they are aware of the situation and the reasons for changes, it is quite possible that they will still consider a project to be a success, even if the final outcome is less than they had originally expected.

# Glossary

### B

*Backward integration.* When a company acquires one of its suppliers.

*Bill of materials.* A list of the parts used to manufacture a product.

*Bottleneck.* An operation that is already operating at its maximum capacity, and so cannot accept any additional work beyond its current production level.

*Bottom-up estimating.* When the estimating process for a project begins at the lowest level of detail.

*Buffer.* Inventory that is positioned in front of the drum operation, and which protects the drum from any stoppage in materials coming from upstream operations.

*Business ecosystem.* A network of organizations, including suppliers, distributors, and even competitors, that are involved in the delivery of goods and/or services.

*Business process diagram.* A graphical depiction of the flow of business processes.

*Business process reengineering.* The revision of workflows to optimize processes and eliminate non-value-added activities.

### C

*Capacity.* The maximum sustainable rate of output that an operation can achieve.

*Cause-and-effect diagram.* A visual layout of the possible causes of a problem.

*Co-opetition.* The act of cooperation between competing companies.

*Control.* The ability to make changes.

*Control chart.* A statistical control used to analyze process variables and monitor their effects on performance.

*Corporate social responsibility.* The viewpoint that a business should be more aware of its impact on society and the environment.

*Cost.* The expenditure required to create and sell products and services.

*Critical path method.* A planning method in which each task is arranged in sequential order, along with a time estimate for how long it will take to complete the task.

### D

*Defects per unit.* The number of defects divided by the number of products.

*Dependability.* Delivering products or services on the expected date specified by the customer.

*Dependent demand.* The demand for component parts or sub-assemblies.

*Diseconomies of scale.* When unit costs increase as the number of units produced increases.

*Disintermediation.* A reduction in the use of intermediaries between producers and consumers.

*Drum.* The operation, person, or materials within a company that prevent the business from generating additional sales.

## E

*Economic order quantity.* A formula used to derive that number of units of inventory to order that represents the lowest possible total cost to the buyer.

*Economies of scale.* When unit costs decline as the number of units produced increases.

*Empowerment.* The practice of giving employees an increased level of information and decision-making responsibility, so that they can take action to improve the performance of a business.

*Ergonomic.* The design of an efficient and comfortable working environment.

*Expediting.* The assignment of an expediter to a specific high-priority job, who then walks it through the entire production process, shifting other jobs out of the way to make room for the designated job.

*Exponential smoothing.* A forecasting method that is based on historical patterns in the data.

## F

*Finite loading.* When only a set amount of work is allocated to a work center, which is capped at its estimated capacity level.

*Flexibility.* Being able to make whatever internal changes are needed to respond effectively to the outside environment within a short period of time.

*Forward integration.* When a company acquires a customer.

## G

*Gantt chart.* A visual portrayal of the task assignments and task durations within a project.

## I

*Independent demand.* The demand for a finished product, which is being ordered by an outside party.

*Infinite loading.* When no attempt is made to limit the amount of work impacting a work center.

## J

*Job analysis.* The process of assembling activities into specific job descriptions and describing how each job relates to the other defined jobs in an organization.

*Job enlargement.* Increasing the number of tasks associated with a job in order to increase the variety of work.

*Job enrichment.* Expanding the amount of responsibility built into an employee's job.

*Job rotation.* The exposure of employees to multiple aspects of an organization through different job postings.

## K

*Kaizen.* A continuous improvement process that targets small, incremental enhancements to existing processes.

## L

*Loading.* The volume of work assigned to a work center.

## M

*Mass customization.* The production of large volumes of goods while at the same time modifying them to the needs of specific customers.

*Material requirements planning.* A computer-driven production scheduling and inventory management system.

*Mean time between failures.* The average time that equipment is operating between breakdowns or stoppages.

*Method study.* The process of subjecting work to systematic, critical scrutiny to make it more effective and efficient.

## N

*Net profit.* Throughput minus operating expenses.

*Normal capacity.* The amount of output that can be reasonably expected over the long term.

## O

*Operating expenses.* All company expenses other than totally variable costs.

*Organization.* A group of people who have been structured and managed to meet a need or pursue a goal.

*Organizational structure.* The set of rules used to delineate how tasks are controlled within an organization.

*Outsourcing.* The practice of sending work to suppliers, rather than completing tasks internally.

## P

*Pareto analysis.* A method of analysis based on the concept that 20% of the variables included in an analysis are responsible for 80% of the results.

*Phase.* A cluster of related activities that result in a deliverable.

*Planning.* The creation and updating of a plan that is targeted at achieving a specific goal.

*Practical capacity.* The highest realistic amount of output that a factory can maintain.

*Process technology.* The knowledge used to create and deliver a product or service.

*Process value analysis.* The review of each step in a process to see if the activity provides value to the customer.

*Product life cycle.* The different stages that a product passes through over time.

*Productivity.* The effectiveness of productive output, as measured in terms of the rate of output per unit of input.

*Project.* A series of tasks that must be completed within a fixed time frame in order to achieve certain objectives.

## Q

*Quality.* Conformance to customer expectations.

## R

*Regression analysis.* A forecasting method that is based on a cause-and-effect relationship between a dependent and independent variable.

*Reorder point.* The inventory unit quantity on hand that triggers the purchase of a predetermined amount of replenishment inventory.

*Return on invested capital.* The comparison of a firm's return on capital to its cost of capital.

*Root cause analysis.* A tool used to identify the root cause of a problem by asking the question "why" multiple times.

*Rope.* The total time duration needed to bring work-in-process to the drum.

## S

*Safety stock.* Inventory that is kept on hand as a buffer to guard against shortages.

*Scientific management.* The careful study of a job to determine the best possible procedures for conducting it.

*Six Sigma.* A set of management techniques that are intended to improve processes by greatly reducing the probability that an error or defect will occur.

*Speed.* The total elapsed time period between when a customer orders a product and when it is delivered.

*Sprint capacity.* Excess production capacity positioned upstream from the bottleneck operation.

*Stakeholder.* Any person or entity that has an interest in a business or project.

*Strategic experiment.* A risky new venture being run within an established business. It is usually intended to be a multi-year investment in a market that is not well defined, and for which there is no obvious way to earn a profit.

*Strategic risk.* The probability that an event will interfere with a company's business model.

*Strategy.* A plan of action that is targeted at achieving a major aim.

*Supply network.* A cluster of suppliers that assist a business in adding value for customers by manufacturing and delivering products.

*Surety bond.* A contract guaranteeing that a legal agreement will be completed. It is commonly used to ensure that construction performance is completed.

## T

*Technology.* The practical application of knowledge to a particular discipline.

*Theoretical capacity.* The output that can be attained if a production facility were able to produce at its peak efficiency level with no downtime.

*Throughput.* Revenues minus totally variable expenses. Also known as the number of units that pass through a process during a period of time.

*Time to market.* The period of time between when the first ideas are formed for a new product and when it is eventually made available to consumers.

*Top-down estimating.* When the estimating for a project is imposed by company management, stakeholders, or the project manager.

*Totally variable costs.* Those costs that vary when one incremental unit of a product is manufactured.

*Triple bottom line.* The reporting of the financial, social, and environmental results of a business.

## V

*Value stream mapping.* The collection of information about the process steps that a business uses to create value.

*Vertical integration.* When a single business controls different stages of the production process within an industry, extending into the distribution of goods.

# Index

Made in the USA
Las Vegas, NV
17 March 2025

19680753R00177